CW00323924

The Storytelling Handbook

A guide for primary teachers of English

Edited by Gail Ellis and Jean Brewster

PENGUIN ENGLISH

PENGUIN ENGLISH

Published by the Penguin Group
Penguin Books Ltd, 27 Wrights Lane, London W8 5TZ, England
Penguin Books USA Inc., 375 Hudson Street, New York, New York 10014, USA
Penguin Books Australia Ltd, Ringwood, Victoria, Australia
Penguin Books Canada Ltd, 10 Alcorn Avenue, Toronto, Ontario, Canada M4V 3B2
Penguin Books (NZ) Ltd, 182–190 Wairau Road, Auckland 10, New Zealand

Penguin Books Ltd, Registered Offices: Harmondsworth, Middlesex, England

Published in Penguin Books 1991
10 9 8 7 6 5 4 3 2

Copyright © Gail Ellis and Jean Brewster, 1991
All rights reserved

The moral rights of the authors have been asserted

Printed in England by Clays Ltd, St Ives plc

Contents

Acknowledgements

The authors would like to thank Geneviève Kergoat and her CM1 class of 1989/90 at the Ecole Primaire Mixte, 216 bis rue Lafayette, Paris 75010 for trying out many of the activities in the story notes and for suggesting additional ideas.

We are also grateful to Elyane Comarteau, editor-in-chief of *Standpoints*, for allowing us to reproduce recordings from volume 3, number 5, 1990. (*Standpoints* is published by Mission Laïque Française and Centre National de Documentation Pédagogique.)

Finally, our thanks to Fréderic Arnaud of Penguin Jeunesse for his help in the initial stages of this project, and to Chris Snowdon of Penguin English and Helen Woodeson of Penguin France for their interest and support.

Penguin English would like to thank the following for permission to make a cassette recording of their publications:
Hamish Hamilton for *The Very Hungry Caterpillar* by Eric Carle, *The Elephant and the Bad Baby* by Elfrida Vipont, illustrated by Raymond Briggs. (*The Very Hungry Caterpillar* is available both as a Hamish Hamilton hardback and Puffin paperback. Eric Carle is also the creator of *The Very Busy Spider, 1,2,3 to the Zoo, Do You want to be My Friend?* and *The Very Quiet Cricket*); Mallinson Rendel Publishers for *My Cat Likes to Hide in Boxes*; Ventura Publishing Ltd for *Where's Spot?* and *Spot's Birthday Party* by Eric Hill. (The ever-popular Spot made his first appearance in Eric Hill's award-winning lift-the-flap book, *Where's Spot?* His adventures have now been translated into more than sixty languages, including sign language, Braille and many lesser-used languages, and are sold in over a hundred countries. For further information, please write to Ventura Publishing Limited, 11–13 Young Street, London W8 5EH).

Introduction

This handbook is for any teacher who is – or who will be – teaching English to young learners at primary school and who is interested in using storybooks. You may be a primary school teacher who has one class and teaches all subjects, or a specialist teacher of English who visits a number of different schools each week, or even a secondary school teacher who has been asked to teach in a primary school. Whatever your situation, the handbook takes into consideration your particular teaching context and provides plenty of ideas. The handbook is also for teacher trainers who are responsible for training different types of teachers.

The story notes refer to a wide variety of stories which will appeal to young learners. They include traditional stories and fairy-tales (which many will already be familiar with in their mother tongue), animal stories, stories about everyday life and fantasy stories. Pupils are even invited to create their own text for *The Snowman* which is told in a series of strip format pictures.

The story notes also suggest a range of related language-learning activities which demonstrate different approaches to language teaching and learning, from the traditional to the more innovative. They can be used with children at various stages in their primary education and in their English-language learning. You will be able to experiment with a wide range of techniques depending on your position.

The cassette includes some of the stories and some of the songs and rhymes suggested in the story notes, and a recording of the phonetic alphabet which uses words from the stories to illustrate the sounds of English.

Part 1
Storytelling, an introduction

1 Why use storybooks?

Children enjoy listening to stories in their mother tongue and understand the conventions of narrative. For example, as soon as they hear the formula 'Once upon a time . . .' they know what to expect next. For this reason, storybooks can provide an ideal introduction to the foreign language presented in a context that is familiar to the child. Stories can also be the starting-point for a wide variety of related language and learning activities which are described in the accompanying notes. Here are some further reasons why teachers use storybooks:

- Stories are motivating and fun and can help develop positive attitudes towards the foreign language and language learning. They can create a desire to continue learning.

- Stories exercise the imagination. Children can become personally involved in a story as they identify with the characters and try to interpret the narrative and illustrations. This imaginative experience helps develop their own creative powers.

- Stories are a useful tool in linking fantasy and the imagination with the child's real world. They provide a way of enabling children to make sense of their everyday life and forge links between home and school.

- Listening to stories in class is a shared social experience. Reading and writing are often individual activities; storytelling provokes a shared response of laughter, sadness, excitement and anticipation which is not only enjoyable but can help build up the child's confidence and encourage social and emotional development.

- Children enjoy listening to stories over and over again. This frequent repetition allows certain language items to be acquired while others are being overtly reinforced. Many stories also contain natural repetition of key vocabulary and structures (for example, the shopkeepers and the phrase 'Would you like ——?' in *The Elephant and the Bad Baby*). This helps children to remember every detail, so they can gradually learn to anticipate what is about to happen next in the story. Repetition also encourages participation in the narrative, thereby providing a type of pattern practice in a meaningful context. Following meaning and predicting language are important skills in language learning.

● Listening to stories allows the teacher to introduce or revise new vocabulary and sentence structures by exposing the children to language in varied, memorable and familiar contexts, which will enrich their thinking and gradually enter their own speech.

● Listening to stories develops the child's listening and concentrating skills via:
a visual clues (for example, pictures and illustrations)
b their prior knowledge of how language works
c their general knowledge.
This allows them to understand the overall meaning of a story and to relate it to their personal experience.

● Stories create opportunities for developing continuity in children's learning since they can be chosen to consolidate learning in school subjects across the curriculum.

● Learning English through stories can lay the foundations for secondary school in terms of basic language functions and structures, vocabulary and language-learning skills.

Storybooks and the curriculum

There are three main dimensions in which stories can add to learning in the whole school curriculum:

1 Stories can be used to reinforce conceptual development in children (for example, colour, size, shape, time, cause and effect, and so on).

2 Stories are a means of developing learning to learn. This major category covers:
   ● reinforcing thinking strategies
     (for example, comparing, classifying, predicting, problem-solving, hypothesizing, planning, and so on).
   ● developing strategies for learning English
     (for example, guessing the meaning of new words, training the memory, self-testing, and so on).

- developing study skills
  (for example, making, understanding and interpreting charts
  and graphs, making and learning to use dictionaries, organizing work, and so on).

3 Carefully selected stories can also be used to develop other
  subjects in the curriculum, in particular:

- *Mathematics* telling the time, numbers: counting and quantity,
  measuring

- *Science* the life-cycle of insects, animals, outer space, how
  seeds grow

- *History* prehistoric animals, understanding chronology/the
  passing of time

- *Geography and the Environment* shopping and shops in the local
  area, neighbourhood parks, sports and games, using a map,
  using an atlas, the weather and climates around the world,
  cultural studies

- *Art and Craft* drawing, making masks, hats, cards, clocks etc.,
  making collages, making puppets

- *Music and Drama* singing songs, playing instruments, role-play,
  miming.

The story notes have many examples of how different aspects of
the curriculum can be developed.

The chart Stories and Learning highlights some of the major
general concepts, Learning to Learn and Curriculum Links in the
storybooks and story notes. Many of the more general learning
strategies – such as guessing the meaning of unknown words
through visual aids or the context, self-testing and reviewing – will
be developed in teaching the stories. (For further information on
Learning to Learn see chapter 4.)

Storybooks and the syllabus

What is a syllabus?

A syllabus is concerned essentially with the selection and grading
of content. For example, if you are using a coursebook in your
teaching, it is the authors who have selected the language items

Stories and learning

CONCEPTS	Where's Spot?	Spot's Birthday Party	I Can Do It!	Having a Picnic	The Very Hungry Caterpillar	Meg and Mog	Don't Forget the Bacon!	The Elephant and the Bad Baby	My Cat Likes to Hide in Boxes	Little Red Riding Hood	Pat the Cat	Mr Gumpy's Motor Car	Mr Biff the Boxer	The Turnip	The Fat Cat	The Snowman
colours	✓			✓										✓	✓	✓
size and shape	✓	✓	✓		✓	✓									✓	✓
time		✓			✓	✓								✓		✓
spatial context	✓			✓					✓			✓				
cause and effect								✓		✓	✓					✓
LEARNING TO LEARN																
comparing		✓	✓		✓	✓	✓				✓	✓	✓			✓
classifying		✓	✓		✓	✓		✓	✓	✓	✓	✓	✓			✓
predicting	✓		✓		✓		✓	✓	✓	✓	✓		✓		✓	✓
sequencing	✓				✓	✓	✓	✓	✓	✓	✓				✓	✓
hypothesizing and problem-solving							✓		✓			✓		✓		
memory training					✓	✓	✓			✓					✓	
charts		✓			✓		✓	✓	✓			✓	✓			✓
surveys and investigations		✓			✓		✓	✓				✓	✓			✓
using dictionaries							✓									
CURRICULUM LINKS																
Mathematics telling the time										✓						✓
numbers and quantity		✓					✓									
graphs		✓					✓									
Science life-cycles					✓											
outer space						✓										
how seeds grow														✓		

This page contains a large checklist matrix. The activity labels (read along the left) are grouped under category headings; the grid to the right records which of thirteen unlabelled story columns involve each activity (✓).

Activity	1	2	3	4	5	6	7	8	9	10	11	12	13
History													
prehistoric animals													
understanding the passing of time	✓												
Geography and the environment													
shops													
food			✓		✓		✓						
parks			✓										
using a map or atlas					✓			✓					
the weather/seasons	✓			✓									
sports and games	✓				✓								
clothes	✓		✓			✓							
Cultural studies													
festivals in other countries	✓			✓		✓							
food and meals in other countries					✓								
famous people from other countries				✓			✓						
CREATIVE ACTIVITIES													
drawing and printing	✓			✓	✓	✓	✓						
making masks, hats etc.		✓	✓	✓	✓	✓	✓						
making collages and friezes	✓	✓		✓									
making puppets and models	✓	✓			✓								
making a theme-based display			✓			✓	✓						
cooking			✓			✓	✓						
making tickets, cards, posters, etc.	✓		✓	✓		✓							
MUSIC AND DRAMA													
singing songs and rhymes			✓	✓		✓		✓					
playing instruments					✓								
role-play	✓												
miming						✓							
dramatization			✓		✓	✓	✓						

you are going to teach and the order in which you introduce them. They, in turn, may have based their selection on guidelines laid down by a Ministry of Education. A syllabus is most likely to include language functions and structures, vocabulary, pronunciation and skills to be practised. It may also include the types of activities and tasks your pupils will be involved in. Various factors are considered when selecting and grading content such as the age and conceptual level of the learners, their needs and interests, their language level and previous language-learning experience, and the degree of difficulty of language and activities.

Storybooks and the coursebook

Storybooks can be used to provide variety and extra language practice by supplementing or complementing another language course. For example, if you have just covered a unit in your coursebook about animals, you may like to read an animal story to your pupils, such as *Pat the Cat*. Or, if you have just covered a unit which has introduced a particular language function and structure (for example, offering and accepting something politely, 'Would you like . . .?', 'Yes, please'), you may like to read a story like *The Elephant and the Bad Baby* to show how this language is used in a different context. In this way learning can be made more memorable and more fun. The linguistic objectives described in each set of story notes highlight the language that is considered relevant to beginner learners to help you decide which stories to use – and when to use them in conjunction with your coursebook.

Storybooks as an alternative to the coursebook

If you do not have to adhere rigidly to a coursebook, storybooks can also be used as short basic syllabuses in their own right, offering a novel alternative to the coursebook. Six or seven stories could be worked on throughout a school year. This would mean spending about four to five weeks on each story and about eight to ten lessons per story, if the class has two hours for English a week. In this way, a storybook provides the starting-point for all kinds of related language activities as described in chapter 5 and in the story notes themselves. (Again, the linguistic objectives are outlined in the story notes for each story and indicate the language items that could be covered.)

A story-based syllabus

The stories in this handbook have been carefully selected both to meet the needs of young, beginner learners and to appeal to them.

They contain language which is traditionally included in most beginner syllabuses, as well as language central to the world of the child. For example, children love stories about witches, so we have included *Meg and Mog*, about a witch called Meg whose spells always go wrong. This story includes vocabulary usually found in most beginner syllabuses related to clothes, food and adjectives of size, but it also includes words like broomstick and cauldron, and those for the ingredients for a witch's spells. Although these words may not be immediate to the everyday needs of the children, they are easy to understand in their context and the illustrations also help.

Below we can see how five stories were used as the principal teaching material throughout a school year with a class of 9–10-year-old beginners in France who had an hour of English twice a week from November until June. The permanent class teacher observed and participated in each lesson so that she could carry out many of the activities mentioned in the conceptual reinforcement and curriculum links section described in the story notes. The diagram breaks down the language in terms of language functions and vocabulary from each story to show how it constitutes a mini-syllabus and to show how a global syllabus was built up for the year with the introduction of new language and other language recycled. Other syllabuses could be planned in the same way, using different storybooks.

A story-based syllabus

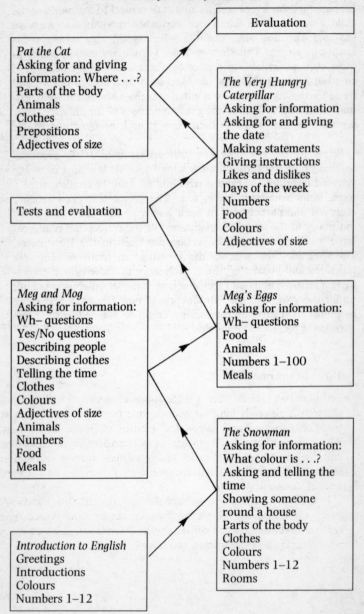

Evaluation

Pat the Cat
Asking for and giving
information: Where . . .?
Parts of the body
Animals
Clothes
Prepositions
Adjectives of size

*The Very Hungry
Caterpillar*
Asking for information
Asking for and giving
the date
Making statements
Giving instructions
Likes and dislikes
Days of the week
Numbers
Food
Colours
Adjectives of size

Tests and evaluation

Meg and Mog
Asking for information:
Wh– questions
Yes/No questions
Describing people
Describing clothes
Telling the time
Clothes
Colours
Adjectives of size
Animals
Numbers
Food
Meals

Meg's Eggs
Asking for information:
Wh– questions
Food
Animals
Numbers 1–100
Meals

The Snowman
Asking for information:
What colour is . . .?
Asking and telling the
time
Showing someone
round a house
Parts of the body
Clothes
Colours
Numbers 1–12
Rooms

Introduction to English
Greetings
Introductions
Colours
Numbers 1–12

2 Selecting storybooks

Authentic storybooks

Many publishers produce simplified storybooks especially for children learning English. However, there are many authentic storybooks written for English-speaking children which are also suitable for those learning English. As these have not been written specifically for the teaching of English as a foreign language, the language is not selected or graded. Many, however, contain language traditionally found in most beginner syllabuses. The advantage of using authentic storybooks is that they provide examples of 'real' language and help to bring the real world into the classroom. Very often simplified stories represent a watered-down version of the English language and can deceive both teacher and learners about the true nature of language. Authentic storybooks can also be very motivating for a child as they experience a strong sense of achievement at having worked with a 'real' book. Furthermore, the quality of illustration is of a high standard, appealing to the young learner, and it plays an important role in aiding general comprehension.

Types of storybooks

Teachers can choose from a wide range of storybooks: those that children are already familiar with in their mother tongue, such as traditional stories and fairy-tales; picture stories with no text, where the children build up the story together; rhyming stories; cumulative stories with predictable endings; humorous stories; stories with infectious rhythms; everyday stories; fantasy stories; animal stories, and so on.

We have classified the storybooks included in this handbook under three headings: narrative features, content and layout. You will see that many of the stories can be classified in different ways according to the classification you have in mind.

PART 1

NARRATIVE FEATURES

rhyming words	*My Cat Likes to Hide in Boxes*
	Pat the Cat
	Don't Forget the Bacon!
	The Elephant and the Bad Baby
repeating structures	*The Very Hungry Caterpillar*
	I Can Do It!
	Where's Spot?
cumulative content and language	*The Elephant and the Bad Baby*
	My Cat Likes to Hide in Boxes
	The Turnip
	The Fat Cat
interactive	*Where's Spot?*
	Spot's Birthday Party
	Pat the Cat
humorous	*Pat the Cat*
	Spot's Birthday Party
	Don't Forget the Bacon!
	The Elephant and the Bad Baby
	My Cat Likes to Hide in Boxes
	Meg and Mog
	The Very Hungry Caterpillar
	Mr Biff the Boxer

CONTENT

everyday life	*Don't Forget the Bacon!*
	Having a Picnic
	Mr Biff the Boxer
	Mr Gumpy's Motor Car
	The Very Hungry Caterpillar
	Pat the Cat
animal stories	*Where's Spot?*
	Spot's Birthday Party
	My Cat Likes to Hide in Boxes
	The Elephant and the Bad Baby
	I Can Do It!
trad/folk/fairy	*The Fat Cat*
	Little Red Riding Hood
	The Turnip

| fantasy | *Meg and Mog* |
| | *The Snowman* |

flap	*Where's Spot?*
	Spot's Birthday Party
cut-away pages	*The Very Hungry Caterpillar*
	Pat the Cat
minimal text	*Having a Picnic*
	Where's Spot?
	Spot's Birthday Party
	I Can Do It!
no text	*The Snowman*
speech bubbles	*Don't Forget the Bacon!*
	Meg and Mog
	Pat the Cat
	Spot's Birthday Party

Criteria for selecting storybooks

Care needs to be taken to select authentic storybooks that are accessible, useful and relevant for children learning English. What criteria, then, can a teacher use? The diagram on pages 12 and 13 breaks down three major objectives of language teaching into criteria which are further translated into questions you could ask yourself. The objectives overlap to some extent as indicated by the arrows.

Stories and language features

Some of the stories in this handbook are linguistically less complicated than others. This is partly to do with the language used in the text, the length of the story, and the use of illustrations and layout. For example *Where's Spot?* is useful for learning spatial context and prepositions. The text consists principally of seven questions which repeat the structure: 'Is he behind the door?' and gives attention to the language of position. Clever use is made of flaps, doors and lids so children can be actively involved opening them in the search for Spot; the illustration of 'behind' really is behind. The short text and the clever use of layout make *Where's Spot?* very accessible to beginners. *Mr Gumpy's Motor Car*, on the

Criteria for selecting storybooks

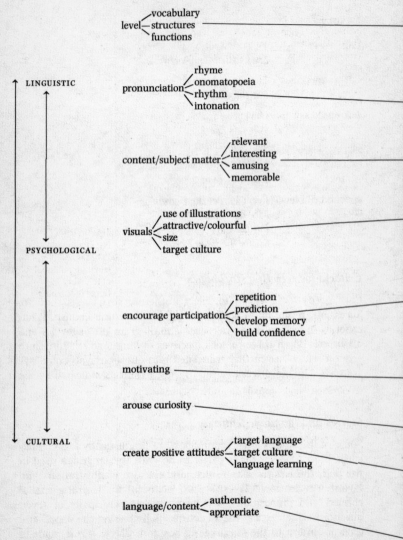

LINGUISTIC

level — vocabulary
— structures
— functions

pronunciation — rhyme
— onomatopoeia
— rhythm
— intonation

content/subject matter — relevant
— interesting
— amusing
— memorable

PSYCHOLOGICAL

visuals — use of illustrations
— attractive/colourful
— size
— target culture

encourage participation — repetition
— prediction
— develop memory
— build confidence

motivating

arouse curiosity

CULTURAL

create positive attitudes — target language
— target culture
— language learning

language/content — authentic
— appropriate

POTENTIAL FOR FOLLOW-UP WORK

Does the story provide a starting-point for related language activities
and lead on to follow-up work such as drama or role-play to reinforce
vocabulary and structures in a meaningful and memorable way?

Is the language level appropriate? Not too easy? Not too difficult? Does the story contain language included in beginner syllabuses? For example, vocabulary, structures and functions? Will it provide pupils with a successful learning experience?

Does the story contain any features such as rhyme, onomatopoeia, rhythm or intonation that pupils will enjoy imitating and so improve their pronunciation?

Will the story interest pupils? Is it relevant to their needs? Is it amusing? Is it memorable?

Do the illustrations relate to the text and support the children's understanding? Are they appropriate to the age of the pupils? Are they attractive and colourful? Are they big enough for all the class to see? Do they depict life in the target culture?

Is there any natural repetition to encourage participation in the text and to provide pattern practice, pronunciation practice, to recycle language items and develop memory skills? Does the repetition allow pupils to predict what is coming next in the story and to build up their confidence?

Will the story motivate pupils by drawing on their personal experience? Will it develop their imagination and appeal to their sense of humour?

Will the story arouse their curiosity and make them want to find out more about the target language and culture and language learning?

Will pupils respond positively to the story and develop positive attitudes towards the target language and culture and towards language learning?

Is the language representative of what is spoken in the target culture? Does the story give any information about life in the target culture? Does it contain any obscure cultural references that may be difficult to understand? Is it too culture specific?

EDUCATIONAL POTENTIAL
What is the learning potential of the story in terms of learning about other subjects, the target culture, the world and learning about learning?

Stories and language features

VERBS	Where's Spot?	Spot's Birthday Party	I Can Do It!	Having a Picnic	The Very Hungry Caterpillar	Meg and Mog	Don't Forget the Bacon!	The Elephant and the Bad Baby	My Cat Likes to Hide in Boxes	Little Red Riding Hood	Pat the Cat	Mr Gumpy's Motor Car	Mr Biff the Boxer	The Turnip	The Fat Cat	The Snowman
Mood																
imperative	✓	✓			✓		✓			✓		✓	✓	✓		✓
Tense																
simple present	✓	✓	✓	✓	✓		✓		✓		✓		✓	✓		✓
present continuous						✓			✓						✓	✓
simple past		✓			✓	✓	✓	✓	✓	✓	✓	✓	✓		✓	✓
past continuous										✓		✓			✓	✓
perfect		✓		✓						✓					✓	
'going to' future												✓				
Modal verbs																
can/could			✓				✓	✓		✓			✓	✓		✓
will/would												✓	✓		✓	
may/might												✓				
must																

	1	2	3	4	5	6	7	8	9	10	11	12	13	14	15	16	17	18
Interrogative forms																		
Yes/No questions	✓	✓	✓	✓	✓	✓	✓		✓		✓	✓		✓	✓		✓	✓
wh– questions	✓	✓	✓		✓	✓	✓				✓	✓		✓	✓		✓	✓
PREPOSITIONS																		
on/in/inside/under																	✓	✓
up/down					✓	✓		✓										
behind/in front of															✓	✓	✓	✓
through/between												✓						
off/into								✓					✓					
at/to/from													✓					
ADJECTIVES																		
word order											✓							
comparative			✓		✓													
superlative				✓														
NOUNS AND PRONOUNS																		
countable/uncountable												✓						
possessive	✓	✓		✓		✓												
ARTICLES																		
a/an										✓		✓						
some/any									✓			✓						
LINKING WORDS																		
first/then/next	✓	✓	✓		✓				✓									✓
but			✓	✓											✓		✓	
so		✓		✓					✓	✓				✓			✓	

other hand, contains much more text and several different tenses which make it suitable for children with a higher language level.

A feature often found in narrative is the simple past. Some teachers may feel that they do not wish to introduce their pupils to this tense in the early stages of their learning. However, many stories begin with the formula 'Once upon a time there was a . . .' which indicates to the listener that the story is going to describe past events and actions. The use of the past tense is a natural feature of narrative and many stories would sound unnatural and distorted if this was changed. Furthermore, children will be concentrating on the meaning of the story, not on why and how the simple past is used. Their previous knowledge of narrative in their mother tongue will have, to some extent, prepared them for its use in the target language.

The chart on pages 14 and 15 highlights some of the main language features used in the storybooks and notes. It also highlights the language pupils will produce through activities described in the story notes. It does not focus on the teacher's language.

Authentic storybooks and language level

The storybooks referred to in this handbook are all authentic. This makes it difficult to give definitive indications for the level of each book. Many can be read with pupils of different ages and levels, depending on the way they are used, the amount of detail you wish to go into and the time you have available, as well as on your pupils' conceptual level and concentration span. For example, *The Snowman* will bring delight to quite young children, as well as to adolescents and adults. As this story is wordless, the type of language work which could be covered can range from simple vocabulary sets related to clothes, rooms in a house, and so on, to a quite sophisticated description of the process of building a snowman. Some story notes contain suggestions on how to use the stories with different levels. For example, see the notes for *Pat the Cat*.

Many syllabuses grade down the input to enable learners to cope with it. When using authentic materials it is the output or response to the authentic input which should be graded down. The story notes in this handbook propose activities which are within the capabilities of beginner learners. Remember that the overall aim of using storybooks with young beginners is to encourage general comprehension which can trigger a wealth of purposeful language-learning activities.

To provide some guidance on levels of difficulty, we have attempted to group the stories into three categories. The first grouping gives an indication of language level and is based on the length and linguistic complexity of the text. The second grouping is based on the difficulty of the activities described in the notes for each story. In this way, you will see that although *Little Red Riding Hood* and *The Turnip* are grouped together under the same category for language level, the tasks and activities suggested in the accompanying notes for *Little Red Riding Hood* are easier than those suggested for *The Turnip*. Similarly, the suggested text for *The Snowman* means that this title has been put in the third category for language level and in the first category for the activities and tasks suggested, thereby allowing it to be handled by near-beginners. Some notes have activities which have been pitched deliberately at a particular level, although activities at other levels could have been devised. Many optional activities suggested for each story can, however, be used with pupils of different levels and are useful if you are working with mixed-level classes.

LANGUAGE LEVEL

Easy	More difficult	Most difficult
Where's Spot?	*The Very Hungry Caterpillar*	*Mr Gumpy's Motor Car*
I Can Do It!	*Meg and Mog*	*Mr Biff the Boxer*
Having a Picnic	*Spot's Birthday Party*	*The Turnip*
Don't Forget the Bacon!	*The Elephant and the Bad Baby*	*The Fat Cat*
	My Cat Likes to Hide in Boxes	*Little Red Riding Hood*
	Pat the Cat	*The Snowman*

DIFFICULTY OF ACTIVITIES

Easy	More difficult	Most difficult
Where's Spot?	*Having a Picnic*	*The Turnip*
The Snowman	*Spot's Birthday Party*	*Mr Biff the Boxer*
I Can Do It!	*The Very Hungry Caterpillar*	*The Fat Cat*
The Elephant and the Bad Baby	*My Cat Likes to Hide in Boxes*	*Pat the Cat*
Little Red Riding Hood	*Don't Forget the Bacon!*	
Pat the Cat	*Meg and Mog*	
	Mr Gumpy's Motor Car	

When selecting storybooks, factors such as time, your pupils' conceptual level and concentration span should also be considered. Generally speaking, authentic storybooks are flexible for use with a variety of levels, depending on how you wish your pupils to respond.

If a story appeals to you but some of the language is too difficult for your pupils to follow, the next section contains suggestions on how to adapt stories.

Adapting stories

There are some features of stories specific to narrative; if we modify and simplify stories too much there is a danger of losing some of their magic. At the same time, this magic may also be lost if the language is too advanced for children to follow. What can the teacher do to make the story more accessible? The guidelines below suggest checking vocabulary and general meaning, grammar, organization of ideas and story length.

VOCABULARY AND GENERAL MEANING

● *check unfamiliar content or words:* is it necessary to substitute familiar words for the more unfamiliar ones?

for example, in *Don't Forget the Bacon!* change 'pounds' to 'kilos',

NOTE: in some stories it is important to keep certain keywords, even if they are a little unfamiliar. In *Meg and Mog*, for example, it is preferable to retain 'cauldron' for its stylistic impact. Here the use of pictures makes its meaning clear.

● *check idioms:* are there any idioms which need to be rephrased in clearer language?

for example, in *Little Red Riding Hood* the sentence 'The beast had a mind to eat her up' could be replaced by 'The wolf decided to eat her up.'

● *check clarity:* would more examples make the meaning of the story clearer?

for example, in *Mr Biff the Boxer* the sentence using 'toughen up' needs examples to clarify the meaning.

GRAMMAR

● *check tenses:* are there too many tenses? Can they be simplified?

for example, in *Mr Gumpy's Motor Car* the past continuous 'everyone was enjoying the ride' can be changed to 'everyone enjoyed the ride'.

- *check use of structures:* the story may use several structures but you may wish to emphasize one or reduce the number of structures.

  for example, in *Mr Gumpy's Motor Car* the characters describe why they cannot push the car using six different structures. These could be simplified so that only one or two are used such as: 'Not me, I'm too ——' or 'He's bigger.'

- *check word order:* in stories the word order sometimes differs from everyday use to create a more dramatic effect.

  for example, 'down came the rain' and 'out popped a dinosaur'.

  NOTE: You will need to decide whether this is confusing or whether the original effect should be kept.

ORGANIZATION OF IDEAS

- *check sentence length and complexity:* a long sentence may need shortening by splitting it into two sentences. You may have to add other words or mime actions to make the meaning more explicit.

  for example, this sentence in *Little Red Riding Hood*: 'At once he fell upon the good woman and gobbled her down in a moment, for it had been more than three days since he had last eaten' could be changed to: 'He grabbed the old woman and gobbled her up. Yum yum! [Storyteller rubs her stomach and licks her lips] It was his first meal for three days.'

- *check time references:* is the sequence of events clear or does it need to be reinforced by time markers such as first, then, the next day, etc?

  for example, see notes for *The Snowman*.

- *check the way ideas are linked:* does the relationship between sentences need to be made clearer?

  for example, a story such as *The Elephant and the Bad Baby* could highlight the use of causes and their effects by using 'so' more frequently.

- *check the way ideas are explained:* if there is a lot of narrative, would more direct speech make the story easier to follow?

19

for example, see notes for *The Turnip*, where more use of direct speech helps to reinforce the repeating sequence of the story-line.

STORY LENGTH

● *check the number of ideas in the story:* in some cumulative stories it is possible to leave out some of the characters or events to reduce the length of the story without spoiling the overall effect.

for example, see the notes for *The Elephant and the Bad Baby*.

Some of the notes, for example, on *The Turnip*, include a revised version of the story, where several of these suggestions have been made use of.

3 Using storybooks

'These storybooks are beautiful but they are written for children who speak English as their mother tongue. I couldn't use them with my pupils.' This comment reflects the attitude of many teachers of English as a foreign language when they first look at authentic storybooks. It is sometimes difficult to imagine how a story can be exploited, or how the time required to plan story-based lessons, and to make all the necessary preparation, can be found. The story notes in this handbook have done this for you and explain how each storybook can be used. Each set of notes contains lesson-by-lesson or activity-by-activity guidelines. In this way the storybooks, used in conjunction with the notes in this handbook, provide you with a novel and useful teaching-kit.

As we have already seen, one of the main reasons for using storybooks is to develop comprehension skills. As children enjoy hearing stories over and over again, they can develop these skills and build up confidence. Gradually, as pupils become more and more familiar with the story, they will participate by repeating key vocabulary and phrases. Very often they are able to memorize almost all of the narrative.

How can storybooks be used?

We have already discussed the ways in which storybooks can be used to supplement or complement a coursebook – or to provide short, basic syllabuses in their own right (see chapter 1). Which-ever way you choose, storybooks will give your pupils plenty of variety.

How long can a storybook be used?
This will depend on the amount of choice you have in selecting your own materials. If you have to work through a syllabus imposed from outside, you may not have a great deal of time to spare. You may, therefore, spend only a couple of lessons on each story. The notes in this handbook, however, contain activities related to each story that could be carried out over several lessons of forty-five to sixty minutes each.

Does each pupil require a copy of the storybook?
For the preparatory work and for many of the activities related to the storytelling, only the teacher requires a copy of the storybook. This is because a majority of the tasks are based on the pupils' predicting what comes next in the story or recapping it from memory. If they see the storybook at this stage much of the surprise element and active involvement is lost. You may find that at the end of a lesson you will have to be especially vigilant to stop your pupils peeping in the book when your back is turned!

When you have completed work on a story, it is a good idea to put some copies of the book into the classroom book corner or class library so that the children can look at them in their own time. This provides a natural introduction to the written word in English and to developing reading skills. Pupils may ask to have their own copy of the storybook. This, of course, will depend on resources available or on the type of contribution parents can make.

How many times should a story be read to the pupils?
The notes will suggest how many times – and when – to read a story. This may vary from reading the whole story once or twice each lesson, after appropriate preparation, to reading the whole story just a few times. Some notes suggest that you begin and finish each lesson by reading the story up to a certain point and that at each subsequent lesson you read a little more (see *The Snowman*). This repetition recycles language previously introduced and pupils learn to predict and to participate in the story and so build up confidence.

Don't pupils get bored if they hear the story over and over again?
Pupils positively enjoy hearing stories over and over again. Their confidence grows as they realize that they can remember more and more. It also presents them with the challenge of remembering new language. Participating in the storytelling becomes a kind of game activity.

What happens to any work pupils produce?
We suggest that every pupil has his or her own story folder or A4-size envelope for each story in which any related work such as language exercises, drawings, masks and so on can be kept. (All this work should be dated.) The envelope or folder can be decorated with drawings inspired by the story and pupils should write the

title of the story on the envelope. In this way children can build up their own personal record for each story. Storing and organizing work in this way teaches pupils important study skills.

Will the teacher have to use the mother tongue?
For stories with beginner pupils you may have to use the mother tongue from time to time. If your class shares a common language, this is quite natural. In fact, you would be denying your pupils a very useful learning strategy if you insisted on always using English. However, you should consider carefully when and why you would use the mother tongue. Obviously, the more you use English and the more your pupils get better at and more familiar with the language, the less you will need to use the mother tongue.

Here are some occasions when you might decide to use the mother tongue:

● Setting the scene by drawing upon the children's experience related to the story or their knowledge about the subject and language.

For example, for *Meg's Eggs*, pupils can complete a dinosaur quiz in English as an introduction to some of the key vocabulary and concepts. However, the mother tongue can be used to help pupils make informed guesses about the English words. Pupils could tell you what questions they would include in a quiz about dinosaurs or what questions they would expect to find. They can also look carefully at the questions and options to work out meaning and use other linguistic clues such as similarities with the mother tongue. Even if the pupils complete the quiz in their mother tongue, it will still prepare them for the story in English.

For example, many pupils are likely to be familiar with traditional stories or fairy-tales. As an introduction to *Little Red Riding Hood*, pupils could use their mother tongue to tell you what they remember about the tale.

● Predicting what comes next in a story.

For example, in *Meg and Mog* there is a flash and a bang after Meg chants her spell. In their mother tongue ask pupils if they think Meg's spell goes right or wrong. If their answer is the latter, ask them what they think happens.

For example, in *The Very Hungry Caterpillar* when you have read 'On Friday he ate through five oranges but he was still hungry', ask what day comes next and what pupils think the caterpillar eats. Alternatively the teacher could use English to ask, 'And on Saturday?' with a rising intonation and questioning expression.

● Providing a gloss of the main storyline beforehand. This is important with the more difficult stories such as *Mr Biff the Boxer* and *Mr Gumpy's Motor Car*.

● Eliciting vocabulary or phrases.

For example, in *The Elephant and the Bad Baby* you could ask pupils to say which food shops they think the elephant takes the bad baby to. If they do not know these words in English, they will need to make suggestions in their mother tongue. This provides you with an ideal opportunity to introduce the words in English as the need to know them has come from the pupils themselves and the context is clear.

● Explaining keywords, a grammatical rule or cultural information.

For example, 'kipper' in *Meg and Mog*. Translating a keyword may be a useful short cut if there are no illustrations to convey the meaning or if it is an abstract word.

● Reminding pupils of what has happened so far in the story.

● Explaining how to do an activity. For example, pair work or a game. The more familiar pupils become with these activities, the less you will need to use the mother tongue.

● Learning to learn. Many activities which require pupils to reflect on their learning or the language need to be carried out in the mother tongue with lower-level pupils.

Supporting children's understanding

How can the teacher help pupils to understand a story?
Using storybooks successfully in the classroom needs careful planning. Simply reading a story to a class without preparation can be disastrous with the loss of pupil attention, motivation and self-confidence. Although children are used to listening to stories in their mother tongue, understanding a story in a foreign language is hard work. Pupils' enjoyment will increase enormously if the teacher ensures that their understanding is supported in several

ways. The following guidelines provide a framework to make story-based lessons more accessible.

● Provide a context for the story and introduce the main characters. Help your pupils feel involved and link their experience with that in the story to set the scene. Relate the story to aspects of their own lives such as where they live, the animals they are familiar with, what they like or dislike, going shopping, having picnics, the people they know, etc. Once the context has been understood and the children can identify with the characters, then elicit key vocabulary and phrases, and involve pupils in predicting and participating in the story.

● Provide visual support: drawings on the blackboard, cut-out figures, speech bubbles, masks, puppets, real objects, flash cards, etc. Can pupils make any of these?

● Explain the context, keywords and ideas in the mother tongue, if necessary.

● Identify your linguistic objectives. Decide which language points your pupils need to recognize for comprehension when the story is told and which would be useful to reproduce such as lexical sets, language functions and structures, etc.

● Relate the story or associated activities to work in other subject areas if possible.

● Decide how long you will spend on the story. Will you use it once or twice or over a period of several lessons?

● Decide when you will read the story. Will you read a little each lesson – or all at once after appropriate preparation?

● Decide in which order to introduce or revise the language necessary for understanding the story. Make sure pupils understand the aims of each lesson and how it relates to the story. For example, learning vocabulary for the different food shops in *The Elephant and the Bad Baby*. Check that each lesson provides variety and the opportunity for recycling language previously introduced.

● If necessary, modify the story to make it more accessible to your pupils. Substitute unfamiliar words with better-known ones and adapt the sentence structure to make the story easier to follow, and so on. (See guidelines in the section, Adapting stories in chapter 2.)

- Find out if there are any rhymes or songs that pupils can learn to reinforce the language introduced. For example, they can learn the action rhyme 'Ten fat sausages' in the notes for *The Very Hungry Caterpillar*. This revises numbers and the words, fat, sausages and pop, from the story.

- Decide which follow-up activities would provide opportunities for pupils to use language from the story in different contexts. See, for example, the role-play in *The Elephant and the Bad Baby*.

Planning story-based lessons

How can the teacher plan story-based lessons?
Most of the notes in this handbook are broken down into lessons. For example, seven lessons are suggested for *The Very Hungry Caterpillar*. The aims of each lesson are defined and suggested procedures are given. However, you may wish to modify these. Whether you follow the guidelines closely or not, it is useful now and again to write out a detailed lesson-plan to help you define and clarify the aims of the lesson, and to think carefully about the types of activities pupils will be involved in to achieve the aims. It will also help you think about the classroom language to use both in the target language and in the mother tongue, and to see what materials (flash cards, real objects, etc.) to prepare or collect. Lesson-plans also give you a written record of what you have done with your pupils. Not only does this allow you to see what language work you have covered but it is also a measure of whether you vary your lessons enough in terms of activity types and interaction.

There are many different ways of writing a lesson-plan and, equally, of conducting a lesson. Below is a list of procedures which you may like to consider:

- Warm-up. For example, an informal chat aimed at building up and maintaining rapport with your pupils. This is especially important if you are a visiting teacher to the school. You could ask what the pupils did over the weekend, comment on work in the classroom, and so on.

- You can review or remind pupils of what they did in the previous lesson. Ask the questions 'What did we do last lesson?' or 'What did you learn last lesson?' This encourages pupils to reflect on what they did and provides you with valuable information about what your pupils found memorable.

- Explain what you are going to do in the lesson. You do not need to go into technical details here. Simply inform your pupils of the overall aim and of how they are going to work.

- Present new language. (See the story notes for a variety of techniques.)

- Controlled practice. Opportunities for pupils to practise the new language in carefully directed activities. (See the story notes for a variety of suggestions.)

- Production. Here your pupils should have the chance to use the new language relatively spontaneously. This may be in a game, an interview or a role-play, and is monitored by you.

- Reviewing at the end of the lesson. Ask, for example, 'What have we done today?' This provides pupils with another opportunity to reflect on the lesson, their participation in it and to confirm its aims.

- Prepare for the next lesson by explaining homework. Tell pupils about any preparation they may need to do for the next lesson.

This set of procedures is only one of many ways to conduct a lesson. However, children do feel secure when there is some kind of routine and established framework to work in, so the first three points and the last two could remain fixed. Your pupils will know where they are, as they are provided with clear signals for the different stages of a lesson.

On pages 28 and 29 there is a lesson-plan for *Pat the Cat* which incorporates the above procedures and which you may like to use as a model.

Improving storytelling skills

How can the teacher improve his or her storytelling skills?
There are a number of techniques you can use when reading stories aloud to make the experience more enjoyable and successful for your pupils. If they are unfamiliar with storytelling, begin with short sessions which do not demand too much from them and over-extend their concentration span.

- If possible, have children sit on the floor around you when you read the story, making sure everyone can see both your face and the illustrations in the story.

- Read slowly and clearly. Give your pupils time to think, ask

Lesson Planning Sheet

Date	11.6.90
Class	CM1 (9–10-year-olds, first year of English)
Length of lesson	50 minutes
Materials	*Pat the Cat*

Aims Structural	There's a cup on the table. There are two pens in the bag. Where's . . .?　　It's on the table. Where are . . .?　　They're under the table.
Functional	Asking for and giving information about location.
Skills	Listening to instructions. Speaking: asking and answering questions.
Phonological	Falling intonation: – Where's the cup? – It's on the table.
Vocabulary	Prepositions: on/in/under Nouns: hat, mat, bag, table (revision) cup, rat, cat, bug, caterpillars
Learning to learn	Reviewing Working independently of teacher (pair work) Self-checking Organizing work
Assumptions	Pupils already know the above nouns.

questions, look at the pictures, make comments. However do vary the pace of your voice when the story speeds up.

● Make comments about the illustrations. When you say a word, point to the illustration at the same time. For example, in *The Very Hungry Caterpillar*, when reading 'In the light of the moon a little egg lay on a leaf', point to the moon, the egg and the leaf. Involve your pupils actively by asking them also to point to the illustrations.

● Encourage your pupils to take part in the storytelling by repeating key vocabulary items and phrases. You can invite them to do this by pausing and looking at them with a questioning expression and by putting your hand to your ear to indicate that

Procedures			
Time of		Activity	Materials
lesson	stage		
1.30	5	Warm-up and review of work covered last lesson	
1.45	10	*Presentation* Show pupils cover of *Pat the Cat* to remind them of the story. Read the story emphasizing the prepositions in the appropriate lines. Repeat these lines and stop. Check comprehension asking a pupil to put a pencil *on* another child's desk/chair, etc. Continue with story, stop again and check comprehension by asking a pupil to put the pencil *in* his/her desk/bag, etc. Continue with story. Introduce *under*. Revise prepositions again by giving instructions.	Cover of book
2.00	15	*Controlled practice* i) *Action game*: Show pupils actions with hands for on/in/under. Call out prepositions at random and children respond by making the appropriate action. ii) *Picture dictation*: Distribute worksheet on p. 220. Dictate descriptions. Children draw and number each object (1–6) in the order described. Check by asking: Where's the cup?, etc.	Work-sheets
2.15	15	*Production*: Distribute worksheet on p. 221. Divide pupils into pairs, A and B. Pupils draw items. Pupil A: 1–4, Pupil B: 5–8. They must not show their partner. Check pupils can produce question and answer 'Where's the cup?', 'It's on the table,' etc. Tell pupils they have five minutes to complete the activity. Pupils draw items on worksheets according to the instructions given. Pupils then check their own work by comparing their drawings.	Work-Sheets
2.20	5	Review work covered in lesson. Pupils organize worksheets in their envelopes. Distribute homework. Ask pupils to prepare for next lesson by collecting magazine pictures of people with different expressions: happy, sad, angry, etc.	

you are waiting for them to join in. The accompanying cassette provides a demonstration of a teacher reading *The Very Hungry Caterpillar* with the pupils participating.

● Use gestures, mime, facial expressions, varied pace and tone. Adapt your voice to the different characters as much as you can to help convey meaning and to keep your pupils' attention.

As pupils enjoy hearing stories over and over again do read a story, or part of it, as often as possible, so your pupils hear English frequently. You can also use the cassette to allow pupils to listen to the story whenever they wish and to reinforce the learning of slower learners.

How can the teacher assess his or her skills as a storyteller?

Reading stories aloud is not an easy task and any teacher, whether a native speaker or not, needs to practise this skill. Use cassette recordings, when possible, to provide you with a model to copy. Try to rehearse at home or with another colleague, record yourself and compare it with the model. This will help develop your confidence and to hear which areas need improving. You may like to use the following self-assessment sheet to evaluate your performance.

PREPARATION

1 Familiarize yourself with the book, the story and illustrations.

2 Decide where you wish to pause in the story to invite your pupils to join in.

Using the cassette

Are the stories recorded on cassette?

The accompanying cassette contains recordings of some of the stories referred to in this handbook. However, we suggest you read each story to your pupils yourself, especially the first time they hear the story. This is important for the following reasons:

● It allows you to develop a personal rapport with your pupils and to involve them actively in the story.

● You can help make the story come alive through use of intonation, gesture, mime, and so on, and by making maximum use of the illustrations to help convey meaning.

● Reading a story to your pupils yourself is more flexible than

Self-Assessment Sheet

Find a private room where you can record yourself. Imagine you are reading the story to your pupils. When you have finished, listen to the recording and ask yourself the following questions:

1 Pronunciation. Did I have any problems with any vowels or consonants?

2 Stress. Did I have any problems with stress in individual words or in sentences?

3 Rhythm. Did I read too slowly or too quickly? Did I pause in the right places?

4 Intonation. Did I sound interesting or boring and did I vary my intonation where appropriate? Did I use the appropriate intonation for questions, statements, lists, and so on?

5 Variation. Did I vary the pace and the volume of my voice where appropriate? Did I adapt my voice enough for the different characters?

6 Pupil participation. Did I pause in the correct places and use appropriate intonation to invite pupils to join in? Did I ask the appropriate questions to encourage pupils to predict what comes next?

7 General impression. How did I sound in general? Clear? Expressive? Lively?

8 What do I need to improve? What shall I focus on this week?

This rehearsal will prepare you for reading a story to your pupils in the classroom. You may also like to record yourself and use the self-assessment sheet again when you do this using a cassette recording as it allows you to stop and ask pupils questions, so they can relate the story to their own experience. You can repeat a part of the story immediately if you sense the pupils have not understood. Encourage them to repeat or to predict what happens next or to join in, to clarify a language item or cultural detail, or to refer to some other work you have covered together.

Using the cassette can be beneficial for the following reasons:

- It provides variety by allowing pupils to hear English spoken by someone other than their teacher, another voice, another accent.

- The voice on the cassette provides a constant model and provides examples of English as spoken by a native speaker.

- Some recordings contain amusing sound-effects which are motivating and can help pupils guess the meanings of unknown words. See, for example, *Meg and Mog*.

- The voice on the cassette provides a model for the teacher to imitate by demonstrating a number of storytelling techniques such as adapting the voice for different characters, intonation patterns, stress and rhythm, altering the pace of the voice, and so on.

It is, however, important to bear in mind that playing a cassette recording of a story can become a mechanical activity unless it is used in a way that actively involves pupils in listening tasks. Where appropriate, these have been suggested in the story notes.

4 Developing language-learning skills

The skills which are emphasized most in the story notes are learning vocabulary, listening and speaking. Learning grammar and learning to read and write are generally not the chief objectives of using the storybooks. Remember that it is you, the teacher, who will read the story to the children. Many of the activities suggested in the section on writing are suitable for children who have been learning English for some time. Although the activities have been listed separately under each skill, there are many opportunities for integrating them.

Learning vocabulary

This section looks at different ways new vocabulary can be introduced and at activities for practising and checking vocabulary, and at those for consolidating vocabulary.

Introducing new vocabulary

The story notes highlight the main vocabulary areas in each story. Some will be for passive recognition only, so pupils will not be expected to produce it. They will be encouraged to repeat other items when the story is told or to use them in the activities suggested in the notes.

Vocabulary in stories is presented in a vivid and clear context and the illustrations help to convey meaning. Both the context and the amusing situations can make the vocabulary easy to remember. For example, you will probably find that pupils have no problem recalling the ten items the caterpillar eats through on the Saturday in *The Very Hungry Caterpillar*. Similarly, pupils are able to learn the vocabulary items necessary for the Bingo game in *Pat the Cat* with relative ease.

Research has shown that words are often remembered in groups which have something in common. Because of this, try to introduce new words in:

- lexical sets (for example, shops, fruit, rooms in a house)
- rhyming sets (see *Pat the Cat*, *Don't Forget the Bacon!*, *My Cat Likes to Hide in Boxes*)

- colour sets (grouping together objects that are green. For example, a pea, a leaf, an apple, a caterpillar, a bird)
- grammatical sets (for example, adjectives, verbs, prepositions, nouns).

Grouping words together in this way can help pupils associate new words with words they already know and can aid retention and recall.

Whenever possible, get pupils to use their senses: touch, smell, taste and sight to help memorize words and understand their meanings. For example, pupils could find something cold or hot in the classroom to touch.

Here are some techniques that can be used to introduce new vocabulary:

● Using objects
Much of the vocabulary at this stage of children's learning will consist of concrete nouns. This means that there are many objects that can be used to show meanings. You can use those in the classroom or bring in examples. Introducing a new word by showing the real object often helps pupils to memorize the word through this visualization.

● Drawing
Objects can either be drawn on the blackboard or on flash cards. The latter can be used again and again in different contexts if you make them on card and then cover them in plastic.

● Using illustrations and pictures in the storybooks
A great deal of vocabulary can be introduced by using the illustrations in the storybooks to help convey meaning.

● Mime, expressions and gestures
Many words can be introduced through mime, expressions and gestures. For example, adjectives: sad, happy; nouns: mime taking a hat off your head to teach 'hat', and so on.

● Using opposites
This technique works well for adjectives. See the examples in the notes for *Little Red Riding Hood* and the game Snap.

● Guessing from context
Encourage pupils to take risks and to guess the meanings of words

they don't know. This will help them build up self-confidence so that they can work out the meanings of words when they are on their own. They are many clues pupils can use to establish meanings for themselves:

a pictures in the storybooks
b similarity of spelling or sound in the mother tongue
c general knowledge.

● **Eliciting**
Once the context is established, you can ask pupils (you may need to do this in the mother tongue) what they would expect someone to say or do in a particular situation. See the notes for *Meg and Mog*, Lesson Four, where this method is used to introduce the ingredients for Meg's spell.

● **Translation**
If none of the above techniques works, translate. There are always some words that need to be translated and this technique can save time.

When using any of the above techniques, you can follow this procedure. Illustrate the word in one of the ways above. If a child knows the word, get him or her to say it and use this as your model if it is correct. If not, say the word yourself. Ask the class to repeat it. Check pronunciation. Say the word again if necessary. Ask individual pupils to repeat the word and then ask the whole class again. You may then want to write the word on the board.

Practising and checking vocabulary
Once a new word has been introduced you will want to provide opportunities for pupils to practise it and for you to check that they understand it. Here are a variety of activities you can use to do this:

● **What's missing?**
This game can be played by using illustrations made by you and stuck on the board, or drawn (or written) straight on to the board. The number of items you include will depend on the level of your pupils, but you may need to limit them to a maximum of ten. Ask pupils to close their eyes. Remove an item from the board. Pupils open their eyes and tell you what is missing. You could ask the rest of the class, 'Is he or she right?' This game can also be played as a team game. Divide the class into two teams. Play as above

with each team taking a turn. Each time a pupil is correct he or she wins a point for the team.

● **Kim's Game**
This works in the same way as the game above, using objects displayed on a tray or a table.

● **Matching words to pictures**
Pupils match words to the correct picture. See *Spot's Birthday Party*, where pupils match prepositions to hiding-places. For example, *under* the mat, *in* the cupboard, and so on.

● **Guessing games**
Hide-and-seek A pupil leaves the classroom while the others hide an object. The child comes back and must guess where it is hidden. For example, 'Is it under the table?' This practises prepositions and nouns. (See *Where's Spot?*)

Mime A pupil can mime an animal, a profession, or anything he or she chooses, and the class must guess what it is or who they are. 'Is it a ——?' 'Are you a ——?'

● **Giving instructions/Picture dictation**
The teacher gives instructions focusing on specific vocabulary. For example, colours and shapes: 'Show me a red square!'; colours and numbers: 'Colour number four red!'; objects: 'Show me a table!', 'Draw a table!', 'Touch a table!', and so on.

● **Sequencing**
Jumble up pictures on the board. The teacher or a pupil gives instructions; 'Put the chocolate cake first!', and so on.

● **Labelling**
Pupils label a picture. For example, see *Little Red Riding Hood* where pupils label the parts of the body.

● **Bingo**
Bingo can take various forms and the board can consist of words or pictures. As words are called out, pupils put down picture cover-cards or word cover-cards.

● **Classifying/Sorting**
Pupils sort words into different categories. For example, hot and cold in *The Snowman*, sweet or salty in *The Very Hungry Caterpillar*.

● **Dominoes**

Here children practise reading and matching words which rhyme. See *Don't Forget the Bacon!*

● **Word stars**

Pupils arrange words which rhyme on a star diagram. This organization provides a rich visual contextualization. (See *Pat the Cat.*) If pupils keep a vocabulary book or a picture dictionary, words could also be organized in this way. (See below.)

● **Memory Games**

Chinese Whispers Give one pupil in a group or team a list of words which they must remember and then whisper to the next child. This child whispers to the next child and so on until the last child is reached. This child must compare the list with the original one and see if it has changed. (See *Where's Spot?* and *Don't Forget the Bacon!*)

Market game A child begins, 'I went to market and bought a pie.' The next child adds an item. 'I went to market and bought a pie and a bun,' and so on. (See *The Elephant and the Bad Baby* for further details.)

Remembering details from a story In *The Very Hungry Caterpillar* pupils remember how many different sorts of fruit the caterpillar ate and work out what it ate through. In *Spot's Birthday Party* pupils recall which animals hid where and match a picture of the animal to a picture of the hiding-place.

● **Word machines**

These can be used to help children develop a working knowledge of possible letter combinations and it also helps with spelling. The machine changes a word by performing one (or more) adaptation(s) to form a new word. (See *Don't Forget the Bacon!* for further details.)

There are, of course, many other activities that can be used to practise vocabulary and you may like to develop some of these yourself: crosswords, hangman, odd word out, card games such as Snap and Happy Families, I Spy, and so on.

Consolidating vocabulary

Many children learn new words relatively quickly but they also forget them quickly too. Once new vocabulary has been introduced and practised, pupils should be encouraged to devise techniques they can use on their own to consolidate and revise vocabulary. Many similar words appear in different stories. For example, food items in *Don't Forget the Bacon!*, *The Very Hungry Caterpillar* and *The Elephant and the Bad Baby*. This provides an ideal opportunity to revise words and to introduce new ones from the same lexical set. What can pupils do with words as they learn them? Many ask to write them down as this aids retention. Here are some techniques you can propose to your pupils which will allow them to build up their own personalized vocabulary-learning strategies.

● **Picture dictionaries/Vocabulary books**

Encourage pupils to create their own picture dictionaries or vocabulary books. Discuss ways of organizing these: alphabetically or by topic. It is useful for pupils to use a ring-folder for this purpose so they can add new pages when necessary. Pupils collect or draw pictures to illustrate the meaning of a word. They can write the word too. Some may want to do so in their own language. Do not stop children doing this, as for some it can be a useful learning strategy.

A class dictionary can also be made in the same way and hung on the classroom wall. (See *I Can Do It!*)

It is a good idea to have a dictionary for classroom use which will enable pupils to find out the meaning of new words themselves and help them develop useful study skills. This could be a picture dictionary (for example, *The Puffin First Picture Dictionary*), a bilingual dictionary, or an elementary monolingual dictionary. Some story notes encourage pupils to make use of a dictionary. (See *Meg and Mog*, where pupils are invited to write their own spells.)

● **Word families/sets**

Encourage pupils to build up their own word sets as an alternative to a picture dictionary. Pictures can be copied from the stories, coloured and labelled, and kept in envelopes which can be labelled, for example, Clothes, Fruit, Toys. (See *The Snowman* for further details.)

● **Vocabulary cards**

Pupils can make their own sets of vocabulary cards for self-testing. Discuss ways of conveying meaning: a picture, a translation, putting the word in a sentence. On one side of the card pupils draw, for example, a picture and on the other they write the word in English. They pick up a card, look at the picture and try to recall the word in English. They can then turn over the card and check if they are correct.

● **Collages**

Making collages is a useful way of revising vocabulary. Pupils collect pictures around a particular theme. For example, hot and cold objects in *The Snowman* or emotions in *Pat the Cat*. They stick these on to a large sheet of paper which can be used to decorate the classroom. More pictures can be added on an on-going basis.

● **Researching**

Encourage pupils to look for similarities between English words and words in their own language and to build up a wall display or collage. Alternatively, they may like to look for English words that are used in their country on food packets, clothes, in the street, and so on, which will provide a language awareness activity. (See *Don't Forget the Bacon!* for further details.)

Learning grammar

Stories introduce pupils to the grammatical structures of English in a natural and authentic way and the rich context helps them understand the meanings they convey. Furthermore, as children enjoy listening to stories over and over again, certain structures can be acquired without being formally or explicitly introduced. The natural repetition in some stories also encourages pupils to join in when the story is being told in a type of pattern practice.

Appropriate language use requires a knowledge of both the form and the functions of a language. The story notes, therefore, outline the structures and functions for each of the stories to be presented to beginner learners and practised by them. Many of these consist of Wh– questions and Yes/No questions, statements, instructions and simple descriptions which arise from the related language activities. For further details regarding stories and language features, see the chart on pages 14 and 15.

Presenting a structure

The following procedure for presenting a structure is one that is used frequently in the story notes.

To present the structure 'Do you like ——?' 'Yes, I do'/'No, I don't':

PRESENTATION

● Revise vocabulary for different food items.

● Hold up a picture and ask, 'Nicholas, do you like sausages?' He will probably reply, 'Yes' or 'No' at this stage.

- Using different pictures, ask two or three other pupils the question. Now say, 'Listen! "Yes I do." Repeat!' The whole class repeats. 'Again!' Now ask individual pupils to repeat until you are satisfied with the pronunciation. Ask the question again and insist on the reply 'Yes, I do.'

- Introduce 'No, I don't' by repeating this procedure.

- Give a picture to a pupil and say, 'Ask me!' The pupil may be able to produce the question 'Do you like cherry pie?', maybe not. If yes, ask him or her to repeat the question and get the class to repeat it. If not, ask the question yourself and get the class to repeat it. Then ask individual pupils as above.

- Now give a picture to a pupil and instruct him or her to ask another pupil: 'Nicholas, ask Sarah!' Nicholas asks, 'Sarah, do you like ice-cream?' Sarah replies, 'Yes, I do,' or 'No, I don't.' Continue in this way until you are satisfied.

- You may or may not wish to write the question and answer on the board.

CONTROLLED PRACTICE

- Now choose a picture but do not let your pupils see what it is. Invite them to ask, 'Do you like salami?' and so on until someone gives the word for the food item in the picture.

- Pupils now play the game in pairs.

PRODUCTION

- Now distribute worksheets (see page 133). This activity involves pupils in interviewing. They go round the class asking about their classmates' likes and dislikes. Monitor or join in the activity yourself. If you find pupils are having problems, make a note of what these are and revise them after the activity.

- To round off the activity, pupils can collate their information on worksheets.

This procedure allows a structure to be presented, practised and produced in a controlled framework. Pupils move from a situation tightly directed by the teacher to one where they direct their own learning.

The procedure can be successfully applied to teaching other

structures. See the lesson-plan on pages 28–9 where prepositions and the question and answer: 'Where's the ——?', 'It's —— the ——' are presented in the same way.

For further ideas on how to present, practise and produce structures see Learning to speak on page 45.

DISCOVERY GRAMMAR ACTIVITIES

Many pupils in Europe are well grounded in formal grammar in their own language and understand the metalanguage (language of a higher or second-order kind) to describe it. Teachers of English can, therefore, capitalize on this by encouraging pupils to compare their own language with English to spot similarities and differences and attempt to work out the rules of English grammar for themselves. This approach turns grammar into a problem-solving activity where pupils consolidate knowledge of a structure that has been introduced as suggested above or establish the structure for themselves without an explanation from the teacher.

Story notes that include discovery grammar activities are *Meg and Mog* (working out word order), *The Very Hungry Caterpillar* (attempting to work out the difference between countable and uncountable nouns) and *The Elephant and the Bad Baby* (working out the use of the indefinite articles a and an). There are many other occasions when these activities could be used and you may like to devise appropriate activities yourself.

Learning to listen

Helping children to listen with understanding is much easier if they are motivated and actively engaged while listening. It is important to remember that listening is not a passive activity. Asking children simply to 'listen and remember' places a great strain not only on their listening skills but also on their memory. Children will be able to listen with understanding more effectively if their attention is directed to specific points to listen for. This can be achieved by using activities which support learners' understanding, such as those which provide some kind of visual support or written framework.

Points to bear in mind when supporting listening can be summarized as follows:

Give the children confidence

Make sure the children know that they cannot always be expected to understand every word. You need to be clear in your own mind if you are asking the children to understand only the general content of a story – the 'gist' of the storyline. Alternatively, you might choose a smaller part of the story and ask the children to focus more on specific details, such as following the exact sequence of events.

Help the children to develop strategies for listening

Linked to the first point is the need to encourage children to use intelligent guesswork when listening. Explain that they can use their background knowledge to work out the meaning of new words, or draw upon any information given in pictures or in charts connected with the story. They may even be encouraged to notice your body language or the way you use your voice to stress important words which might give them some clues about the meaning. The most important listening strategies include:

- predicting: it is useful to encourage children to predict what they think might come next in a story. This means that they then listen to check whether their expectation matches the reality of what they hear. Many of the stories have repeating sequences which make prediction much easier. Children's success in this task makes them feel more confident.

- inferring opinion or attitude: an awareness of stress, intonation and body language – such as facial expressions or gestures – will help the children work out if a character is angry, happy, sad and so on. This contributes to understanding the story. (See the notes for *Pat the Cat*.)

- working out the meaning from context: although keywords might be glossed before the story is told, children need to be encouraged to use pictures and their general knowledge about a topic to work out the meaning of unfamiliar words.

- recognizing discourse patterns and markers (words such as: first, then, finally or: but, and, so) gives important signals about what is coming next in a story. Again, the repeated sequences of stories help the learner to predict from such discourse markers what might be coming next.

Explain why the children are listening

Make explicit the reasons why the children are listening. This means spelling out what they need to focus on and what they are going to do while they listen or afterwards. For example, the children could draw as they are listening. They will need to know that the words to focus on will be key nouns, along with adjectives, which describe colour, size or shape, and prepositions, which describe their position in relation to each other. Different kinds of listening purpose are described below:

- listening to improve general listening attitude: this includes listening for enjoyment, listening to improve concentration span, or listening to develop the memory. Various listening games are useful here such as Simon Says.

- listening to develop aspects of language: this includes listening to improve the pronunciation of sounds, stress and rhythm, and intonation in English, as well as becoming familiar with new words and structural patterns. Listening to learn songs and rhymes provides important pronunciation practice, while listening to stories may provide practice in the simple past tense or with vocabulary connected to the topic of weather.

- listening to reinforce conceptual development: many stories will act as useful revision for reinforcing concepts such as colours, size, or cause and effect, which will have been covered in other areas of the school curriculum.

- listening to interact with others: listening is an important part of communicating with others. Activities which encourage children to work with others, for example, when carrying out surveys in pairs or playing games in groups, require the learners to negotiate meaning by listening and asking questions, checking meaning, agreeing and so on.

Set a specific listening task

To make listening an active process, teachers need to develop a repertoire of different activity types which 'fit' different types of language. When listening to a series of actions in a narrative, for example, a listening task which asks the children to rearrange a series of pictures, or put numbers by pictures describing different actions, supports the child's understanding very well. If learners are asked to listen to something (without visual support) and simply to recall the facts, they are being 'tested' rather than 'taught'. It is important, therefore, to teach listening by making explicit to children all the strategies outlined earlier, as well as by using a range of tasks which the learners complete while they are listening. The while-listening activities which follow should give you an idea of the different possibilities. You will probably be able to add some of your own.

- **Listen and repeat**

  Examples of this are found in games such as Chinese Whispers, which is described in *Don't Forget the Bacon!*, or in memory-training games used in *The Elephant and the Bad Baby*, *Meg and Mog*, among others. Other games focus the learners' attention by asking them to repeat something only if it is true.

- **Listen and discriminate**

  In this kind of activity the learners' attention is often focused on pronunciation features, such as listening for words which rhyme, or on selecting phrases which have the same rhythmic pattern. Examples can be seen in the notes for *Don't Forget the Bacon!*, *Pat the Cat* and *My Cat Likes to Hide in Boxes*.

- **Listen and perform actions/follow instructions**

  This kind of activity is used with action songs, rhymes or games such as Blind Man's Buff or What's the Time, Mr Wolf? Examples can be seen in *Having a Picnic* and *Little Red Riding Hood*. Following instructions can also be used as a listening activity when the learner is asked to trace a route on a plan or map. This is a good exercise to practise: left, right, next to, first, second, third, etc. If the children find this very difficult to do even in their mother tongue, do not attempt it in English.

- **Listen and draw/colour**

  Picture dictation is often used to help children focus on key nouns and on adjectives which describe colour, size, shape, and so on. The picture can be drawn in its entirety or one which has missing items can have these added as children listen. These activities can be seen in *The Snowman*, *The Elephant and the Bad Baby*, *Pat the Cat* and *Meg and Mog*.

- **Listen and label**

  This activity is used with drawings, maps or diagrams where the learners are asked to listen to a description of an animal, person or place in order to label key parts. The written labels can be provided for the children to match up or words could be on the blackboard for the children to write themselves. This approach is explained in more detail in *Spot's Birthday Party*.

- **Listen and guess**

  This listening is often based on the description of something whose identity the children have to guess. It is used in *Meg and Mog*.

● **Listen and predict**
This has already been described in some detail and can be seen in many of the story notes.

● **Listen and match**
This usually involves matching pictures to spoken words and is common in games such as Bingo. More details can be found in *Pat the Cat*, *Where's Spot?* and *Spot's Birthday Party*. For older children listening can involve matching pictures or words – such as those in speech bubbles – to other written texts. Examples can be seen in the notes on *The Turnip*.

● **Listen and sequence**
As described earlier, this activity is usually based on pictures or written phrases which the children rearrange into the correct order while they listen to a narrative. Examples of this activity are in the notes for *The Snowman* and *Mr Biff the Boxer*.

● **Listen and classify**
This activity is also usually based on pictures; the children listen carefully to a series of descriptions and sort pictures into different sets.

● **Listen and transfer information**
This usually involves interaction in pairs or groups. The children carry out a survey or complete a questionnaire where they ask each other questions and listen carefully for the answers. The responses are recorded on a chart to help the children remember details and to consolidate understanding. You can see examples of surveys of likes and dislikes, using charts, in *The Very Hungry Caterpillar*, *Don't Forget the Bacon!* and *The Snowman*.

Learning to speak

Expectations

Most children equate learning a foreign language with learning to speak it and, because learning to speak their mother tongue was a seemingly easy task, they expect it to be the same with the foreign language. They want immediate results and even after their first lesson will want to show other children in the school or members of their family that they can speak some English. The comments below from young beginners in France, who were asked what they hoped to be able to do in English by the end of the year, reflect this

45

attitude. The comments also reveal that they expect to learn quickly in order to communicate with other people: 'I hope to speak it', 'I want to speak well', 'I want to understand well and reply without hesitating' and 'I want to have conversations with English people.'

The comments show a strong motivation to learn. If children are to sustain this, they need to be given opportunities to speak English as soon as possible, and as much as possible, so they feel they are making progress and fulfilling their expectations.

The initial stages

It is important that children leave their first few lessons with some English to 'take away'. It is useful to begin an English programme by teaching vocabulary for simple concepts such as numbers, colours, etc., which can provide the basis for subsequent activities. First lessons often focus on simple greetings and introductions. For example, Hello! What's your name?/My name's ——/This is——. Pupils can be given 'English' names, although they should be allowed to keep their own names if they choose. Where possible, give the closest English equivalent or anglicize a name, for example, Mehdi/Meddy. Learning English names provides pronunciation practice. Teaching pupils a few rhymes and songs at the beginning of their course will also give them the impression that they are learning to speak English quickly.

Many language programmes begin with a lesson to help pupils understand why they are learning English. For example, they may be asked to think of famous people who speak English; where English is spoken in the world, etc. They may also be asked to think of any English words they know such as hamburger, steak, sandwich, tennis, football, jeans, hotel, taxi, television, etc. They can compare how these words are pronounced in their own language as an introduction to the features of English pronunciation. This type of reflection heightens children's awareness of the use of language and builds up their confidence by making them realize how much English they know already.

Formulaic language

In the early stages of learning you cannot expect much spontaneous speech from your pupils. The English they will learn to produce will be what is known as formulaic language. This consists of routines or patterns which children memorize and which enable them to communicate with a minimum of linguistic competence. As this type of language is repeated regularly, children learn it quickly and feel they are making progress. Such language consists of:

- Simple greetings: Hello! How are you?/I'm fine, thank you. And you?

- Social English: Did you have a nice weekend?/Have a nice weekend!

- Routines: What's the date?/What's the weather like today?, etc.

- Classroom language: Listen!/Repeat!/Sit down!/Work in pairs! Good!/It's your turn!/Be quiet!, etc.

- Asking permission: Pupils can be encouraged to do this if you prepare five or six cards with common requests written on them. For example, Can I/May I go to the toilet?/Can I clean the board?/Can I wash my hands?/Can I put the book away?, etc. Attach these to a board at the front of the class. Each time a child wishes to ask one of the above questions, he or she must take the appropriate card and ask you the question. This will combine reading with speaking practice and can also be used throughout the school day and not just during the English class.

- Communication strategies: If you want children to use English as much as possible in the classroom, it is important that they learn a number of phrases to participate in and maintain communication in English. Here are some of the phrases they could learn: Can you say that again, please?/How do you say —— in English, please?/What does —— mean, please?/I don't understand!/Can I have a —— please?, and so on.

As children hear this language over and over again they soon learn to use it and realize that certain questions and requests can be made in English. Very often pupils will tell other pupils to listen if they are chatting or to sit down if they are moving about! These phrases could also be written out in speech bubbles and stuck around the classroom.

Speaking activities
Speaking practice in the early stages of learning will mainly be initiated by the teacher and will consist of simple questions and answers. However, pupils can be given opportunities to initiate conversation too by playing games such as Kim's Game or guessing games.

Features

Below is a list of the activities described in the story notes which provide opportunities for pupils to learn to speak in English:

● Activity type: those which offer opportunities for very controlled practice or communication practice. (See, Learning grammar and the lesson-plan on pages 28–9 which show how pupils move from a very controlled activity to one where they can move on to real communication.)

● Fun: games, songs, rhymes.

● Interaction patterns: these include: teacher/whole class; teacher/individual pupil; pupil/pupil (pupils speaking in turn in front of the class); whole class works in pairs or groups at the same time.

● Response: activities range from those which require a one-word response to those which need whole sentences or dialogues.

● Confidence building: the variety of activity types allow all pupils to participate according to their ability and stage in learning.

● Accuracy/fluency: some activities allow for practice in accuracy, others for fluency. It is important that children know which aspect an activity is developing and why you will correct pupils more in activities focusing on accuracy than in those concentrating on fluency.

● Amount of talking time: each pupil in an average class of twenty-five pupils will have very little time to speak English if exercises are always done round the class where one pupil says one sentence each. This would also become very boring. Pupils will have many more opportunities to practise speaking if you build into your lessons opportunities for pupils to work together in pairs or groups where all the pupils are working at the same time. This also helps them feel much more involved in a lesson and helps them learn to work together. For details on organizing, pair and group work see chapter 6 'Classroom Management'.

Activities

The following activities progress from tightly controlled practice to freer communication. (See Learning grammar for suggested procedures for presenting new structures.)

● **Look, listen and repeat**

This technique is used to introduce new vocabulary and characters in the stories. The teacher shows a picture, says the word and pupils repeat. 'Look! An elephant. Repeat!' When the teacher is satisfied with the pupils' pronunciation he or she will move on to another word. Once several animals have been introduced, the teacher can check by asking, 'What's this?' and pupils repeat, 'A dog' or 'It's a dog', etc. The same technique, using a word card instead of a picture card, will provide basic reading practice.

● **Listen and participate**

When a story is told, children are encouraged to participate by repeating key vocabulary and phrases to involve them actively in the storytelling process. Techniques for encouraging pupils to participate are described in chapter 3.

● **Reading aloud**

Certain games require pupils to read words or sentences aloud. For example, in Phonetic Bingo, described in *Pat the Cat*, the winner must read back the words on his or her cover-cards. In the Emotion Game (also described in *Pat the Cat*) pupils read sentences conveying different emotions and their partner shows a picture with the matching facial expression.

● **Memory games**

Games like 'I went to market and bought ——' and Chinese Whispers require pupils to memorize and repeat.

● **Dramatization**

This involves pupils in learning lines for their role and can provide them with a memorable occasion to practise English.

● **Rhymes, action rhymes, songs, chants**

Children learn to speak by imitating. Repeating rhymes, songs or chants provides an ideal context in which to practise English pronunciation and consolidate or introduce new language. Rhymes or songs with actions also provide exercise and encourage body control.

● **Retelling a story**

When a story is retold, children can be allocated a different character's lines and say them when appropriate. (See *The Turnip* and *Spot's Birthday Party*.)

● **Look and ask**

As a preparation for freer activities such as pair work or questionnaires and surveys, the teacher can use picture prompt cards. In *The Very Hungry Caterpillar*, after introducing the question, 'How many plums are there?' and getting the answer, 'There are three plums', the teacher gives a picture card (five oranges) to a pupil and instructs him or her to ask another pupil: 'Benjamin, ask Mary!' Benjamin shows Mary the picture and asks, 'How many oranges are there?' Mary replies. The teacher can then ask the class, 'Is that right?' This provides controlled practice where the pupils are focusing on producing the correct form and pronunciation.

● **Guessing games**

These games usually involve pupils in asking questions or describing something or someone. For example, pupils draw a picture of an animal they would like to have as a pet, without showing the class. The class must guess what it is. 'Is it a cat?', etc. Pupils can also describe someone in the class without saying her (or his) name. 'She's got long hair. She's wearing a red pullover', etc. and the other pupils must listen and guess, 'It's Sarah!' Examples of this game can be found in *Meg and Mog*.

● **Information gap**

These activities are usually carried out in pairs or groups and often involve pupils in asking and answering questions. One partner has some information that the other does not. The aim is to find out what this is so as to complete a task. (See *Pat the Cat* and *Spot's Birthday Party*.)

● **Questionnaires and surveys**

The aim here is to interview other classmates about, for example, their abilities, their likes and dislikes, and to collate the information on a chart. Examples can be found in *I Can Do It!*, *The Very Hungry Caterpillar* and *Meg and Mog*.

● **Role-play**

Role-play provides an opportunity for language that has been presented in a story to be used in a different context. For example, pupils act out a shopping dialogue inspired by *The Elephant and the Bad Baby* and *Don't Forget the Bacon!*

Learning pronunciation

Inevitably, there will be many differences in pronunciation between the pupils' mother tongue and English. Children are generally good at imitating and will pick up your model of pronunciation more easily than adults would. Some remedial work may be needed but usually pronunciation teaching forms an integral part of your presentation of new words and sentence patterns, and of subsequent practice activities. The use of songs and rhymes will be particularly important to develop a feel for English and an awareness of the way it sounds. The use of pronunciation drills, especially those which contrast words with different sounds, is not appropriate for young learners. The practice is meaningless and de-contextualized and the children will easily become bored. Many practice activities, such as making surveys using Yes/No questions, or games, will more naturally involve repetition to create opportunities for pronunciation practice.

A brief overview of the main areas of pronunciation difficulties which teachers need to be aware of is shown below:

Individual sounds

The accompanying cassette provides a recording of all the sounds of English, using words taken from the storybooks which you can use as a model. Here is the list of phonetic symbols used in the notes and a list of the words used on the cassette.

STORY-BASED PHONETIC ALPHABET

/ɪ/	as in witch	/ɪə/	as in ear
/e/	leg	/eə/	pear
/æ/	bat	/a/	park
/ɒ/	pop	/ɔ/	ball
/ʊ/	book	/ʊə/	pour
/ʌ/	bun	/ɜ/	bird
/ə/	butcher	/tʃ/	cherry
/i/	cheese	/dʒ/	jam
/eɪ/	cake	/ŋ/	sing
/aɪ/	pie	/θ/	thin
/ɔɪ/	boy	/ð/	they
/jʊ/	new	/ʃ/	shop
/aʊ/	house	/ʒ/	television
/əʊ/	snow	/j/	you
/u/	blue		

There may be some consonant sounds which are not present in the mother tongue but which occur in English. There will not necessarily be problems in articulating them, although some may present difficulties. One example is /ð/, which occurs in English but not in French. In cases like this, it will be useful to demonstrate how these sounds are made by showing what should be happening to the lips, tongue and teeth.

The pronunciation of vowels is more likely to cause problems; again the teacher needs to demonstrate the way in which these sounds are made. For example, whether the mouth is quite open or closed, and whether the lips are rounded or spread out. Try, wherever possible, to demonstrate the word on its own first of all, but move quickly to putting it in a sentence so that pronunciation practice is more meaningful. It may be necessary to spend a little time making the children aware of the differences between /ɪ/and /i/. For example, using the technique of ear-training. Children may find it difficult to distinguish between two sounds if they cannot hear first that the sounds are actually different. Listening exercises and games where the children learn to hear these differences can include listening for sounds which are the same or different, or by spotting the odd man out in a series. Examples can be seen in Phonetic Bingo as described in *Pat the Cat*.

Sounds in connected speech

It is important that pronunciation teaching does not concentrate exclusively on the production of individual sounds. How sounds blend together in informal speech is equally important. One feature present in English is 'linking', where certain sounds are run on together to avoid a jerky, staccato sound. This happens particularly where a word ending in a consonant is followed by a word beginning with a vowel. Four examples can be seen in the following rhyme:

CHARLIE THE CHIMPANZEE

Charlie has a cheerful face,
He loves to chatter, chuckle, chase,
The children come to watch him too,
For Charlie Chimp is in the zoo.

Linking the words in this way helps to keep the smooth flow of English. This rhyme is also useful for practising the consonant /tʃ/; long vowels such as /a/ and /u/; short vowels such as /æ/ and /ɪ/ and diphthongs such as /eɪ/.

Stress and rhythm

English is a stress-timed language in that stressed beats occur at roughly equal intervals of time, regardless of how many syllables there are between each beat. A useful way of demonstrating this is to ask the children to clap to the strong beats, while adding more and more syllables between the claps (strong beats are in capital letters):

ONE		TWO		THREE		FOUR
ONE	and	TWO	and	THREE	and	FOUR
ONE	and a	TWO	and a	THREE	and a	FOUR
ONE	and then a	TWO	and then a	THREE	and then a	FOUR

Songs and rhymes are an excellent illustration of the way in which stress and rhythm work in English. Again the children can be asked to clap the rhythm.

Words which tend to be stressed are important 'content' words including nouns, verbs, adjectives, adverbs. When a word is stressed three things tend to happen: the stressed word sounds slightly louder than the others, the vowel in the stressed word is clearly articulated and so it tends to sound longer than the other words. Try to notice this with the two rhymes above. What also happens is that the words which do not have stress often have to be said rather quickly to fit them in. This means that they sound shorter and the vowel sounds are not so clearly articulated. In fact the vowels often change to an easily pronounced vowel such as /ə/; /ʊ/ and /ɪ/. When this happens these words are said to be 'weak' forms. These occur most commonly with 'grammatical' words in a sentence such as the articles, auxiliary verbs or modals, and pronouns or prepositions, when they are not a very important part of the message. Weak forms in 'Charlie the Chimpanzee' are: a, to, the, for, which are pronounced /ə/; /tə/; /ðə/; /fə/.

Intonation

Some of the most important functions of intonation in English are to help emphasize the most strongly stressed word in a sentence, to show the grammatical function of what you are saying (for example whether something is a statement or question) and to show feelings and emotions. The story notes, such as those for *Don't Forget the Bacon!* and *Pat the Cat* show many examples of particular intonation patterns and their meaning. The most usual intonation pattern in English uses a falling tone. This is used to make:

● a short statement

for example, 'We can't pull up the turnip'

- questions with words such as who, what, why, etc.

  for example, 'Where's Spot?'

- commands
  for example, 'One, two, three, PULL!'

- exclamations to show surprise, anger or give a warning.

  for example, 'Look out!'

The rising tone is used:

- to make requests
  for example, 'May we come too?'

- to make questions from statements

  for example, 'A pile of chairs?'

- in Yes/No questions
  for example, 'Would you like a ride?'

- in clauses or phrases that come before the main clause in the sentence.
  for example, 'But when the woman had gone, the gruel looked so good that the cat ate it all.'

Improving your own pronunciation
The cassette will provide a useful model for pronunciation. When you listen to the recorded stories, try to become more aware of some of the features discussed above. Listen to as much 'authentic' English as possible, such as radio broadcasts. You might like to record yourself speaking and note your main strengths and weaknesses in pronunciation. If you pick one area at a time to work on, you should gradually build up confidence and fluency. For further suggestions see the section on Self-assessment on page 31.

Learning to read

The process of comprehension when listening to the spoken word is similar in many respects to understanding the written word. Learners need to know, for example, why they are reading something. Are they reading for general understanding or reading for detail? In the first case, learners might be asked to follow the written version of the story while they listen to it again for reinforcement of comprehension. In the second case, they might be asked to scan a chart quickly while listening to a description so that they can tick certain columns, or to read written statements to check if something is true or false. Learners also need to develop confidence in applying similar sorts of strategies as those used in listening to work out the meaning of words from context. The use of pictures and general knowledge of a topic may help young learners to guess the meaning of unfamiliar words. Recognizing discourse markers (such as but and so) also helps the children to anticipate that the next statement will explain some kind of difference or the result of something happening. The benefits of prediction in aiding comprehension are as important in reading as in listening.

It is wise not to place too many reading demands on younger learners at an early stage of reading development. Children in many countries will have a working knowledge of the Roman alphabet, although those from Greece or Turkey will need to spend more time learning to form and recognize letters which differ from their alphabets. Early work could be carried out on noticing similarities and differences between alphabets, such as the absence of accents for French speakers or tildes for Spanish speakers. It is also a good idea to encourage children to notice any examples of written English in their local environment. There may be signs, notices or advertisements in English which they could collect. This kind of reading awareness is a useful prelude to encouraging children to think about text types and different reading purposes such as reading stories for enjoyment and signs for information.

Reading in English in the early stages will usually remain at the word level, where children play simple games such as Dominoes, Snap or Bingo to become familiar with typical letter combinations and thereby to reinforce word recognition. The learners at this stage will still need to rely on pictorial information to provide a context for understanding the word. Other activities such as labelling pictures or reading lists help them to recognize keywords in a story. Gradually the children will become more confident in reading the written word on its own.

The use of charts provides an intermediate stage in reading development and a framework to support children's speaking skills. Reading practice may also be derived from listening work or may lead to writing. In this way reading becomes integrated with other language skills.

The following activities summarize the kinds of reading activities which are used in the story notes:

Reading, word recognition and pronunciation practice

- playing games such as Rhyming Dominoes, Bingo and Snap: here the children learn to recognize words and match words which rhyme (for example, *Don't Forget the Bacon!*, *Little Red Riding Hood*)

- matching words in sentences: the children match two halves of a sentence so that they rhyme (for example, *Don't Forget the Bacon!*, *My Cat Likes to Hide in Boxes*)

- reading aloud: the children practise reading sentences aloud using the appropriate stress and intonation (for example, *My Cat Likes to Hide in Boxes*, *Pat the Cat*).

Reading as a prompt for speaking

- using vocabulary prompt cards to make statements: the use of pictures as prompts rehearses sentences patterns such as 'I can skate' (for example, *I Can Do It!*, *The Elephant and the Bad Baby*)

- reading and ticking a chart to make sentences or ask questions: this also provides a guided context for rehearsing specific structural patterns

   I Can Do It!, *Don't Forget the Bacon!*, *The Very Hungry Caterpillar*, *The Turnip*, *My Cat Likes to Hide in Boxes*, *Mr Biff the Boxer*, *The Snowman*

- reading words and rearranging them to make sentences: a useful way of checking comprehension and the understanding of word order (for example, *Meg and Mog*)

- reading a clock face to tell the time: this reinforces mathematical concepts of telling the time (for example, *Meg and Mog*, *The Snowman*)

Listening and reading

- matching pictures to speech bubbles: as the children listen to the teacher or to a cassette they read a selection of speech bubbles and choose the correct one (for example, *The Turnip*)

- sequencing: while the children listen to a stretch of narrative or to a description they arrange the sentences in the right order (for example, *The Turnip*)

Reading and thinking/problem-solving

- verifying written statements: the children read statements in a quiz, or sentences derived from a calendar, or a graph written by other children, and check whether they are true or false. In *The Turnip*, for example, a graph made by the children has sentences for the children to answer such as 'Ten people like chocolate cake. Is this true?' (for example, *The Turnip*, *Don't Forget the Bacon!*, *Meg's Eggs*)

● reading lists, sentences or food packets to classify, for example, where different kinds of food are bought or produced (for example, *The Very Hungry Caterpillar*, *Don't Forget the Bacon!*, *The Snowman*, *Meg and Mog*)

Once a story has been told, copies of the book can be placed in the classroom book corner or school library. This will provide a useful introduction to the written word and reading in English. For further details about the book corner, see page 75.

Learning to write

The writing process

When supporting children's writing skills, the teacher should help to make writing purposeful and contextualized wherever possible. The first point implies that the children should know why they are writing; it may be to help them to spell, to use specific structural patterns to form sentences or to produce different text types which allow their imagination to run free after having been provided with written models. Much of the writing produced by children is clearly an opportunity to provide language practice in selecting and using words and structural patterns, spelling, organizing ideas and practising handwriting and layout. These are all components of the writing process which teachers hope will become more and more automatic. However, it is useful to bear in mind that writing to communicate is also an important aspect of the writing process. With this dimension in mind it becomes increasingly important for teachers that they create opportunities for children to have a specific context and audience to write for, one which goes beyond this kind of practice. Here is where the teacher can encourage the older child to experiment with different text types, such as writing cards, letters, invitations, menus or stories which someone other than the teacher will read.

An important part of this process is collaboration between children during which they discuss ideas, plan the writing, and revise their work after further consultation with the teacher to produce a polished product. Some of this may, of course, need to take place in the mother tongue. Developing a sense of audience in order to communicate with someone else is possible even at a relatively early stage of learning English. Children can be encouraged to write sentences which, for instance, other children have to decide are true or false or which act as riddles for children to guess the answer to.

Writing activities

Writing activities can be divided into those which encourage copying and those which encourage creativity. Copying at word or sentence level can be more or less guided by support frameworks such as pictures, written models, charts and so on. Guided copying is often used to practise handwriting, spelling and new grammatical constructions. The support frameworks give learners guidance on producing written work within clearly defined constraints; the use of a chart, for example, can provide a simple sentence pattern such as 'Jacques likes hot dogs but Louise likes sandwiches' which the children can adapt according to the information on the chart. Less guided copying is sometimes used to help children to learn new vocabulary, group new words into word families and generally consolidate word meanings. Lists of words can be provided for children to classify under different headings which allows them to bring some of their own ideas into play. Freer still are more creative writing activities which encourage and support the children in composing sentences or texts and which provide practice in planning, organizing ideas and understanding the conventions of different text types, such as layout. Designing a seed packet, invitation or advertisement, for example, requires a child to focus on the most important pieces of information and present them in a way which is eye-catching yet clear. All these activities are necessary and build upon one another; it is impracticable to imagine that one can encourage creativity without specific skills practice at word or sentence level, but not all writing should remain at the practice level.

Text types

The following table shows some of the different writing activities which learners practise in the story notes. You might like to add ideas of your own.

Common writing functions children will practise include:
- describing people, animals and places
- comparing people, animals and places

Writing activities in the story notes	
Writing at word level • labels for pictures/diagrams • shopping lists • dictionaries	*Purpose* learning new vocabulary handwriting and spelling
Writing at sentence level • diaries • captions for pictures • speech bubbles for cartoons • charts for surveys and questionnaires	all of the above and practising new structures and functions
Writing at text level • food/seed packets • advertisements • Christmas/birthday cards • invitations • tickets • books for other children to read	all of the above and planning, drafting, editing and understanding layout

- asking questions
- giving information in response to questions
- describing present actions
- narrating past events
- describing cause and effect
- giving reasons

The description of specific language-learning skills outlined so far in this chapter now leads on to a discussion of strategies for learning to learn.

Learning to learn

As we have seen, stories can provide a useful context in which to develop learning to learn. The aim of learning to learn is to focus the pupils' attention on how to learn, as well as on what to learn. It is concerned with the process of learning and aims to help pupils understand themselves and eventually lead them to a conscious development of their own learning strategies in English, as well as in other subjects. For this reason, it is important that learning to learn is built into the curriculum in an overt and explicit way and demonstrated with transfer in mind. If learning to learn is too specifically tied to a subject its potential for transfer may be hidden. For example, making two-sided cards for self-testing can be useful for learning English vocabulary. However, its potential for also learning and practising times tables or countries and their capitals, and so on, may not be perceived by learners if the teacher does not point this out.

Virtually any class activity may be used for learning to learn. All that is necessary is to focus attention upon the learning process aspect of an experience, which always exists side by side with the content. Below is a description of some of the strategies that can be developed through storybooks:

An awareness of visual and audio clues

We make use of a variety of clues to help work out meaning in our mother tongue usually at a subconscious level. When deciphering meaning in the foreign language, pupils will need to use these clues to a greater extent and they have to become aware of what they are. Many of the story notes focus pupils' attention on developing this awareness. *Pat the Cat*, for example, shows how facial expressions and intonation can give clues to meaning; *Meg and Mog* shows how sound-effects can help pupils guess the meaning of Meg's breakfast ingredients and how visual clues can help convey meaning. This conscious knowledge will in turn enhance the pupils' performance in their mother tongue.

Predicting

Because pupils are familiar with the conventions of narrative and many of the contexts and characters described, they can be encouraged to predict the storyline or specific vocabulary. This helps them feel more involved in a story and develops their self-confidence.

Classifying

Many activities get pupils to classify items into different groups. For example, 'hot' and 'cold' in *The Snowman*, 'sweet' or 'salty' in *The Very Hungry Caterpillar*, etc. This revises a basic concept for pupils and can also be used as a memory aid when learning vocabulary. Pupils can also classify words into parts of speech:

nouns, verbs, adjectives, lexical sets (for example colours, fruits, clothes, rooms in a house and words that rhyme).

Problem-solving and hypothesizing
Pupils are encouraged to work out the rules of grammar for themselves. This can be done by looking at examples of the language and making hypotheses as to why, for example, 'a' or sometimes 'an' is used in front of certain nouns in *The Elephant and the Bad Baby*; or to reflect on the use of countable or uncountable nouns in *The Very Hungry Caterpillar* or on word order in *Meg and Mog*.

Comparing
You might like to encourage pupils to spot similarities and differences between English and their mother tongue. This can arouse curiosity and develop language awareness.

Self-questioning
Pupils can be taught how to ask themselves questions about their learning. They can be asked about parts of the lesson they found easy or difficult and why; about activities they enjoyed and didn't enjoy, and how they helped or didn't help them learn; about how they guessed the meaning of an unknown word, and so on. Through this form of interrogation the teacher is modelling for the learners the type of questions they can eventually ask themselves. This will help them identify their weak and strong points and reach a greater understanding of why certain aspects of learning may be more difficult for them than others.

Working independently of the teacher
Pair work and group work give pupils opportunities to work on their own and take on responsibility for their own learning.

Risk-taking
The teacher can encourage pupils to take risks by guessing the meaning of words they do not know; attempting to pronounce a new word; hypothesizing; putting forward a point of view for discussion, and so on. This will help build up their confidence.

Organizing work
Work related to each story can be organized in a folder or envelope; work can be labelled and dated; personal vocabulary sets can be made as described in *The Snowman*; personal picture dictionaries, rhyme or song books can be made; pupils can also collect pictures

and make collages of specific language examples, for example, food packets, clothes labels, shop signs, and so on.

Self-assessment

This can be done after a storybook is read. For example: Did you enjoy this story? Why?/Why not?/ What did you learn from the story?, and so on. Questions can also be asked about particular activities: pupils' points of view can be recorded and they can listen to them afterwards; a lesson can be video-recorded and questions asked about their participation, etc. when they view it. Pupils can record themselves in English, listen and judge their performance as suggested in *I Can Do It!*

Reviewing

Pupils can learn to review systematically if they are asked at the beginning of each lesson, 'What did we do last lesson?', and at the end of the lesson, 'What did we do today?' This consolidates work and helps pupils become aware of what they do and don't know, and can help them know what to revise.

Using reference materials

Pupils can learn how to use a dictionary in English. This may be a picture dictionary, a bilingual dictionary or a dictionary with simple definitions in the mother tongue. They can learn to use a book corner efficiently and to look for other books related to a particular subject, for example on dinosaurs, butterflies, and so on.

Selecting activities

Some notes provide a selection of activities for children to choose from. This allows pupils opportunities to work independently of the teacher, to decide for themselves what to do and to plan their own work.

Self-correction

Some activities allow pupils to check their own work individually or in pairs.

It is important to remember that the strategies described above for learning English can also be applied to other subject areas. The children should be reminded of this when appropriate, so that they learn to transfer the strategies and develop an overall awareness of their learning across the curriculum.

5 Story-based activities

Preparation activities

In chapter 3 we discussed the need to prepare pupils for the time when the teacher will read the story, or part of it, for the first time. There is a wide range of preparation activities which the teacher can use to do this. Most of the notes suggest that at least one lesson be spent preparing for the story, while some suggest spending more time. Preparation activities are used to introduce the content, language and concepts contained in the story.

The suggestions below provide a variety of ideas and the teacher should select those which are most suitable for the language level of the pupils and for the particular story.

1 Make the children more familiar with the content of the story:

- remind children of other stories with similar content

  for example, stories connected with food (see *Don't Forget the Bacon!*, *The Very Hungry Caterpillar*, *The Elephant and the Bad Baby*)

- set the scene by drawing upon the children's experience related to the story

  for example, eliciting from them their experience of shopping, making lists, forgetting and remembering things (see *Don't Forget the Bacon!*); asking children about going to the park, having picnics (see *Having a Picnic*)

- provide a summary of the main storyline beforehand, if necessary in the pupils' mother tongue, especially for more difficult stories

  for example, *Mr Biff the Boxer*, *The Snowman*, *Little Red Riding Hood*

2 Make the children more familiar with the concepts in the story:

- remind pupils of any related concepts or aspects of the curriculum covered in other classes

  for example, using a map, interpreting a graph

- remind pupils of other stories which draw upon the same or a similar concept

  for example, size in *Meg's Eggs*, *The Turnip*, *The Fat Cat*, *Little Red Riding Hood*; telling the time in *Meg and Mog*, *The Snowman*

3 Teach or revise some of the key language items in the story:

- introduce and explain keywords using the appropriate technique (see the section on presenting new language on page 39).

- introduce or revise key structural patterns using the appropriate technique (see above)

  for example, using 'Do you like ——?' for surveys

  for example, discuss ways children talk about the concept of size in their mother tongue and how to do this in English

  compare *grand*, *plus grand*, *le plus grand*,
  grande, *mas grande*, *el mas grande*,
  big, bigger, biggest

It is also useful to remind children of some of their learning strategies. For example, how they learn new words, how they can make use of the context to make informed guesses about unfamiliar language or how they can organize their work. It is also motivating to let pupils know what they will work on after they have listened to the story. In other words, tell them that after they have listened to this story they are going to:

- make some masks/invitations/posters, etc.
- write a book for another class to read
- do some acting
- do some cooking (and so on).

The next section looks in more detail at follow-up activities.

Follow-up activities

It is important that after several lessons working on a storybook there is some kind of outcome, so pupils know that all their hard work has been leading somewhere. Informing pupils of possible outcomes will make their work more meaningful and motivating, and will provide them with an extra incentive. Most story notes suggest a variety of follow-up activities. Some can be chosen by the pupils themselves according to their own interests. Alternatively, one particular activity, such as developing the story into a play, can be developed as a project for the whole class.

Follow-up activities provide opportunities to bridge the gap between language study and language use and to link classroom learning with the world outside. Some of the activities do not always have a very large language element but are nevertheless important in creating a feeling among the pupils that learning English means fun, activity and enjoyment.

Characteristics
The essential characteristics of follow-up activities are:

1 **Consolidation**
They provide opportunities to extend and consolidate language introduced through a story. (See, for example, the role-play in *The Elephant and the Bad Baby*.)

2 **Final product or collective event**
The options include:
● Making something. For example, a frieze, a book, a greetings card, a model, a puppet, a collage, a cassette-recording of the story, and so on
● Organizing an event. For example, a tea-party; turning a story into a play. This can also involve pupils in some of the above activities such as making costumes and masks, posters, programmes, tickets, invitations, and so on
● Researching a topic and gathering information. For example, pupils are invited to discover what caterpillars really eat in *The Very Hungry Caterpillar* or to find out about winter climates in other English-speaking countries around the world in *The Snowman*.

3 **Integrated skills work**
They involve pupils in skills such as writing, note-taking, interviewing and using reference materials which give pupils integrated practice in all the language skills.

4 **Independent learning**
Very often pupils have the chance to pursue an area that interests them; to present their work in different ways: for example, a poster, a collage, a cassette-recording and can be based on individual work, group work or a class project.

5 **Short-term or long-term**
The activities can be short-term, such as a role-play completed

in one or two lessons or they can be long-term developing a story into a play. The latter allows pupils to pick up language without its being formally or explicitly introduced.

6 Enjoyment

Follow-up activities provide enjoyment and satisfaction as they allow pupils to complete a piece of work in English. They can also gain self-confidence which, in turn, can create a more positive attitude to learning English.

7 Creativity

Many of the follow-up activities provide opportunities for pupils to express their own ideas. Creativity should be encouraged.

Classroom organization and resources

Some follow-up activities may necessitate moving classroom furniture around for more space or to allow pupils to work together in groups. It is also a good idea to have a supply of paper, scissors, glue, coloured pencils, etc., and old magazines for pupils to cut up. Creative activities may be done in collaboration with the art teacher to allow you to use facilities in the art room. End-products can be used to decorate the classroom or English corner. The follow-up activities you or your pupils choose will ultimately depend on your time and the resources available.

Many follow-up activities can be integrated into other subject areas such as maths, music and drama, geography, and so on. The chart Stories and Learning, in chapter 1, indicates possible links that could be made with each story. If you are a visiting teacher to the school, you will need to liaise with the appropriate teacher about such collaboration. (See the following section on integrating language work across the curriculum for further guidelines on this.)

Integrating language work across the curriculum

Teachers of English are likely to be of two types: the first kind is the class teacher who teaches all subjects to one class; the second is the specialist English teacher who teaches English in different classes at different age-levels. If you are the permanent class teacher you have the ideal situation for integrating English with other subjects, as you will know exactly what your class has been studying. Using the chart Stories and Learning, you can select a story which fits in with some of the concepts and content areas covered in other classes.

If you are a visiting teacher to the school you will need to liaise with the appropriate class teacher to find out what the pupils have been studying and whether the teacher would be willing to collaborate with you. The ideal situation for you in this context is one where the permanent class teacher is interested in what you are doing and may observe or even participate in the class with you, so that he or she knows when to integrate and to follow up the activities that you have begun. Some teachers may even use your language class as an opportunity to learn English themselves!

In practical terms this may be difficult to organize because the permanent teacher may be too busy with other duties, may not be interested in or may not speak English. In this event some information about the children's work may be available from several other sources such as:

- the school syllabus, forecast or programme for different classes for a term or year
- the class record of work carried out in the previous week
- the textbooks used with the children.

However, if you are very keen to integrate your English work with other areas of the curriculum it is worth building up a close working relationship with another teacher in the school or another English-teaching colleague who is able to do this. Starting from small beginnings often bears fruit when the benefits of such collaboration become obvious. Teachers who initially may be a little reluctant to liaise in this way are most likely to be persuaded by results and may in the end even approach you to find out what you have been doing.

Although the primary curriculum in most countries is usually very full it can be beneficial to integrate language work with other subjects for the following reasons:

- It gives children a broader perspective on why they are learning English, so that they do not always see it in isolation from other subjects. Relating English language learning to other subjects can help children see they are increasing their general knowledge instead of simply learning a language divorced from any real context.

  for example, learning about famous people (see notes for *Pat the Cat*).

- It reinforces certain key content areas and concepts which cross subject boundaries and underpins more general learning across the curriculum.

for example, learning about dinosaurs, (see notes for *Meg and Mog*); using maps (see notes for *My Cat Likes to Hide in Boxes, Pat the Cat*)

● It can maximize the limited time often given to foreign language learning by offering opportunities briefly to revise or review relevant language as the opportunity arises.

for example, taking two minutes to revise numbers in English in the maths class.

You do need to be careful that this language integration is done in a way which does not take too much time from other subjects.

The notes describe in detail a range of activities which relate to other areas of the curriculum. The chart Stories and Learning describes in detail the particular curriculum and conceptual links possible with each story. If you have the time, these links can, of course, be added to. It would be great fun to experiment with other areas.

6 Classroom management

Classroom management includes the practical organization of human and material resources. Good management can positively influence the way in which your pupils participate in classroom activities and so can improve their learning. In this section we will look at:

- Organizing storytelling
- Using audio-visual aids
- Collecting and organizing resources
- Managing pair and group work
- Displaying children's work
- Organizing a book corner.

Organizing storytelling

When telling a story for the first time try to create a relaxed, informal atmosphere which mirrors storytelling in children's homes. You can do this by gathering pupils around you in a semicircle; this arrangement also makes it easier for them to hear you and to see any visuals you wish to use. The children will be more comfortable if there is a small carpeted area in a corner of the classroom where they can sit. Some old blankets spread out for storytelling time would be a good substitute. Make sure you have rehearsed the story beforehand so that you are able to look at the children frequently while you read or tell the story. You should also know where you are going to pause or break up the text to ask questions, and so on. (See chapter 3 for further suggestions for improving your storytelling skills.)

Using audio-visual aids

When listening to a story in a foreign language children rely heavily on their eyes to help them understand. The use of visuals and other support for listening is consequently very important to the child's comprehension and enjoyment of the story. The aids you use when telling stories can take many forms, both visual and aural, and are often referred to as story props. These might include pictures, real objects, models, or pre-recorded or teacher-made cassettes.

Examples of story props are given below. Some of these are suitable when telling the story for the first time; others are suitable for the children's use in follow-up activities.

Visuals

REAL OBJECTS

These can add an air of authenticity to the story and are one of the easiest ways of making the details of a story accessible to all children. An example can be seen in *Little Red Riding Hood* where a basket and items of clothing are used.

PUPPETS

Puppets are especially useful for younger children and can be used by the teacher when telling the story for the first time and in later lessons by the children to produce short dialogues or when retelling the story themselves.

PICTURES AND GAMES

These can be mounted on card and covered in plastic film to make them durable. When using pictures make sure they are large enough for all the class to see and use afterwards, individually or in small groups. You might like to produce line drawings of different characters or scenes that you can reproduce for classroom use. One set can then be coloured in and mounted on card, perhaps by the children themselves. Scenes from the story can be put on to a rectangular shape, but characters should be stuck on to card and then cut round to make them more realistic. The use of pictures and games is demonstrated in all the stories in this handbook.

MOVABLE PICTURES/MAGNETBOARDS

There are many advantages in having movable pictures, especially in stories with repeating sequences such as *The Turnip* and *The Elephant and the Bad Baby*. Here the effect is more dramatic if the scene can be gradually built up before the children's eyes. With a commercially produced magnetboard or a sheet of clean metal, pictures can be attached to the metal background with magnetic tape stuck on to the back of the picture. If you do not have a magnetboard you can achieve a similar effect by using Blu-Tack and the blackboard or a feltboard. These visual aids are especially useful for the children to use in groups when retelling the story. Free-standing cut-out figures on movable bases (wood, Plasticine etc.) are also useful for showing movement and action.

MASKS

These can be made by the children, using faces drawn on paper bags and then put over their heads; or faces cut out and mounted on a stick to hold in front of the face or attached to the head with elastic. These are useful for children to create their own dialogues, use for miming activities, retell the story or create new stories. Masks are used in *The Turnip* and *Little Red Riding Hood*.

WRITTEN CAPTIONS/SPEECH BUBBLES

Speech bubbles mounted on to card can be shown when recapping a story or for pupils to use in small groups. A group task might be to match pictures of characters with the appropriate speech bubble (see the notes for *The Turnip* for an example). Written captions can also be used for picture-matching exercises, sequencing or classifying activities. When the children know the story well they might like to produce their own written captions for other children to match or sequence.

Aural support

Some of the stories in this book are recorded on the accompanying cassette. This can be used as a model for the teacher when telling the story and for pupils to listen to afterwards. As we saw in chapter 3, it is usually better for the teacher to tell the story the first time rather than play the cassette. This can be used in later sessions to recap or for the children to use in groups. If the story you want to use has not been recorded on cassette you could do this yourself, perhaps with a colleague. In this case you might like to tell the story all the way through and then record the story broken into smaller chunks. This is useful for children working independently in small groups. A sound signal, such as tapping a glass, can show where the children have to stop the cassette and carry out a listening activity such as sequencing or matching pictures. An example of this can be seen in *Don't Forget the Bacon!*

For more suggestions about making and using audio-visual aids, see page 278 for a list of helpful books.

Collecting and organizing resources

The resources for stories can be built up gradually with aids produced both by yourself and by the children. Keep any story props in a clearly labelled envelope or container for ready access. These story packs could be shared by other colleagues so that you have a wide range of audio-visual aids. You might like to share your ideas with colleagues at meetings or workshops so that other ones can perhaps be added by them.

Managing pair and group work

Once the children have become more familiar with the story there are many suggestions in the notes for encouraging them to work independently using pair and group work. You may need to rearrange the classroom furniture but if the children are working in pairs, they can simply move their chairs so that they work with the person next to or behind them. You will have to think carefully about the composition of these groups and decide which children will work together. You may like the children to choose their own groups; occasionally you may have to intervene to ensure that children of similar language ability work together. Alternatively you may decide that it would be useful for a slower learner to work with a more able child. In this case you will need to ensure that all the children in the group have access to the materials used and play a specific role to avoid possible domination by some children.

You will also need to match the task to the language level of the child; a matching task is often easier than a sequencing or classifying task, for example. You may also need to spend some time talking to the children about how to work in groups if they are not used to doing so. It will probably be important to spell out certain ground rules, such as:

- independent learning in pairs or groups requires cooperation not competition. Children should be encouraged to help each other, provide explanations where necessary and avoid ridiculing others if they do not understand.

- the children need to share materials so they all have access to the task. The teacher must ensure, therefore, that there are enough copies and that visuals are clear and large enough for all to see.

- children should be encouraged to listen to each other and to take turns in speaking. This can be developed through information gap activities where the children are compelled to listen to

each other and through games where turn-taking is emphasized.

● children must not raise their voices or shout

Preparing for group work
The teacher's preparation for independent learning in small groups
is very important. Most activities such as games and information
gap require some demonstration or modelling by the teacher. The
language to perform the activity must also have been taught
beforehand. If the children are carrying out a survey by asking
questions, make sure that they have had adequate rehearsal of the
appropriate question forms beforehand. Try to provide some kind
of visual framework, such as a chart, to help them cope with the
response to the questions. When carrying out an investigation
such as measuring, check that the concepts involved are familiar
to the children in their own language. Instructions for tasks
should be clearly explained, using the mother tongue if absolutely
necessary. It will usually be helpful to have instructions written
down or even recorded on to tape for slower learners who have
difficulty in reading. Written instructions should consist of short,
simple sentences which are clearly numbered. You might like to
have these written first in English, with a version in the children's
mother tongue next. If the task is new, or a little complicated, you
may need to check that the children have understood what to do
by asking them to explain the task to each other, probably using
the mother tongue. Assuming that the class has been carefully
prepared and that sufficient visual or aural support is provided,
avoid paraphrasing your instructions if the children have difficulties. Encourage them to work out the details together by referring
them to the materials.

   If some pupils complete an activity before others they should be
trained to use their time effectively. For example they could read a
book in the book corner, revise vocabulary in their personal
dictionary, look at the classroom displays of work and answer any
accompanying questions, and so on.

FREE-CHOICE ACTIVITIES
If you decide to allow the pupils free choice in activities, as
suggested in some of the notes, a careful record needs to be made
of the work that has been done. A simple checklist, where children
sign their names against the activity chosen, will help you to keep
track of the work covered. Activities requiring audio-visual support

such as charts or captions need to be stored in envelopes and labelled or colour-coded so that the pupils can easily find the materials and put them away.

THE TEACHER'S ROLE IN GROUP WORK
One of the most important things to remember when using group work is that it should be set up so that you are free to monitor the groups and provide support for individuals, especially the slower learners, where necessary. While moving around the room listening to the children, try not to intervene too much unless you are asked for help or if they are obviously having difficulties. You will need to make a mental note, however, of common language difficulties which you can revise with the whole class afterwards.

You will also need to provide some form of feedback about the groups' activities to your pupils. Correction of any problem-solving activities or written work can either be done by the children, using answer cards, or by yourself. You can also, of course, verbally round off or summarize what the children have been doing. Alternatively, the groups can report to the class, if appropriate, showing and describing any products or outcomes of their work; these might be a book, a tape, some masks, pictures and so on.

Displaying children's work

It is very motivating for children to display their work. Displays also make the classroom brighter and can encourage a purposeful working atmosphere. The standard of children's work is often pushed higher if they know it is to be made public. Displays can take many forms and might include models, pictures, a chart of word families, mobiles, mounted written work or pupil-made books.

When setting up a display keep the following points in mind:

● try to arrange the work at children's eye-level: you want to encourage them to look at it

● titles and lettering should be large and attractive

● always try to stick pictures on to a coloured background or mount

● link or coordinate work through colours

● use boxes covered in brightly coloured cloth (or paper) to create differences in height for models and also cover tables for display with similar materials.

- use attractive wallpaper as cheap backing material for written work or pictures

- displays should encourage skills such as reading and listening, as well as simply looking: you could try writing some questions about the display for the children to answer.

- ensure that all the children have something on display

- write the child's name on all displayed work

It is a good idea to link artwork with written work; if written work centres around a topic, see if you can build some aspect of the topic into the display. For example, if the children collect vocabulary connected with dinosaurs, write the words on a large chart cut into the shape of a dinosaur. If the children do some writing about witches, mount the work on to a cut-out shape of a witch, a cauldron or a witch's hat.

Other ideas for linking artwork with topics in the storybooks include:

Time   (clocks, cogs and wheels)
Dinosaurs (large drawings, dinosaur footprints)
Witches   (hats, witches on broomsticks, cauldrons)
Space   (rockets, the solar system)
Shops   (market stalls, giant cut-outs of food)
Money   (lettering in the shape of coins)

The final section looks at ways of setting up a book corner.

Organizing a book corner

Most primary school classrooms have a book corner where pupils can read books of their own choice and at their own pace. Once a story in English has been completed in class, it is a good idea to put extra copies of the book in the book corner. This will provide an introduction to the written word in English. Furthermore, as the child will have memorized much of the story, he or she will be able to make the connection between what he or she has heard and memorized and what he or she sees written and illustrated on the page. A stimulating book area will also promote a positive attitude towards reading and create enthusiasm among children for books.

Setting up the book corner

If you do not already have a book corner in your class, or would prefer to set up a special one for English, you may find the following tips useful:

- A bookcase or shelving is ideal but a table or cardboard boxes covered in coloured paper can be used to display and store books.

- Flowers, plants, a carpet and cushions will make the book corner cosy, attractive and inviting.

- If possible, display books with the cover showing. This is more attractive and makes selection much easier.

- Try to involve your pupils as much as possible in the organization of the book corner. Looking after a book corner encourages children to take responsibility for the care of books. The class could elect book corner monitors/librarians each week or month to keep the book corner tidy.

- Decorate the corner with any artwork or writing inspired by stories read to pupils in class. They could also write comments about different books and stick these on the wall. Get the children to organize a Top Ten book chart and display the results in the corner.

- Bring your pupils' attention to other books in English or in the mother tongue related to a topic you are covering. For example, magic, dinosaurs, butterflies, witches, animals, etc.

As far as possible, allow pupils to have open access to the book corner. This will encourage them to visit it as often as they can, without feeling they have to use it at specific times.

If your pupils can borrow books, you will need to devise a lending system. A simple one is to use an exercise book in which pupils write their name, the title of the books, the date borrowed and the date returned. Decide how long the lending period should be: one week, two weeks? The book corner monitors/librarians can take responsibility for this.

It is useful for the pupils to keep a personal record of books they have looked through or borrowed. You could design a record card which enables pupils to do this. The amount of detail you include will depend on the age, level and interests of your pupils, but noting down even basic information will help pupils learn useful study skills. On pages 78–9 are two examples of record cards. The information recorded can be written in English or in the mother tongue.

Similarly, you could design a poster to keep a class record of books read. You will need a large sheet of paper. Write the titles of books horizontally and the names of your pupils vertically to form a grid. This can be designed by the pupils themselves. When they have read a book, they put a tick in the corresponding box. At the end of a school term or year, pupils can collate the results: Eight pupils read *The Very Hungry Caterpillar*; ten pupils read *Meg and Mog*, etc. The most popular book was ——.

Effective organization and imaginative display of your book corner both play a vital role in helping your pupils develop a positive attitude towards books, reading and the foreign language.

(⊙) PENGUIN JEUNESSE (⊙)

Class Library – Pupil Record Card

Name _____

Class _____

Title/author	Date borrowed	Date returned	Comments	Title/Author	Date borrowed	Date returned	Comments

PENGUIN JEUNESSE

Class Library — Pupil Record Card

Name _____

Class _____

Title/author	Date borrowed	Date returned	Type of book	Problems	Useful vocabulary and information	Comments

Part 2 Story notes

1 Where's Spot?

Author: Eric Hill

Description: It's dinner-time and Sally can't find her puppy, Spot, anywhere. She searches the house for him.

Layout: An interactive book which demands reader involvement because of its clever use of lift-up flaps. This device is an integral part of the narrative: the illustration of 'behind' really is behind, so children can be actively involved in the search for Spot, learning spatial context. Each double-spread contains brightly coloured illustrations and a short text printed in large black letters on the left-hand page.

Linguistic features: A simple text based on the repetition of the question form: 'Is he in/under/behind/inside the bed?' etc.

Linguistic objectives

SKILLS
- Listening to the story, to instructions and statements, questions and answers, words in games and songs
- Speaking: asking and answering questions, games, role-play, rhymes and songs
- Reading: words and sentences, reconstructing the story, sequencing
- Writing: spelling, copying, gap-filling

FUNCTIONS/STRUCTURES
- Asking for and giving information using Yes/No and Wh– questions
- Making statements using the verb to be

VOCABULARY
- Animals, birds: dog, puppy, bear, snake, hippopotamus, lion, monkey, crocodile, penguin, tortoise
- Furniture: armchair, door, clock, piano, stairs, wardrobe, bed, box, rug, basket, table, telephone, vase

● Prepositions: in, under, behind, inside, on, in front of

PRONUNCIATION
● Intonation: Is he in the wardrobe?

CONCEPTUAL REINFORCEMENT/CURRICULUM LINKS
● Spatial context
● Music and drama; singing songs and rhymes, role-play

LEARNING TO LEARN
● Predicting; sequencing, memory training, making charts

Suggested procedures

The work related to the story is divided into three stages:

1 Preparation: Introduction or revision of vocabulary and structures used in the story
2 Using the storybook
3 Follow-up activities

The activities you choose to cover will depend on time available and on the level and interest of your pupils.

Materials
● A pack of alphabet cards
● Pictures of the animals
● Pictures of the furniture
● Cards with the names of animals
● Cards with the names of furniture
● Bingo boards and cover-cards (see page 87)
● Worksheets (see pages 90–91)
● Large cards with the questions from the story written on them

Preparation

1 *Aim:* To introduce or revise vocabulary for animals

Show the pictures of animals to your pupils one by one and ask, 'What's this?' Children may reply in their mother tongue. Say, 'Yes, it's a monkey! Repeat!' First have the whole class repeat and then ask individual pupils so that you can check pronunciation. As you introduce each animal, stick its picture on the board. To check comprehension, give the following instructions: 'Pierre, point to the snake!' The pupil must come to the board and show you the snake. Ask the rest of the class, 'Is that right?' Then say, 'Marie, give the monkey to a boy!' She must take the picture of the monkey and give it to a boy and say, 'Here you are.'

GAME: MY FAVOURITE ANIMAL!
Arrange four of the animal pictures on the board. The pupils must listen to you carefully and work out what your favourite animal or bird is through a process of elimination.
Teacher: It isn't a monkey. It isn't a snake. It isn't a lion. What is it?
Pupils: It's a penguin!
When the pupils feel confident enough, you can invite them to take your place.

MIME
A pupil selects a picture of an animal or bird without showing the rest of the class and mimes it. The class must guess what it is. 'Is it a ——?' or 'Are you a ——?'

KIM'S GAME
Stick the pictures on the board or on a table. Tell pupils to close their eyes. Remove a picture. Tell pupils to open their eyes and ask 'What's missing?'

SONG
'The Animals Went in Two by Two' (traditional)
(See *This Little Puffin* and *The Zoo* for other songs and rhymes on the topic of animals.)

2 *Aim:* To introduce or revise vocabulary for furniture
Follow the same procedure as above.

3 *Aim:* To introduce or revise the prepositions: on, in/inside, under
Show pupils the following actions to help them visualize and memorize the prepositions. Make a C shape with your left hand and put
 i) your right hand *on* your left hand
 ii) your right hand *in/inside* your left hand
 iii) your right hand *under* your left hand.

SIMON SAYS
Using vocabulary related to the body and the classroom give commands. For example:

● Simon says put your hands on your head
● Simon says put your hands under the table, etc.

Pupils should only carry out commands preceded by the words 'Simon says . . .' Those who mime when they shouldn't are out.

4 *Aim:* To revise vocabulary for animals, furniture and prepositions.

CHINESE WHISPERS

Divide pupils into two groups and get them to sit one behind the other. Whisper to the first child in each group the name of an animal or a complete sentence like 'The lion is in the bed.' Count to three. The first pupil in each group whispers the words to the child behind him or her, and so on. The child at the end of the line must run to the board and either say the word or sentence, find the picture on the board, or write the word or sentence on the board.

WRITING GAME

Divide the pupils into two teams. Select the cards from the alphabet pack with the first letter of animals or furniture that the pupils know. A pupil from team one takes any card and says to team two:

● 'Give me an animal beginning with M.' (Monkey)
● 'Yes. Can you spell monkey?'

The pupil from team two must spell monkey and the pupil from team one writes it on the board.

TEAM GAME

Draw pictures of the furniture on the board and number each one. Revise vocabulary by asking, 'What's number three?', etc.

Now stick the pictures of the animals on the board. Divide the children into two teams. Instruct a member from each team to 'Put the lion under the piano!', etc. If the pupil carries out the instruction correctly, he or she wins a point for the team. The team to get the most points wins. Then individual pupils can take your place and give instructions.

Keep the pictures on the board and take the cards with the names of animals written on them. A child from one team chooses a card. Pupils from the other team must guess which animal it is by asking, 'Is he in the clock?' 'Yes, he is,' or 'No, he isn't.' After three negative replies, the children must ask, 'Where is he?' 'He's in the basket.'

'Who is he?' 'He's the hippopotamus.'

5 *Aim:* To introduce or revise the prepositions behind/in front of

Using your hands and your head, mime the above prepositions and repeat the words. Get your pupils to copy you. Check their pronunciation.

SIMON SAYS
Play as described above.

ACTION GAME
Instruct pupils to put the pictures of animals in different places in the classroom. 'Louis, put the lion behind the cupboard!', etc.

HIDE-AND-SEEK
Ask two children to go outside the classroom while the others hide the picture of an animal. The children come back and must guess where it is. 'Is it under the table?', etc.

ACTION SONG   Put your hands in your pockets

| me | fa | soh | me | ˋla | la | | la | so | fa | fa | so ˋ | soh |
Put your | hands in your pockets, put your | hands on your toes,

| so | fa | ˋme | me | me | do | ˋfa | fa | me | ˋní | so | la | si ˋ | do |
Put your | hands between your legs, put your | hands under your nose,
p

| me | so | soh | me ˋ | la | la | so | fa | fa | ní ˋ | soh |
In | front of your eyes, put your | hands, one and two,
s   d

| me | me | me | do | ˋfa | | ˋso ˋ | la——si ˋ | ˋdo |
Turn around and guess | . . . . who's behind YOU.
d   o

This song is accompanied by the following actions: one child stands in the middle and carries out the actions. At 'Turn around and guess' he or she turns his or her back to the other pupils. Choose a child to stand behind him or her. The first child must guess who's behind him or her by asking, 'Are you Pierre/Patricia?' The other child must reply, 'No, I'm not!' or 'Yes, I am!' The game can be adapted for pupils to guess the name of an animal. The second child takes a picture of an animal and shows it to the other children. The first child asks, 'Are you a monkey?', etc.

OPEN AND CLOSE
Using the vocabulary related to the body and the classroom, give pupils the following instructions; for example, 'Alice, open the door!' 'Richard, close the window!' Continue in the same way with: eyes, mouth, book, bag, table, box, basket.

PART 2

Using the storybook

TEAM GAME
Draw pictures of furniture on the board and write up the vocabulary in the following way:

Animals/Birds	Prepositions	Furniture
lion	behind	piano
penguin	under	bed
snake	on	stairs

etc.

For each set of vocabulary have a different coloured pack of cards and arrange them on a table. Divide pupils into two teams. A pupil from team one takes a card from each pack (for example: lion, under, piano) and must make a sentence 'The lion is under the piano.' A pupil from team two takes the animal card and sticks it on the board in the place described.

BINGO
Give each pupil a Bingo board and eight cover-cards (see page 87). Tell pupils to cover any three illustrations. Describe each illustration:

- The crocodile is under the piano
- The bear is in front of the door
- The snake is behind the clock
- The monkey is in front of the cupboard
- The tortoise is on the rug
- The hippopotamus is in the armchair
- The penguin is in the bed
- The dog is behind the box.

When pupils hear a description that matches an illustration on their board, they put down a cover-card. The first pupil to cover all the illustrations on their board is the winner and calls 'Bingo!'

STORYTELLING
Show pupils the cover, point to the dog and then at the box and ask 'What's this?'

First double-spread. Cover the text and ask the following questions: 'What's the dog's name?', 'Who is she looking for?', etc. Now show pupils the text and read it. Mime looking for Spot by putting your hand above your eyes and looking around. Sally is

86

Bingo

looking for Spot. Ask, 'What is she saying?' 'Spot, where are you?'
Encourage your pupils to repeat this.

Second double-spread. Cover the text. Ask, 'What's this?' 'It's a
door.' Ask, 'What colour is it?' Ask pupils to tell you what they
think Sally is saying: 'Is he behind the door?' Ask a pupil to open
the classroom door. Ask, 'Is he behind the door?' 'Yes, he is,' 'No,
he isn't.' Ask, 'Who's behind the door?' 'It's the bear.' Continue in
this way for the other pages.

Read the story again, ask questions and invite pupils to open the
flaps.

Optional follow-up activities

● Revise the story and read it again

● RECONSTRUCTING THE STORY
Write the seven questions from the story on pieces of card big
enough for the whole class to see. Jumble them up and stick them
on the board. In the middle of the board write the numbers one to
seven in a column. Divide the class into two teams. Cover the text
in the book. One pupil from each team comes to the front of the
class. Open the book at the page with the door and give it to the
pupil from team one. He or she shows it to the pupil from team
two who must find the corresponding question on the board: 'Is he
behind the door?' and stick it next to number one in the middle of
the board. The first child now opens the door and asks his team,
'Who's behind the door?' Each team wins a point if they reply
correctly. Continue in this way until the text has been recon-
structed.

ROLE-PLAY

Roles: A child, a mother and a dog who follows the child every-
where.

You have lost your dog. You can't find it anywhere and ask
your mother questions. She is very busy and replies to your
questions without looking at you.

Child: Mummy, where's ——?
Mother: I don't know. Is he in the bed?
Child: (*mimes looking in the bed*) No, he isn't.
Mother: Is he under the piano?
Child: (*mimes looking under the piano*) No, he isn't.

Mother: (*Looking at child*) Look!
   He's behind you.
Child: Oh! So he is.

When pupils are confident they can add other lines.

● WRITING

a Write three lists on the board as on page 86. As you do this, ask pupils questions like, 'Give me an animal beginning with C!', 'Give me an animal which is small and black and white!'

b Distribute the worksheet A on page 90. Pupils look at the board and find the word and write it in the corresponding speech bubble.

c Distribute worksheet B on page 91. Pupil A chooses an animal and asks, 'Where is the lion?' Pupil B replies, for example, 'The lion is under the piano.' Both pupils draw the lion on their worksheets and write the sentence under the picture or on a separate piece of paper. Pupil B then chooses an animal and the activity continues as above.

● Read *Spot's Birthday Party.*

   (*Where's Spot* is on cassette.)

Story notes by Eileen Sorley

Worksheet A   Who is number one?

Worksheet B   Where is the ———?

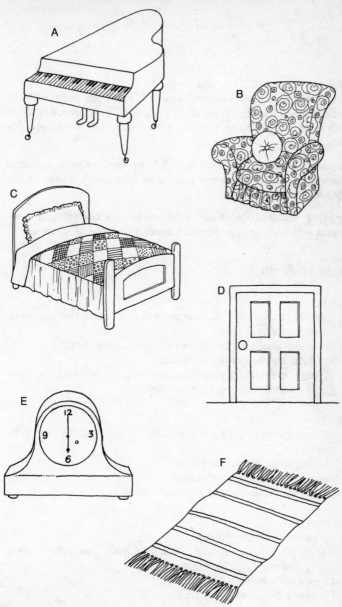

2   Spot's Birthday Party

Author and illustrator: Eric Hill

Description: Spot plays hide-and-seek at his birthday party with the same animals friends we met in *Where's Spot?* This story follows on well from *Where's Spot?*, revising animal vocabulary and prepositions.

Layout: An interactive book with lift-up flaps, brightly coloured illustrations and a short text printed in large black letters on the left-hand pages.

Linguistic features: Questions, suggestions, statements and commands which encourage pupils to interact with the illustrations.

Linguistic objectives

SKILLS
● Listening to the story, to instructions, to questions and answers, words in Bingo
● Speaking: questions and answers, interviewing, singing
● Reading: charts, graphs, matching
● Writing: completing charts, statements, descriptions, birthday cards, birthday party invitations, labelling

FUNCTIONS/STRUCTURES
● Asking for and giving information using Yes/No and Wh– questions
● Making suggestions using let's
● Describing using the verb to be
● Giving instructions using the imperative

VOCABULARY
● Animals: see *Where's Spot?*
● Hiding-places: rug, curtain, cupboard, bath, coat, plant, door, table, cushion
● Prepositions: behind, in, under
● Numbers: cardinals and ordinals
● Months

PRONUNCIATION
● Intonation: When's your birthday? Let's play hide-and-seek.

CONCEPTUAL REINFORCEMENT/CURRICULUM LINKS
● Spatial context
● Maths: numbers and quantity, making a grid and graph
● History: understanding the passing of time
● Geography and the environment: using a map, sports and games
● Creative activities: drawing, making masks, making a birthday card
● Music and drama: singing songs and rhymes, dramatization

LEARNING TO LEARN
Comparing, classifying, predicting, memory training, making charts, surveys and investigations, using dictionaries

Materials
● Pictures of animals
● Pictures of hiding-places
● Worksheets
● Bingo boards and cover-cards

Suggested procedures

Preparation
Show pupils the cover, but do not let them see the title. Ask, 'Who's this?' Then say, 'It's Spot.' Point to the balloon, the bone and the paper hat and ask in turn, 'What's this?' Introduce the vocabulary and practise pronunciation. Can they guess why Spot is wearing a paper hat, why he is playing with a balloon and why he has a bone with a ribbon around it? If no one guesses, tell pupils that it's Spot's birthday party.

BIRTHDAY SURVEY
Revise dates (ordinal numbers and months). Ask one pupil, 'When's your birthday?' and check the reply. For example, 'It's the 7th of June.' Ask several pupils. When they feel confident, tell a pupil to ask you or another pupil. For example, 'Brigitte, ask me!' or 'Michel, ask Carole!'

Each pupil will need a worksheet. You can either prepare these in advance yourself or get pupils to make their own. This will involve them in listening to instructions to make a grid. Write the months horizontally along the top of the page and pupils' names vertically along the left-hand side. Pupils ask each other, 'When's your birthday?' (If you have a large class, divide it into two groups for this activity.) Pupils write down the names of the pupils they interview and tick the month of their birthday.

When's your birthday?

Names \ Months	January	February	March	April	May	June	July	August	September	October	November	December
André	✓											
Sarah					✓							
Quentin								✓				

MAKING A WALL CHART OR A GRAPH
Information can then be transferred to a large wall chart or a graph and collated in the following way:

Five pupils have birthdays in January
Two pupils have birthdays in February
etc.

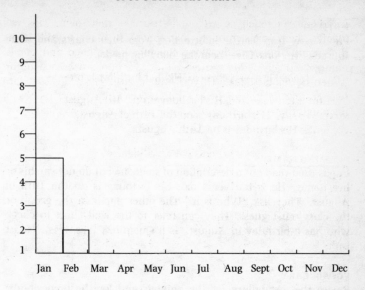

GROUP WORK

Show pupils the cover again and ask them how old they think Spot is. Revise the numbers one to twelve. Teach or revise the question and answer, 'How old are you?', 'I'm nine,' etc. Revise the questions and answers, 'What's your name?' and 'When's your birthday?' Divide your class into groups of four to five. Pupils must ask each other the above questions and complete the chart.

Name	Age	Birthday
Quentin	10	14th August
André	9	9th January

WRITING

Pupils now transfer the information from their charts and write short descriptions. Give them the following model:

[*name*] is —— years old. His/her birthday is on——

Quentin is ten years old. His birthday is on 14th August.
NOTE: We say, 'His birthday is on the 14th of August.'
We write: His birthday is on 14th August.

GUESSING GAME

Pupils then read out a description of someone but do not say his or her name. 'He is ten years old. His birthday is on the 14th of August.' They ask, 'Who is it?' The other pupils in the group or the class must guess. They can refer to the wall chart to check who has a birthday in August. 'Is it Quentin?', 'Yes, it is.' 'No, it isn't.'

VOCABULARY

Revise the vocabulary for the animals and for the prepositions: behind, in, and under (see *Where's Spot?* for a variety of activities).

To check comprehension, stick the animal pictures on the board and instruct pupils in the following way: 'Gary, put the crocodile under your table!' Gary must take the picture from the board and put it under his table. Continue giving instructions in this way and then invite individual pupils to come to the front of the class and give instructions themselves.

PAIR WORK

Give children pictures or models of the animals. Alternatively, they could bring these in from home or prepare small pictures on card for homework. In pairs, pupils give each other instructions: 'Put the lion in your bag!', etc.

HIDE-AND-SEEK

Show pupils the cover again. Ask pupils either in English or in their mother tongue what games they play at birthday parties. (For typical games played in Great Britain, see *Copyparty*.) If no one suggests Hide-and-Seek, show pupils the first double-spread but cover the text. Direct their attention to Spot hiding his eyes and counting one, two, three. If they still don't guess, tell them. Ask someone to explain the rules of the game.

Ask pupils to suggest hiding-places if they were playing Hide-and-Seek at home. As they suggest them, probably in the mother tongue, introduce the English words in the book – rug, curtain, cupboard, bath, coat, plant, door, table, cushion – and stick the corresponding illustration on the board in a column. Get pupils to repeat each word for pronunciation practice. Play Kim's Game or give instructions: 'Paul, point to the cupboard!', and so on, to check comprehension.

MATCHING

Now write the prepositions: under, behind and in in another column opposite the illustrations of hiding-places. Ask pupils to come to the board and match the prepositions with the hiding-places by drawing a line connecting them. (See page 98.)

NOTE: You could hide both *under* or *behind* a coat, *under* or *behind* a cushion, *in* the bath or *behind* the shower-curtain. These alternatives are acceptable.

Reading the story

Make sure all the pupils can see you and the book clearly. (When you read the speech bubbles under the flaps, try to vary your voice for each of the animals.) Show pupils the cover and read the title. Get pupils to repeat it. Read the first double-spread.

Read the text for the second double-spread. Ask, 'Who's under the rug?' You may need to direct your pupils' attention to the tail peeping out. Encourage pupils to guess and reply in the following way. Either: 'The crocodile!', 'It's the crocodile!' or 'The crocodile's under the piano!' It's best to ask one pupil the question to avoid everyone shouting out. If the pupil replies correctly invite him or her to lift up the flap. Say to the other pupils, 'Is he (or she) right?' 'Yes, he (or she) is,' or 'No, he (or she) isn't.' If no, repeat the question, 'Who's under the rug?' Continue in this way, reading the text and asking pupils questions.

NOTE: 'Who's *in* the bath?' or 'Who's *behind* the shower-curtain?'

When you read, 'Somebody giggled', giggle yourself to make the meaning clear and tickle the nearest child to demonstrate the meaning of tickle. Whisper when you read, 'Ssh! Don't tell Spot.'

At the final double-spread sing 'Happy Birthday'.

Happy birthday to you, Happy birthday to you,
Happy birthday dear Spot, Happy birthday to you.

Read the story again.

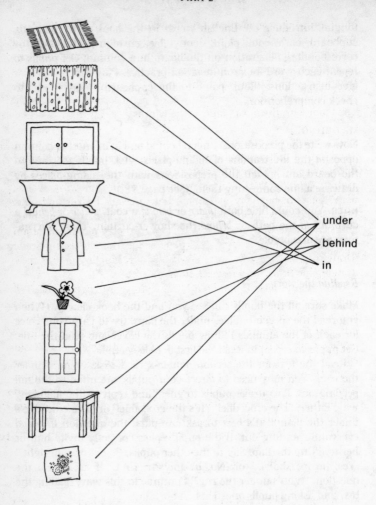

under

behind

in

Optional follow-up activities

MEMORY GAME

Divide the class into two teams and appoint one monitor. Stick the pictures of the animals and the hiding-places on the board. Can pupils remember who hid where? A pupil from team one comes to the board and you ask, for example, 'Where did the lion hide?' The pupil must take the picture of the lion and put it next to the plant. Ask the monitor, 'Is that right?' He or she checks in the book and replies, 'Yes, it is'/'No, it isn't.' If not, a pupil from team two comes to the board. Repeat the question. NOTE: The monitor only shows the illustration in the book to the class if the answer is correct. The pupil who remembers correctly wins a point for his or her team. The team with the most points is the winner.

SPOT'S BIRTHDAY BINGO

Show pupils the last double-spread. They may like to sing 'Happy Birthday' again. Direct their attention to the different objects by asking, 'What's this?' Revise or introduce the following words; bone, balloon, birthday card, ball, hat, present, basket and jelly. Practise pronunciation. To check comprehension, use the book and say, 'Richard, show me a hat!', etc. Also play picture dictation by dictating the following instructions for the pupils to draw: 'Draw a ball!', 'Draw a hat!', etc. Make sure pupils number their drawings so that you can check them afterwards.

Give each pupil a Bingo board and eight word cover-cards. Tell pupils to cover any three squares with the matching cover-card *face down*. Each board should now have five different words showing. Tell pupils to arrange the remaining five cards on their desks *face up*. Call out the words, keeping a record of each one. Call out each word once only. When pupils hear a word that is on their board they must place the matching word cover-card face up on their board. It is a useful idea to make the word cover-cards on different-coloured paper. The first pupil to cover all the squares on his/her board calls out 'Bingo!' and must read back the words that are facing up. If correct, he or she wins.

Spot's Birthday Bingo

a bone	a balloon	a birthday card	a ball
a hat	a present	a basket	a jelly

The Bingo board could be made using illustrations instead of words.

MAKING A BIRTHDAY CARD

This will give pupils practice in the following skills:

- thinking about layout, shape and size: square, rectangular, a cut-out card in the shape of a number, etc.
- thinking about the design: illustrations, decorations (glitter, wool) etc.
- thinking about the message: Happy Birthday [*name*] Love from [*name*]

For further ideas see *Copycard*.

Optional follow-up activities

CREATING A STORYBOOK

Pupils can make their own Spot book with lift-up flaps.

BIRTHDAYS

Return to the birthday wall chart or graph and find out who has a birthday soon. Revise the question (and answer) 'When's your birthday?' Organize a typical birthday party. Pupils can write invitations, make cards and hats, organize games, write menus, etc. (See *Copyparty* and *Copycard* for ideas.) Don't forget to sing 'Happy Birthday'.

DRAWING AND LABELLING

Pupils can draw a plan of Spot's house and label the different rooms and furniture. Encourage pupils to use a dictionary to find out any words they don't know. If this is not possible, they should ask you in the following way: 'How do you say/write [pupil says word in mother tongue, for example, *cuisine*] in English, please?'

LISTENING, LABELLING AND DRAWING

As an alternative to the above, give pupils a plan of Spot's house such as the one on page 101. As you describe it, pupils label the various rooms and draw the different pieces of furniture. For example: 'Room number one is the living-room. In the living-room there is a green armchair, a yellow rug, a plant, a green curtain and a table. Room number two is the kitchen. There is a big cupboard in the kitchen. Room number three is the bathroom. There is a pink bath. Room number four is the hall. There is a brown coat and hat hanging up.'

GAMES PERIOD

English games could be played in the gym on a Friday afternoon or on wet days when children can't play outside. Refer pupils to the first double-spread of *Spot's Birthday Party* and read to 'Let's

Spot's House

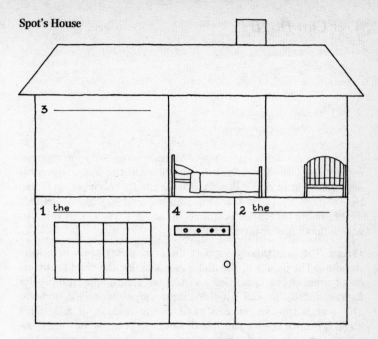

play Hide-and-Seek'. Get pupils to repeat this. Ask them to suggest games using 'Let's play——' and list these on the board. For example, Simon Says, Blind Man's Buff, Kim's Game, What's the Time, Mr Wolf?, and so on.

INVESTIGATING WHERE ANIMALS COME FROM
Get pupils to find out where the animals in the story come from and then stick their pictures or name labels on a world map. They could then make statements or write sentences: 'Crocodiles come from Australia and Africa', 'Lions come from Africa and India', and so on.

DRAMATIZATION
Pupils could learn the animals' lines in the speech bubbles under the flaps and repeat them as you read the story. Masks for each animal could also be made.

   Other stories in the Spot series: *Spot's First Walk, Spot's First Christmas, Spot Goes to School, Spot Goes on Holiday, Spot Goes to the Circus, Spot Goes to the Farm.* (*Spot's Birthday Party* is on cassette.)

Story notes by Hilary Cormack

101

3   I Can Do It!

Author: Shigeo Watanabe
Illustrator: Yasuo Ohtomo

Description: An amusing and easy-to-understand story for any age, telling how Little Bear, the only character in the story, shows his determination to ride a bicycle, drive a car and even pilot a plane. He succeeds by using his own amusing and ingenious methods which, based on Shigeo Watanabe's toddler's typical experiments, will be familiar to readers of any age.

Layout: The illustrations support the text, giving clues to understanding. The details in the illustrations enable the child to understand more about Little Bear, as well as giving opportunities for further discussion and extension into the reader's environment. The text is one sentence a page, facing a page of full-colour illustration, except for the fourth double-spread, where the illustration spreads across both pages, and the last page, where text and picture are on the same page. The pages are not numbered.

The print is the same as in handwriting: ɑ not a, ɡ not g, y not y. This makes copying easier, especially for children whose mother tongue is not written in Roman letters.

The pictures and language content are a-cultural and fit into any society or environment with little or no necessity for cultural explanation.

Linguistic features

Repetition and rhythm: The text uses twenty-one words in thirteen sentences or phrases. The story can be divided into four parts. Each part repeats the statement 'I can ——'. These words in parts one, two and three are followed by confirming statements, including 'nearly' and 'I can do it', which give the opportunity to repeat language in the same rhythm. The repetition and short text help non-native-speaker children to memorize the text.

Linguistic objectives

SKILLS

- Listening to the story, discussion and instructions
- Speaking: asking and answering questions
- Reading aloud/silently
- Writing: copying, creative writing, spelling

FUNCTIONS/STRUCTURES

- Discussing and listing learned abilities using 'I can' and verb and noun, 'I can' and noun and 'too', 'I can't'
- Confirming degree of ability using 'nearly'
- Confirming ability using 'I can do it'
- Conversational expressions using 'well'/'see'
- Asking for information using Yes/No and Wh– questions

VOCABULARY

- In the text:

To ride	To drive	To pilot	To skate
tricycle two-wheeler skateboard	car bus	plane	roller-skates

- Extension:

bicycle trike/bike motor bike horse camel	van truck tractor crane bulldozer	helicopter balloon airship boat	ice-skates

- To play:

    Games: football, tennis, judo, Snap, Ludo, etc.
    Instruments: piano, violin, trumpet, drums, keyboard, etc.

PRONUNCIATION

As young children learn by imitation, it is important to decide how the text is to be read. Use exactly the same intonation and stress for each reading.

- Intonation and stress: Now I can do it.

    See! I CAN do it.

    Well, Nearly.

- Individual sounds: /cən/ as in I can drive a car.

CONCEPTUAL REINFORCEMENT/CURRICULUM LINKS
- Geography and the environment: sports and games
- Creative activities: drawing
- Music and drama: singing songs and rhymes, miming, dramatization

LEARNING TO LEARN

Comparing, classifying, using charts, surveys and investigations, using dictionaries, training the memory, reviewing, self-assessment

Suggested procedures

Preparation
- Introducing key vocabulary words
- Discussing bears, revising parts of the human body, etc.

Projects

Use the story for:
- mini-projects (one or two lessons)
- projects (several lessons)
- games
- rhymes and songs

(details are given in each lesson)

Time

This will depend on the activity and the time taken for organizing the number of children in the class. The time length needs to be adjusted to the children's attention span in the actual lesson. Storytelling and mini-projects could last from five to twenty minutes and projects from twenty to thirty-five minutes. Details of suggested time length are given as a guide with the project descriptions in each lesson. Teachers will need to adapt these for their own classroom situations.

Materials
- Magazine pictures of what is listed in the vocabulary section. Other pictures of local transport and of the people who control it
- Materials to make visual aids
- Reference books

Lesson One (Mini-project: up to twenty minutes)

Aims
- Introduce bears, discussing and comparing parts of the body
- Ask children if they know the names of any famous bears. For example, Paddington, Winnie the Pooh, etc. If they have a bear at home, ask them to bring it to the next lesson.

Introduction
Bring a toy bear or a picture of a bear to the classroom. Group children round the bear to discuss the bear's face and then its body. It is important to note that it has no arms but four legs, no hands but paws. Ask children to touch parts of the bear's body: 'Touch its nose', 'Now touch its left paw', etc.

PICTURE DICTATION
Give each child a piece of paper. Draw a bear's face (side-view) on the board.

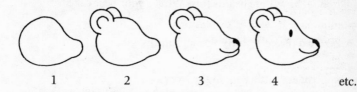

1   2   3   4   etc.

Instructions
- Copy the bear's head.
- Draw two ears.
- Now add a nose and a mouth.
- Now add two eyes and colour them.

- And now draw a body.
- And now four legs: one, two, three, four. Add the paws: one, two and the feet, one, two.
- Colour your bear and put a big label round his neck.
- (The teacher draws a label on the board.) What's your bear called? Write his name on the label.

Ending

Children stand round, holding their bear picture in front of them, so that everyone can see it. The first child says, 'My bear's called ——.' Turning to the next child he or she asks, 'What's your bear called?' The next child says,' My bear's called ——.' He or she turns to the next child and asks, 'What's your bear called?' The chain continues until all the children have told the name of their bear.

If possible, display all the pictures or get children to cut them out and stick them on a big card to make a bear show. Title of the display: Class —— Bear Show.

Follow-up

Next lesson arrange a bear show of toy bears brought in by children. Ask, 'Whose bear is this? What's your bear called?'

Lesson Two (Project: thirty-five minutes)

Aims

- To introduce Little Bear in the story
- To introduce vocabulary: tricycle/two-wheeler/bicycle/skateboard

  Can you ride?/Yes, I can/No, I can't

  I/he or she/you can ride a —— too

- To introduce the first two pages (not the cover or the front page) of the story.

106

Introduction
Show a picture of a tricycle/three-wheeler (the front page of the book) and discuss wheels, bell, handlebars, seat (saddle), pedals.

Say, miming the action, 'I can ride a tricycle.' Ask children in turn, 'Can you ride a tricycle?' At first they will reply, 'Yes' or 'No'. Build on to this, 'Yes, I can,' or 'No, I can't.'

Activity
Show children the tricycle on the front page and let them point to the wheels, the seat (saddle), the handlebars etc.

Children copy from the blackboard: 'I can/can't ride a tricycle' – whichever is appropriate. Children can colour the picture and the older ones can label the parts of the tricycle.

Ending
Recap on bears and then introduce the first picture of Little Bear on the tricycle: 'Look, this is Little Bear. He can ride a tricycle.' Read the text with a special voice for Little Bear. Turn the page and look at the next picture. The children will say 'bicycle'. Reply, 'Yes it is a bicycle but Little Bear calls it a two-wheeler.' Then read the text. Turn to the next page. Again the children will call out 'skateboard'. Read the text maintaining the special voice for Little Bear. Give back the bears from the bear show, asking the children in turn, 'Can your bear ride a tricycle?, and so on. Reply, 'Yes, he can'/'No, he can't.'

Follow-up
For the next lesson prepare a class chart for children to complete.

Can you ride a tricycle?	Can you ride a two-wheeler?	Can you ride a skateboard?
Yes, I can	No, I can't	No, I can't

Complete the chart with each child drawing his or her face and then filling in the speech balloon.

Lesson Three (Mini-projects: including story and rhyme, ten minutes each)

Aims
- To introduce: I can roller-skate
                 I can do it
                 NOTE: *some* roller-skates/*a pair of* roller-skates
                 a bow/I can tie a bow
                 Well, nearly; Now
- To extend vocabulary into the environment and what children can ride
- To transfer 'I can do it' to classroom use in answer to 'Can you do it?'

Introduction
Show pictures of roller-skates and ice-skates and discuss. Reread the story from the beginning up to the page where Little Bear is on the floor with four skates.

Activity
Introduce the chart from the last lesson and complete. Discuss what children can ride and make a list. For example: a bicycle, a horse, and so on. Write the name by the picture, etc. Get children to collect pictures at home for the next lesson.

Ending
Introduce the action rhyme/song: 'Can you walk on two legs/hop on one leg?' in *This Little Puffin*, page 143. It can be sung in two groups with one group asking and the other replying. The replies can be sung, 'I can walk on two legs', etc.

Follow-up
Next lesson teach additional verses of the song. Add children's pictures to the list: What we can ride.

Lesson Four

Aims
- To introduce vocabulary and to practise: I can drive a car; I can't ——
- To transfer and extend language

Introduction
Reread the list: What we can ride, and introduce a new list: What we can drive. Place a picture of a car on the list, write the word 'car' next to it and discuss. Introduce other vehicles. For example: bus, truck, tractor (see Vocabulary list).

Reread the story as far as: I can drive a car. Discuss the picture and the front cover where Little Bear is driving a racing car. Discuss sports/racing cars.

Activity

CARD GAME
Each child is given four cards. On each card they write one object that can be driven or ridden. Two cards are for what can be driven, two cards for what can be ridden. These names can be copied from the lists. Children divide into pairs and play the game with two sets of cards (eight cards).

The cards are placed face down in two groups. The first child picks up one of the other player's cards and reads, for example, 'a bus' and says, 'I can/can't drive a bus.' If he or she reads correctly, he or she can take the card. The second player then picks up one of the first player's cards, reads it and adds the word. The winners are the children who have won four cards.

a bus	a tank	a horse	a donkey

Ending
Repeat the song/rhyme 'Can you Walk on Two Legs?' adding new verses.

Follow-up
For the next lesson develop the game by adding new cards to include: roller-skates and pilot a ——

Lesson Five (Game: fifteen minutes)

Aims
- To finish reading the story
- To transfer and extend language

Introduction
Reread the two lists and add one more: What we can pilot, listing a plane and a helicopter.

Reread the story from the beginning right to the end. Reread straight through once more, remaining silent towards the end of each phrase so that the children can complete them in turn.

Game
Give the children two cards each. They can choose to write either roller-skates or ice-skates on one, and on the other, a plane or a helicopter. Children divide into different pairs and play the game as in Lesson Four. The children with six cards are the winners.

roller-skates	a plane

Ending
Reread the story again, letting the children complete the ends of the phrases. Repeat the song/rhyme, adding new verses.

Follow-up
Ask children to collect pictures of people who drive/ride/pilot objects in their environment. Ask any interested child to prepare reading the story for the next lesson.

Lesson Six (Own projects thirty minutes and some to be finished at home)

Aims
● To let children read the story
● To discuss the names of people who drive/pilot, etc.
● To let children follow their own interests and develop independence.

Introduction
Show children a picture of a pilot and say, 'He can pilot a plane. He's a pilot.' Use other pictures (from their environment) to introduce driver/taxi-driver/bus-driver/lorry-driver, etc.

Free choice
Children working individually or in groups can choose between:
● playing the game
● drawing a picture of Little Bear
● copying the story and pictures to make their own book

- making their own book (four pages folded and stapled together): writing their own text and illustrating it with what they can, or can nearly, do
- children can read the story aloud and record it. They can play it back and then reread and re-record it, making improvements where appropriate.

Quick game

The teacher passes a card to a child with the word car written on it. The teacher asks, 'Can your father drive a car?' The child replies, 'Yes, he can' or 'No, he can't.' The child then passes the card to another child and asks, 'Can your mother drive a car?' The child replies, 'Yes, she can' or 'No, she can't.' The game continues with the child asking questions using the words father or mother and other vehicles to drive, ride or pilot.

Ending

Reviewing children's workbooks and displaying work. Checking games for winners. Listening to story-reading/recording by children.

Further activities

- Words can be added to a picture dictionary.

- A collection of names of professions can be made, using words from this lesson as a starting-point.

- Creating a story and making a book. A class story or individual stories can be written about other animals and what they can do. For example, a monkey or an elephant. Let children suggest animals and discuss some of the things they can, or can nearly, do, before writing a text. Try to bring out some of the humour but do not comment directly on how the humour is used in Little Bear's case. Useful words can be written on the blackboard or in a special large class book, A Book of Useful Words.

- Mime game. The teacher mimes an activity. For example, taking a child's temperature, looking in its mouth and asking, 'What am I?' The first child who replies 'a doctor' takes the turn to mime and ask the question.

- Make two more lists: Instruments we can play and Games we can play. (see Vocabulary).

This story can be followed up by other Little Bear books. Titles are:
How Do I Eat It?, How Do I Put It On?, Ready, Steady, Go!, Hallo! How are You?, I'm Going for a Walk!, I'm Playing with Papa!', I'm Having a Bath with Papa!

Other useful books are:
Big Wheels, Bikes, Boats, Cars, Fire Engines, Planes, Trains, Trucks.
All by Anne Rockwell

Story notes by Opal Dunn

4 Having a Picnic

Author and illustrator: Sarah Garland

Description: A mother, her daughter and baby go for a picnic in the park. The theme, which may seem childish, can be exploited in many ways, especially as the illustrations are rich and evocative.

Layout: The pictures are very realistic, reflecting everyday life in Britain. Each picture covers two pages, which means that they can be easily seen by the whole class. Your pupils will have no difficulty in identifying with all of the characters. The text is short and printed in large type at the top of each page. There are five pages without any text at the beginning and at the end of the book.

Linguistic features

Prediction: You can encourage the use of prediction techniques since the context of the story is so familiar. The text and illustrations encourage the reader to guess what happens next.

Linguistic objectives

SKILLS
- Listening for general comprehension and listening for details via instructions
- Speaking: asking and answering questions, giving instructions
- Writing: labelling

FUNCTIONS/STRUCTURES
- Describing location using prepositions
- Asking for information using Wh– questions
- Giving information using 'Here it is!'
- Giving warning using 'Look out!'
- Well-wishing using 'Have a good picnic!'

VOCABULARY
The vocabulary in the text is limited but it can be extended,

113

depending on the level of your class, by using the illustrations. Vocabulary falls into the following areas: family, colours, house, clothes, weather, street, park, animals, food, prepositions: up, down, off, into, at, to.

PRONUNCIATION

● Intonation: Where's the picnic?

   Who's this?

● Individual sounds: /a/ as in park
                    /ju/ as in view
                    /ɒ/ as in pond
                    /ʌ/ as in ducks, up and buns
                    /ɪ/ and /i/ as in hill and feed
                    /aʊ/ as in down

● Stress: **Picnic**
         Have a good **Picnic!**

CONCEPTUAL REINFORCEMENT/CURRICULUM LINKS

● Colours and spatial context
● Geography and the environment: parks, using a map, seasons, clothes
● Creative activities: drawing
● Music and drama: singing songs and rhymes, miming

LEARNING TO LEARN
Memory training, predicting

Cultural interest
The illustrations depict typical scenes of life in a big town in Great Britain. The mother seems to be bringing up her children alone in this story, as well as in the others in the series (see page 119).

Materials
● The cover
● A tray
● Familiar objects
● A scarf for Blind Man's Buff
● Maps of the local area

Lesson One

Aims
- To introduce the characters and context of the story: place, season, and so on
- To revise or introduce vocabulary for colours and clothes

Show pupils the cover and ask the following questions:
- How many people are there?
- Who are they?
- What's this? (pointing to the dog)
- Are they in a town or in the country?
- How do you know?
- What can you see in the park?
- What do you think they are going to do?
- Is it summer or winter?
- How do you know?

Depending on the level of your pupils, you may need to ask some of these questions in the mother tongue but use English words for picnic, park, mother, baby, dog, hill, and so on. Pupils may reply in English or in their mother tongue. Accepting one-word answers will facilitate the use of English. If you don't want to use the mother tongue, use illustrations to help convey meanings. For example, use photographs of the countryside and of a town.

Revise or introduce vocabulary for colours and clothes and ask the following questions:

- What colour is the mother's coat?
- What colour is the daughter's coat?
- What colour is the baby's suit?
- What colour are the mother's trousers?
- What colour are the daughter's trousers?
- What colour are the baby's boots?
and so on.

COLOUR DICTATION
Give each pupil an outline drawing of the cover of the book and ask them to:
- Colour the mother's coat green
- Colour the daughter's coat blue
  and so on

You can, of course, change the colours and use other parts of the picture (the trees, the sky, the lawn) for your dictation.

Optional follow-up activity:
Ask your pupils to write the names of the objects they know in English. They should write the word next to the item.

Lesson Two

Aims
● To revise the keywords from Lesson One
● To tell the story aloud for the first time
● To present up and down

Procedure
By referring to the cover again, make sure your pupils have remembered the keywords in the text.

Show the class the first two pages without text and then the following two pages. Ask them the following questions:
● What are they?
● What time is it?
● What are they doing?
● What's in the basket?

When you tell the story for the first time, ask your pupils to sit down facing you. Make sure all can see the book. Read the text from the beginning to the end. Introduce pauses after each double-spread so that your pupils have time to reflect on the illustrations, and to give them an opportunity to ask questions. Point to the relevant parts of the illustrations when introducing new words such as ducks, pond, buns, and so on.

PREDICTING
When you reach the page starting 'Up the hill . . .', try to encourage your pupils to guess why the family is climbing up the hill. Use the illustrations and ask questions to help them. In the same way, stop reading after 'Down to the pond . . .' and ask your pupils why the family is going down to the pond.

Ask the following questions about the last double-spread:
● Where are they?
● What time is it?
● How long have they been in the park?
● How do they feel?

116

SONG

To reinforce the use of up and down, introduce the following nursery rhyme:

Up I stretch on tippy toe
Down to touch my heels I go
Up again my arms I send
Down again my knees I bend.

The tune to this rhyme can be found in *This Little Puffin* on page 142. (It is also on cassette.)

Lesson Three

Aims
● To tell the story a second time
● To aid comprehension of action words by using games

Procedure
Read the whole story again. Introduce regular pauses to encourage participation and to make sure that your pupils remember the text. For example, 'Up the hill . . .', 'Down to the pond . . .', 'They've taken the . . .', 'Have a . . .'.

SIMON SAYS

Introduce the game Simon Says to revise the action words used in the text:
● Up the hill!
● Look at the view!
● Down to the pond!
● Feed the ducks!
● Eat a bun!
    Depending on the level of the class, you could use other instructions to review other vocabulary items:
● Put on your boots!
● Put on your coat!
● Call the dog!
● Eat an apple!
and so on.
    You could invite one or several pupils to replace you in giving the instructions.

SONG

To end this lesson, sing the song your pupils learnt in Lesson Two. You could vary this activity by dividing the class into two groups. One group sings while the other group mimes the actions. You can, of course, reverse the roles subsequently.

Optional follow-up activities

PICTURE DICTATION

Each pupil is given a pencil and a sheet of paper. Explain that they must use the instructions you give them to trace someone's route. For example: Off for a walk. Into the park. Draw one, two, three, four trees. Up a hill. Stop at the top. Sit on a bench. Down to a pond. Draw one, two, three, four ducks. Once the drawings have been completed, put them up on the wall, so that your pupils can take pride in their work.

PARKS

- My dream park: Get children to list the different components found in parks: paddling pools, swings, slides, roundabouts, trees, flowers, ponds, sweet shops, and so on, and to devise their dream park. Pupils could draw this and label the various features.

- Using maps and giving directions: Let children work in pairs and groups and distribute a map or plan of your local area. Pupils must mark all the different parks and say which is the best and why. They can then choose a park without saying where it is and give directions to the rest of the class who follow on their own maps. Do this with your pupils yourself first.

- Cultural studies: If possible, show pictures or slides of other parks in large towns in English-speaking countries, for example, Hyde Park, Regent's Park, Central Park. Pupils can compare parks they know in their own country with these.

- A picnic: Organize an English picnic where children can eat buns, drink tea or orange juice. Use this opportunity to revise vocabulary and expressions introduced through the story.

LANGUAGE WORK

To practise using the two questions 'Where's the picnic?' and 'Who's this?' pupils can play the following games:

118

- Hide-and-Seek: To play this game, you need a tray on which you place a number of objects. Use small objects, the names of which your pupils are familiar with in English (pencil, rubber, key, button, and so on). If necessary, write a list of the words on the board. One pupil comes forward and picks up one of the objects, without showing it to the other pupils. The class must identify the missing object by asking questions, such as, 'Where's the pencil?' If the pupil has the pencil he or she says, 'Here it is!' The pupil then puts the object back on the tray. Another pupil comes forward and the game continues as before until the class has gone through all the objects.

  This game could also be played in groups of five or six pupils.

- Blind Man's Buff: The rules of this game are well known and it can be played by the whole class or in groups. When the pupil wearing the blindfold catches a classmate, the class or the group must ask, 'Who's this?' The pupil replies, 'It's Michael.'

DRAWING

Using the pictures in the book, pupils, either individually or in groups, can draw other scenes in parks as they imagine them. These drawings could be used to decorate the classroom.

Having a Picnic is part of a series by the same author which features the same characters. Other titles are: *Doing the Washing, Going Shopping, Coming to Tea.*

Story notes by Anne Feunteun

5 *The Very Hungry Caterpillar*

Author and illustrator: Eric Carle

Description: An amusing story about growth and change. A very tiny and very hungry caterpillar grows from a small egg to a beautiful butterfly.

Layout: Bright, colourful illustrations on double-page spreads with cut-away pages through which the very hungry caterpillar manages to nibble his way.

Linguistic features: A repeating story illustrating the use of counting and sequencing. What the caterpillar did each day is repeated. On [*Monday*] he ate through [*one apple*] but he was still hungry, and so on.

Linguistic objectives

SKILLS
- Listening: for general understanding via visual clues and by recognizing highlighted keywords and phrases when the story is told, for specific information via statements and instructions
- Speaking: repetition of key vocabulary and phrases when the story is told, asking and answering questions, song, action rhyme
- Reading: recognition of key vocabulary and phrases, charts, diaries, calendars
- Writing: vocabulary sets, labelling, simple sentences, diaries

FUNCTIONS/STRUCTURES
- Asking for and giving information using Yes/No and Wh– questions
- Asking for and giving the date using Wh– questions and word order. For example, It's Friday the 2nd of March
- Making statements using the verb to be
- Giving instructions using the imperative
- Asking about and expressing likes and dislikes

VOCABULARY
Includes items from the following lexical sets:

- Days of the week
- Numbers (cardinals and ordinals)
- Fruit
- Colours
- Food
- Life-cycle of the butterfly: egg, caterpillar, cocoon
- Adjectives: little, tiny, hungry, big, fat, beautiful

PRONUNCIATION
- Intonation: The 1st of March is a Tuesday.

    Do you like chocolate cake?

    rising and final falling intonation in lists:

    one piece of chocolate cake,

    one ice-cream cone . . .

    and one slice of watermelon.

- Individual sounds: /ɜ/ as in first, third
    /θ/ as in fourth, fifth, etc.
    /tʃ/ as in cherry, cheese, chocolate
    /i/ as in cheese, cream

- Stress: **Mon**day, **Tues**day, etc.
    But he was **still** hungry.

CONCEPTUAL REINFORCEMENT/CURRICULUM LINKS

- Colours, size and shape and time
- Maths: numbers and quantity, using calendars and diaries, making a grid
- Science: life-cycles
- Geography and the environment: food
- Creative activities: drawing, making masks, models
- Music and drama: singing songs and rhymes, role-play, dramatization

LEARNING TO LEARN
Comparing, classifying, predicting, sequencing, hypothesizing and problem-solving, memory training, using charts, surveys and investigations

Materials
Page from a diary; photocopies of fruit and food or plastic facsimiles.

Lesson One

Aim: To introduce or revise days of the week, cardinal numbers one to seven and ordinal numbers for dates.

Show pupils the cover of the book and tell them that they are going to hear a story about a very hungry caterpillar. Ask some general questions about caterpillars to motivate the children and to contextualize the story. For example: What do caterpillars eat? How long do they stay caterpillars?, etc. You will probably need to do this in the mother tongue.

Days of the week

Ask 'What day is it?' Teach or revise days of the week, starting with the day of this lesson. Check pronunciation by asking pupils how many syllables each word has and which syllable is stressed.

MONDAY, TUESDAY
This song is on the cassette (© Eileen Sorley). Introduce the following song and teach the corresponding actions:

2/4	■ Monday do do C C 1	■ Tuesday sol sol G G 2	■ Wednesday la la A A 1	■ Thursday mi mi E E 2
	■ Friday fa fa F F 1	■ Saturday sol sol G G 2	■ Sunday do do C C 1	X X X X 2 . : Twice

ACTIONS
In pairs, pupils stand opposite each other. For each stressed syllable, they make the following actions:

One	Two	Three	Four
Hands on thighs	Clap hands	Clap partner's hands	Clap hands
Monday Friday	Tuesday Saturday	Wednesday Sunday	Thursday X X

GAME

Once the children know the song and actions well, they can sing it, leaving out every other day. For example, Monday . . . Wednesday . . . Friday . . . Sunday . . . Little by little, other days can be left out. The class can also be divided into two groups to sing the song: each group singing an alternate day.

Cardinal numbers

Revise the numbers one to seven. Starting with the thumb of your left hand count one to seven. Do the same for the days of the week so that each day corresponds to a number. Ask, 'What day is number 4?' and teach the reply, 'It's Thursday.' Repeat this several times, asking individual pupils.

PAIR WORK

Pupils in pairs repeat the activity above.

Ordinal numbers

Ask 'What's the date today?' Introduce or revise ordinals. For example, 'It's Friday, the 2nd of March.' Practise pronunciation of /ʒ/ as in first, third and /θ/ as in fourth, fifth, etc.

NOTE: We say, 'It's Monday, the 12th of March.' We write: Monday, 12th March.

JANUARY							FEBRUARY							MARCH						
M	T	W	T	F	S	S	M	T	W	T	F	S	S	M	T	W	T	F	S	S
						1			1	2	3	4	5			1	2	3	4	5
2	3	4	5	6	7	8	6	7	8	9	10	11	12	6	7	8	9	10	11	12
9	10	11	12	13	14	15	13	14	15	16	17	18	19	13	14	15	16	17	18	19
16	17	18	19	20	21	22	20	21	22	23	24	25	26	20	21	22	23	24	25	26
23	24	25	26	27	28	29	27	28						27	28	29	30	31		
30	31																			

APRIL							MAY							JUNE						
M	T	W	T	F	S	S	M	T	W	T	F	S	S	M	T	W	T	F	S	S
					1	2	1	2	3	4	5	6	7				1	2	3	4
3	4	5	6	7	8	9	8	9	10	11	12	13	14	5	6	7	8	9	10	11
10	11	12	13	14	15	16	15	16	17	18	19	20	21	12	13	14	15	16	17	18
17	18	19	20	21	22	23	22	23	24	25	26	27	28	19	20	21	22	23	24	25
24	25	26	27	28	29	30	29	30	31					26	27	28	29	30		

ACTIVITY

Give out the worksheet above. Pupils discuss dates together first.

Ask a pupil to tell you the date: 'It's Monday, the 2nd of January', while another writes the date on the board: Monday, 2nd January. Repeat with the other dates.

Optional follow-up activities
To introduce the written form, write the days of the week on pieces of card big enough for all the class to see. Show a card to the pupils and ask, 'What day is it?' Teach the reply, 'It's Tuesday.'

Show the cards again and ask, 'Is this Monday?' Encourage the reply, 'Yes, it is!' or 'No, it isn't!'

WHAT'S MISSING?
Using the same cards (either in the correct order or jumbled up), ask pupils to close their eyes. Remove one day of the week, then ask, 'What's missing?'

SEQUENCING
● Stick the cards on the board in a jumbled order and ask pupils to put them in the correct sequence.
● Pupils make their own set of weekdays. Ask them to jumble them up on their desks. Give the following instructions, 'Put Tuesday first!', 'Put Wednesday second!', and so on.

TRUE OR FALSE?
This activity provides a very simple listening and reading exercise. Copy a page from a diary for each pupil or make one (see page 125). Make true or false statements:'The 1st of March is a Tuesday! True or false?' Pupils reply, 'False, it's a Thursday!'

PAIR WORK
Pupils repeat this activity in pairs.

Lesson Two

Aim: To introduce or revise vocabulary for fruit and colours

Begin this lesson by asking pupils the date and revising the days of the week.

Use plastic fruit or copy the pictures in the book (Monday–Friday) on large sheets of paper. Cut them out, so you have individual flash cards. Show pupils the strawberry, pear and plum first and ask, in turn, 'What's this?' Teach the English word and check pronunciation. Encourage the reply, 'It's a strawberry.' Stick the corresponding picture on the blackboard.

February 1990	**1990 March**
26 Monday	Thursday **1**
27 Tuesday	Friday **2**
28 Wednesday	Saturday **3**
	Sunday **4**

A OR AN?

Now introduce an apple and an orange, emphasizing the use of
an. Repeat the sentences or write them on the board and ask
pupils, 'Why is it *a* strawberry but *an* apple?' Encourage pupils to
discover the rule themselves (*an* comes before a vowel sound). If
appropriate, give examples using other words the pupils may
know. For example, egg, bun, apricot, etc.

TRUE OR FALSE?

Pointing to the pictures of the fruit, make true or false statements to check comprehension. 'It's a strawberry! True or false?',
etc.

125

Colours

Revise colours by showing the strawberry and asking, 'What colour is it?', etc. Introduce or revise purple for the plum.

Give each pupil an envelope containing drawings of the five different fruits or they can do their own pictures. Ask them to arrange these on their desks. Then give the following instructions: 'Colour the strawberry red!', 'Colour the plum purple!', etc.

If this colouring in takes too long, ask pupils to mark each fruit with the corresponding colour and to finish at home.

Optional follow-up activities:

LABELLING

Pupils may like to label their pictures either with the corresponding word: apple, or with the sentence: 'It's an apple', etc.

SIMON SAYS

Pupils use the pictures above to play Simon Says:
'Simon says show me a plum!', 'Simon says put the plum down!', 'Show me an orange!', etc.

GROUP WORK

After a few games led by you, pupils could play in small groups with one pupil calling out the instructions. Finish this lesson by singing 'Monday, Tuesday'.

Lesson Three

Aim: To read part of the story and practise asking for information

To encourage pupils to predict some of the vocabulary in the story, ask them some general questions, probably in the mother tongue, about caterpillars.

Show pupils the first double-page spread. Teach or revise moon, leaf and egg, pointing to the illustrations. Read the first two lines. Next double-page spread, teach or revise sun and the adjective, tiny. Read the next two lines. Go back to the beginning and read all four lines. Pause at the keywords and point to the illustrations to encourage pupils to say the words.

STORYTELLING

Read the next part of the story up to Friday, encouraging pupils to repeat the days of the week, the quantity and names of the fruit. After they have heard 'But he was still hungry' two or three times, encourage them to repeat this with you, making sure they stress *still*.

HOW MANY?

Using the illustrations from the book for Monday to Friday ask, 'How many oranges are there?' Teach the reply, 'There are five oranges', etc. For further practice use the names of other fruit the pupils may know. Copy the drawings of pears, plums, strawberries and oranges. Give one to a pupil and ask him or her to ask another pupil, 'How many —— are there?' Teach or revise lemons, bananas and cherries.

PAIR WORK

Divide the pupils into pairs, A and B. Give out the worksheets on page 128 and tell them not to show their partner. Revise vocabulary. Pupil B begins and asks, 'How many lemons are there?' Pupil A replies, 'There are seven lemons.' Pupil B writes seven in the empty box. Pupil A then asks, 'How many strawberries are there?', and so on. When they have finished they can compare their worksheets to check they have the correct numbers.

Counting

MEMORY GAME

Ask pupils the following two questions, in the mother tongue if necessary:

- How many different sorts of fruit did the caterpillar eat? (Answer: five)

- How many pieces of fruit did the caterpillar eat all together? (Answer: fifteen)

RHYME: HOT POTATO

This is a traditional English counting rhyme which is acted out with hand actions.

One potato, two potatoes, three potatoes, four.
Five potatoes, six potatoes, seven potatoes, MORE!

Demonstrate the actions as follows with one group of three to five pupils who form a circle. They place clenched fists outstretched into the centre of the circle. One pupil counts each fist in turn, chanting the rhyme on each beat. The fist that is tapped on MORE! (every eighth fist) is 'out' and must be placed behind the player's

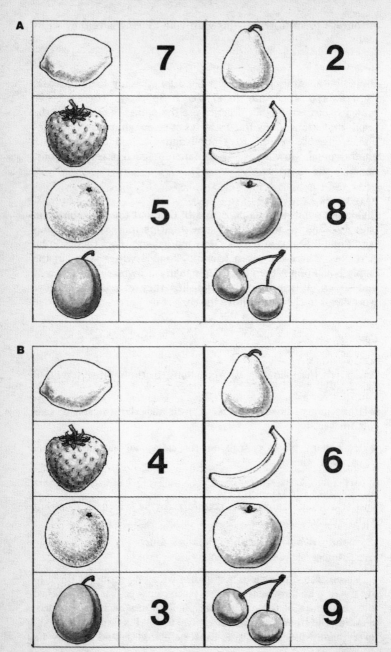

back. When both fists are counted out, that player leaves the game. The winner is the last player remaining.

Divide the class into groups to recite the rhyme as described above. Read the story again up to Friday and ask pupils what they think the caterpillar eats on Saturday.

Lesson Four

Aim: To introduce food items for Saturday

Copy the pictures in the book on large sheets of paper. Cut them out to make flash cards. Ask pupils to tell you again what they think the caterpillar eats on Saturday. If they predict any of the items start with these. If not, show a picture and ask, 'What's this?' Teach or revise the vocabulary. For example, 'It's chocolate cake', 'It's ice-cream', etc. Practise pronunciation. You may need to introduce the vocabulary over two lessons.

To check comprehension, play What's Missing?, True or False? or Sequencing. As you introduce the vocabulary ask, 'Do you like ice-cream?', etc. but don't spend too much time on it at this stage.

SORTING: SWEET OR SALTY?

Draw two columns on the blackboard and teach the difference between sweet and salty. If possible, allow the pupils to taste something sweet and then something salty. Jumble up the pictures and arrange them on a table. Ask individual pupils to sort them into the two groups. For example, say, 'Mary, choose something salty', etc. The pupil selects an item and puts it in the appropriate column.

STORYTELLING

Read the story again including Saturday and encourage the pupils to participate. Make sure they can see the picture of the caterpillar. You may need to walk around the classroom or let the pupils pass the book around. Ask how they think the caterpillar feels after all it has eaten. Ask what they think it eats on Sunday.

Lesson Five

Aim: To introduce the concept of countable and uncountable nouns

Although this can be a difficult concept for pupils to grasp, the distinction between countable and uncountable nouns (sometimes

129

referred to as count or mass nouns) is important for the correct use of articles (a or an) and singular or plural forms. Uncountable nouns are not normally preceded by 'a' or 'one' and do not have a plural. One example of an uncountable noun can be indicated by:

- a/one piece: for example, one piece of chocolate cake
- a/one slice: for example, one slice of Swiss cheese

The suggested problem-solving activity below encourages pupils to work out and discover the rules of grammar for themselves. They will learn much more thinking about the language in this way. Once they have worked out the rule, they can practise the structure by using it in the activity suggested in Lesson Six.

NOTE: Often a word can be used as an uncountable noun when it refers to something in general, but as a countable noun when it refers to one separate unit or a portion composed of that substance, for example, ice-cream, chocolate cake, etc. We have not highlighted this here and have used the above two items as uncountable.

PROBLEM-SOLVING: SPOT THE DIFFERENCE!

Revise vocabulary for Saturday by asking, 'What's this?' Insist on the reply, 'It's chocolate cake.' Now ask, 'Do you like chocolate cake?' and teach the reply, 'Yes, I do' or 'No, I don't.' Continue in this way with the other items.

Give out the worksheet on page 135 and explain the instructions. You will probably need to use the mother tongue for this activity. It is important for the pupils to understand the rule. They must first sort the sentences into two groups and then justify the reasons for their classification.

They may suggest groupings according to colour, whether the food is sweet or salty, etc. You will need to guide the pupils to focus their attention on the structure of the sentences and to formulate their hypotheses.

They should notice that the nouns which take the indefinite article (a or an) also need to take the plural form in the question, 'Do you like . . .?' This is because these items can be counted, whereas the others can't and have no plurals. To be counted, they need to be cut up into pieces or slices.

If possible, bring some concrete examples of countable and uncountable items into the classroom. For example, bread, lollipops, apples, cheese, sweets, milk, chocolate, etc. Ask pupils, 'What's this?' to elicit the reply, 'It's bread', 'It's an apple', etc.

Give the item to a pupil and ask him or her to ask another pupil, 'Do you like bread?', 'Do you like apples?', to see if they can apply the rule.

Lesson Six

Aim: To practise asking about and expressing likes and dislikes

This activity could be integrated into a maths class. The pupils make their own worksheet in the form of a grid to interview others. Making this will provide practice in drawing horizontal and vertical lines according to instructions given by the teacher. Pupils will also be cutting, pasting and colouring.

Copy and, if necessary, reduce the size of the pictures of the food items for Saturday for each child. Alternatively, children could draw their own.

Dictate instructions in the mother tongue or in English to draw a grid. Once this has been completed, revise vocabulary for Saturday. Pupils cut out and stick the pictures on the grid or draw their own (see example on page 133). They can colour them in class or at home. You may or may not wish your pupils to write in the vocabulary.

Revise the question and reply. For example, 'Do you like watermelon?' 'Yes, I do', 'No, I don't.'

INTERVIEW/SURVEY
In pairs or in small groups, pupils interview each other. According to their replies, they put a tick for yes or a cross for no in the corresponding box.

Time allowing, pupils could collate their findings on a chart. This would revise numbers and the question, 'How many . . .?' For example, 'How many pupils like chocolate cake?'
- ten pupils like chocolate cake
- eight pupils like pickles

and so on.

Lesson Seven

Aim: To read the story and encourage pupils to participate by repeating key vocabulary items and phrases

Ask pupils to tell you what they can remember about the story, especially what the caterpillar ate. Ask them what they think it eats on Sunday.

Read the story up to Sunday. Fold the book in half so pupils can see only the caterpillar. Ask, 'Is he tiny?' Teach or revise big and fat. Ask pupils to tell you what they think happens next in the caterpillar's life to elicit the word cocoon. Ask how long they think it stays inside the cocoon and what happens when it comes out.

Read the story again from beginning to end, encouraging the maximum participation. (Listen to the cassette for a demonstration.)

Optional follow-up activities

ART AND HANDICRAFTS
This book leads into a range of art and handicraft activities related to the following concepts: shapes, textures, colours, sizes, parts of the body
● drawing caterpillars and butterflies
● making caterpillars and butterflies (see *Copytoys*)
● making fruit

DRAMATIZATION
The story could be acted out using the props made above. Pupils could also create sound-effects.

NATURE AND SCIENCE
● Pupils could investigate what different types of caterpillars really eat.
● They could select a butterfly or moth of their own choice and draw the different stages of its life-cycle and label keywords.

WRITING
Using the diary page from Lesson One, pupils could write a record of the fruit they ate that week. For example, 'On Monday I ate two bananas,' or simply list vocabulary day by day.

SONGS AND RHYMES
To revise days of the week, see Solomon Grundy on page 140 in *The Mother Goose Treasury*. For numbers, see Number Songs and Rhymes in *This Little Puffin* on page 131 and especially the action rhyme 'Ten fat sausages sitting in the pan' on page 132. (This is on cassette.)

MEMORY GAMES
● To revise the food items, play the game, 'I went to market and

PART 2

Do You Like . . .

	sausages	watermelon	chocolate cake	salami	cherry pie	pickles	cupcakes	lollipops	Swiss cheese	and ice cream
me	✓	✗	✓	✗	✓	✓	✓	✓	✗	✓
Jo	✓	✗	✓	✗	✓	✗	✓	✗	✓	✓
Sarah	✓	✗	✓	✓	✓	✗	✓	✓	✓	✓

PART 2

bought an apple . . .' The next pupil adds an item, 'I went to
market and bought an apple and a chocolate cake', and so on.

● Get pupils to work out how many things the caterpillar ate
through all together. Pupils try to remember and draw or write
each item, or set of items, starting with Monday and going
through to Sunday.

CREATING A STORY AND MAKING A BOOK
Pupils could choose other food that the caterpillar might eat and
build these ideas into new stories of their own. The book could be
made in the shape of a caterpillar.

ROLE-PLAY: THE FOOD SHOP
Props: a table, some plastic fruit
Roles: a very hungry child (A)
       a shop assistant (B)

Pupils memorize the following lines:
A Good morning. Oooh! (*holding his/her stomach*)
B Good morning, what's wrong?
A I'm hungry. Give me an apple, please.
B Here you are. (*Child begins to eat the apple.*)
A How much is that?
B That's ten pence.
A Here you are.
B Thank you.

EXPANSION OF ROLE-PLAY
A I'm still hungry. Give me three bananas, please.
B Here you are. (*Child eats them.*)
A How much is that?
B That's twenty pence.
A Here you are. Oooh!
B What's wrong?
A I've got a stomach ache! Goodbye!
B Goodbye!

Associated book: *Butterflies*
Other books by Eric Carle: *The Bad-Tempered Ladybird, Do You Want
to be My Friend?, The Mixed-Up Chameleon.*

Spot the difference

Look carefully at the two sets of phrases and compare them. Then sort them into two groups using the potatoes on page 136 and justify your classification.

1		It's chocolate cake	Do you like chocolate cake?
2		It's ice-cream.	Do you like ice-cream?
3		It's a pickle.	Do you like pickles?
4		It's Swiss cheese.	Do you like Swiss cheese?
5		It's salami.	Do you like salami?
6		It's a lollipop.	Do you like lollipops?
7		It's cherry pie.	Do you like cherry pie?
8		It's a sausage.	Do you like sausages?
9		It's a cupcake.	Do you like cupcakes?
10		It's watermelon.	Do you like watermelon?

Colour one of the groups of phrases which have something in common.

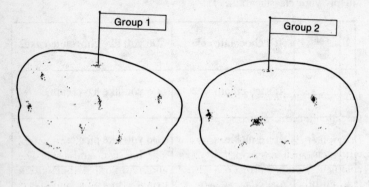

Story notes by Eileen Sorley

6 Meg and Mog

Other titles: *Meg's Eggs, Meg at Sea, Meg on the Moon*

Author: Helen Nicoll

Illustrator: Jan Pienkowski

Cassette: Read by Maureen Lipman

Description: The zany adventures of three friends: Meg, the witch, who gets spell after spell wrong: Mog, her cat, and Owl. The colourful pictures provide a visual representation of the written text, and the cassette contains a spectacular score of sound-effects which interpret the illustrations. Both features play an important role in aiding the child's comprehension.

● *Meg and Mog:* Meg prepares for a wild Hallowe'en party at which a spell changes her friends – Jess, Bess, Tess and Cress – into mice.
● *Meg's Eggs:* Another of Meg's spells goes wrong when the eggs she makes for supper hatch out as dinosaurs.
● *Meg at Sea:* Meg, Mog and Owl go to the seaside and are becalmed in a boat.
● *Meg on the Moon:* Meg and Mog go to the moon in a spaceship.

Layout: The bright, clear pictures in vibrant colour, speech bubbles, and comic-style presentation have great appeal for the young learner.

Each title in the Meg and Mog series (see page 156) can be used independently, or several titles can be used as part of a project around the topic of witches, magic and Hallowe'en. We suggest you begin with *Meg and Mog*, as this provides a general introduction to the series and to the characters. The other titles introduce vocabulary related to dinosaurs, the seaside and outer space. The vocabulary learnt in *Meg and Mog* can be revised.

These notes provide detailed lesson-by-lesson guidelines on how to use *Meg and Mog*. The other stories are dealt with in less detail as many of the techniques and activities suggested can be repeated. Certain ones, however, have been listed for each story.

Using the cassette

The books can be used with or without the cassette, but there are suggestions for activities that do make use of the cassette and involve pupils in active listening tasks.

Linguistic features

Rhymes: Meg's spells are a recurring feature in the Meg and Mog series. They represent short, contextualized rhymes which children can learn and imitate. This provides them with pronunciation practice in rhythm and individual sounds.

Linguistic objectives

SKILLS
- Listening for general understanding via visual and audio clues and by recognizing highlighted keywords and phrases when the story is told; listening to instructions
- Speaking: asking and answering questions, describing, imitating spells
- Reading: word cards, food packets, dictionaries
- Writing: labelling, copying

FUNCTIONS/STRUCTURES
- Asking for and giving information using Yes/No and Wh– questions
- Describing clothes: word order of adjectives and nouns
- Describing people using the present continuous tense
- Asking for and telling the time
- Giving instructions using the imperative

VOCABULARY
The vocabulary falls into the following lexical sets:

Clothes and accessories	Food	Animals	Adjectives	Verbs
stockings	eggs	cat	black	to hoot
shoes	bread	spider	big	to make/
cloak	kipper	frog	long	to chant a
hat	milk	beetle	tall	spell
broomstick	jam	worm	straight	
cauldron	cocoa	bat	curly	
		mice	striped	

PRONUNCIATION
- Intonation: Is it a cat? ↗
  - Meg's spell
- Individual sounds: /e/ as in Meg, spell, Jess, Bess, Tess, Cress
  - /o/ as in frog, bog, pop
  - /æ/ as in bat, hat, snap, crackle, fancy, that
- Stress: AbracaDABra

CONCEPTUAL REINFORCEMENT/CURRICULUM LINKS
- Colours, size and shape, time
- Maths: making a clock and telling the time
- Geography and the environment: food, clothes
- Cultural studies: festivals in other countries, Hallowe'en, food in other countries
- Creative activities: drawing, making masks, making a collage, making a theme-based display, cooking, making hats
- Music and drama: singing songs and rhymes, playing instruments, miming, dramatization

LEARNING TO LEARN
Comparing, classifying, predicting, sequencing, hypothesizing and problem-solving, memory training, using dictionaries

Cultural knowledge
While Meg is probably representative of witches in many different cultures, there are certain aspects of specific cultural interest such as the breakfast ingredients.

Suggested procedures

Materials
- Drawings from the book of:
  Meg putting on her clothes
  the animals put in the cauldron by the witches
  the breakfast ingredients
- Blu-Tack
- Clothes for dressing up (optional)
- Black sugar-paper (optional)

Lesson One

Aims
- To introduce the main characters: Meg, the witch, Mog, her cat, and Owl

139

● To introduce or revise vocabulary for animals and to practise asking for and giving information.

Show pupils the cover or the first page. Pointing to Meg say, 'Who's this?' Pupils may read the name from the cover and say, 'That's Meg.' Say, 'Yes, this is Meg. She's a witch.' Ask pupils if they know of any other witches (for example, the witch in *Snow White*). Point to Meg again and ask, 'Who's this?' Children will probably reply, 'Meg.' Encourage them to repeat the whole phrase, 'That's Meg. She's a witch.'

To introduce 'called' ask, 'What's she called?' and elicit the reply, 'She's called Meg.' Point to a girl in the class and ask, 'What's she called?' to get the answer, 'She's called Barbara.' Repeat with another girl. Now point to a boy and ask, 'What's he called?' Emphasize the difference between he and she and encourage the reply, 'He's called Paul.' Repeat a few more times, alternating between boys and girls. Now point to Mog and say, 'Who's this?' Say, 'Yes, this is Mog. He's a cat.' Ask, 'What's he called?' and encourage pupils to answer, 'He's called Mog.' Now point to Owl and ask the same questions.

Activity: ten guesses

Ask pupils to draw a picture of a pet they may have. If they don't have one, they can draw a picture of a pet they would like to have. They must decide whether their pet is male or female and give it a name. Tell them not to let the other pupils see their pictures. Ask a pupil to come to the front of the class with the picture which must not be shown to the rest of the class. Individual pupils then ask up to ten questions. For example:

Is it a cat?
Is it a fish?   } Yes, it is! or No, it isn't!
Is it a dog?
etc.

The pupil who guesses correctly asks, 'What's he (or she) called?' and the other pupil must reply, 'He (or she) is called ——' The winner then comes to the front of the class and the game is repeated.

Lesson Two

Aim: To introduce or revise vocabulary for clothes and simple adjectives and to give practice in describing people.

Using the cover or the front page say, 'Look at Meg. Look at her hair. Is it straight or curly?' Teach the meaning of the adjectives through opposites, mime and drawings. For example, draw a straight and curly line on the blackboard and point to pupils in the class who have straight or curly hair.

Ask, 'What's she wearing?' Pupils will probably answer in their mother tongue. Repeat in English the words of the clothing items the pupils suggest. For example, 'Yes, she's wearing a hat. What colour is it?' Encourage pupils to reply, 'It's black.' Ask, 'Is it tall or short?' Mime the meaning of tall and short. Get pupils to repeat the phrase, 'She's wearing a tall black hat.' Point to her shoes and ask, 'What are these?' Ask, 'What colour are they?' Encourage pupils to reply, 'They're black.' Ask, 'Are they big or small?' Mime the meaning, if necessary. Get pupils to repeat the phrase, 'She's wearing big black shoes.' Continue in the same way for the cloak and the stockings. Emphasize the pronunciation of cloak /əʊ/ which pupils may confuse with clock /ɒ/.

PICTURE DICTATION
In order to check comprehension of the above items, give each pupil a drawing of the illustration below. Dictate the following descriptions for the pupils to draw:
- Meg's got straight black hair
- She's wearing black stockings

MEG

a big black hat →

MEG

the broom ↓

She's got straight hair

She's wearing a cloak

a big black cauldron

black stockings

two long black shoes

141

- She's wearing big black shoes
- She's wearing a long black cloak
- She's wearing a tall black hat.

If necessary, use mime to remind the pupils of the meanings.

Going back to the cover illustration, point to the broomstick and ask, 'What's this?' Pupils will no doubt reply in their mother tongue. Introduce the English word broomstick. Do the same for cauldron. Ask pupils to add these to their drawings.

Optional follow-up activities

LABELLING

Pupils may like to label their drawings. (See completed picture dictation.)

GUESSING GAME

A pupil describes another pupil in the class without saying his or her name. The others must try to guess who it is. For example:

- She's got curly hair
- She's wearing red shoes
- She's wearing blue trousers
- She's wearing a yellow pullover.

It's Mary!

Lesson Three

Aim: To revise language items introduced in Lesson Two and to encourage pupils to focus on word order.

CASSETTE: LISTEN AND SEQUENCE

Draw copies of the four pictures of Meg getting dressed. Cut them up, so you have four individual pictures. Stick them to the blackboard (using Blu-Tack, for example) in the wrong order. Ask a pupil to come to the blackboard and play the extract from the cassette, using the pause button after each clothing item. The pupil must select the corresponding picture and put it in the correct order. Ask another pupil to come to the blackboard for the second clothing item and so on. Repeat two or three times.

WORD ORDER

To encourage pupils to reflect on word order in English and to make comparisons with their own language ask the following questions in their mother tongue. Use the text from the above pictures.

- Which words are adjectives?
- Which words are nouns?
- Where do adjectives go in English?
- Where do adjectives for colour go?
- Where do adjectives for size go?
- Where do they go in your language?

JUMBLED WORDS

To provide further practice, write the following words: her, black, stockings, big, shoes, long, cloak, tall and hat on individual pieces of paper in large letters. Jumble them up and stick them on the blackboard. (See the illustration below.) Ask a pupil to come to the front of the class and to make a phrase by putting the words in the correct order.

HOMEWORK

Write and copy the following four phrases for each pupil:

- her black stockings
- her big black shoes
- her long black cloak
- her tall black hat

Cut out the fifteen words, jumble them up and put them in envelopes. For homework each pupil reconstructs the four phrases and sticks them on to a piece of paper.

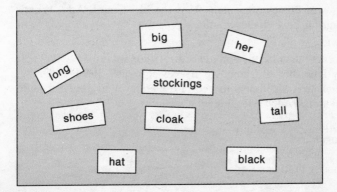

Optional follow-up activities

DRESSING UP

If you have clothes for dressing up, one pupil can pretend to be Meg. Pupils give instructions. For example:

● Put on a tall black hat!
● Put on big black shoes!
● Put on a long black cloak!

etc.

If clothes are not available, pupils could mime the actions.

Lesson Four

Aim: To introduce and teach Meg's spell.

To contextualize the lesson ask pupils in their mother tongue, 'What do witches do?' They should answer, 'They make spells.' Tell them they are going to learn one of Meg's spells.

Draw and, if necessary, enlarge the five animals the witches put in the cauldron and cut out the shapes. Get someone to draw a large cauldron on the blackboard and ask pupils in their mother tongue what they think Meg puts in it to make her spell. They will, no doubt, suggest all kinds of things, including the items from the book: a frog, a beetle, a worm, a bat, a spider. Accept all suggestions but as they mention the above ingredients, say the word in English and stick the corresponding illustration on the blackboard just above the cauldron as in the book. Check pronunciation each time and get pupils to repeat the words correctly.

WHAT'S MISSING?

To check comprehension, play What's Missing? Tell pupils to close their eyes. Remove one item from the blackboard. Ask, 'What's missing?' Repeat this several times.

CASSETTE: LISTENING FOR SPECIFIC INFORMATION

Tell pupils they are going to hear Meg's spell. Before listening, mention that Meg refers to two of the animals on the blackboard in her spell. Which ones? Play the spell.

Frog in a bog
Bat in a hat
Snap crackle pop
And fancy that!

144

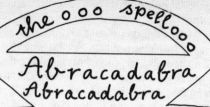

the ooo spellooo

Abracadabra
Abracadabra

Frog in a bog
Bat in a hat
Snap crackle pop
And fancy that

ABRACADABRA

Frog in a bog
Bat in a hat
Snap crackle Pop
And Fancy That

Check that pupils heard frog and bat. If necessary, play the recording again.

Now teach the spell. Explain that abracadabra is a magic word the witches say before chanting the spell. Using the pause button, play the spell, pausing after each line for the pupils to repeat it. Concentrate on pronunciation at this stage: rhythm, individual sounds /ɒ/ as in frog, bog, etc., and /æ/ as in bat, hat, etc., and /h/ as in hat. Explain the meaning of bog, Snap crackle pop and And fancy that! (Snap crackle pop are sounds often associated with breakfast cereals and And fancy that! is an expression of surprise.) Repeat this procedure as many times as necessary until the pupils have memorized the spell. Play the spell all the way through.

IMITATING AND MIMING

As pupils become more familiar and confident with the words and the rhythm, ask them to imagine they are witches and to imitate Meg's voice. They can also mime the action of casting a spell. These two techniques will help make the spell easier to remember.

Optional follow-up activities

WRITING

Cut out a large cauldron from black paper and write the spell inside with coloured crayons to decorate the classroom wall. Each pupil could also make their own smaller versions. (See below.)

MAKING HATS

Chanting spells will be a recurring activity with other stories in the Meg and Mog series. Your pupils could make hats to wear each time they chant a spell. They could make black witches' hats and coloured wizards' hats with stars and moons. (See *Copyparty* for instructions.)

Lesson Five

Aim: To introduce or revise telling the time.

Make a clock by cutting out a cardboard circle of approximately 20-cm diameter (big enough for all the class to see). Write on the twelve numbers. Cut out two hands and attach these to the clock with a paper fastener.

Revise the numbers one to fifteen. Move the hands on your clock to one o'clock. Ask, 'What's the time?' Elicit the answer, 'It's one o'clock.' Continue in this way. Now move the hands to twelve o'clock and ask, 'What's the time?' Teach, 'It's midnight.' Now put the hands to 12.15 and teach 'It's 12.15.' You may prefer to teach, 'It's a quarter past twelve.'

TIME DICTATION
Give pupils a worksheet like the one below. Pupils ask, 'Number one, what's the time?' and you reply, for example, 'It's two o'clock.' Pupils draw in the time on their clock faces. Pupils can also show the time on your clock for you to check their accuracy.

Optional follow-up activities
Children could make their own clocks to involve them in activities related to mathematics and handicrafts. As an alternative to the time dictation described above, dictate different times and then pupils can move the hands on their own clocks.

TIME DICTATION

What's the time?

It's . . . .

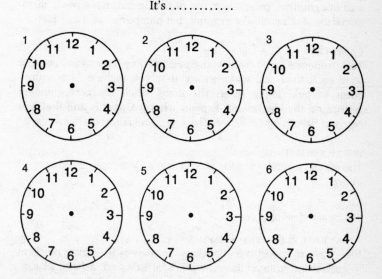

Lesson Six

Aims

- To introduce or revise vocabulary for breakfast foods and to develop an awareness of audio clues as an aid to meaning.

- To read part of the story and to encourage pupils to predict the ending.

Ask pupils when they have breakfast each day: 'What time do you have breakfast?' Then ask them what they eat: 'What do you have for breakfast?' Draw a chart on the blackboard and write in the items under each name:

Benjamin	Sarah	Nicholas	Mary
cornflakes	muesli	bread	cereals
milk	milk	butter	milk
hot chocolate	orange juice	jam	hot chocolate
		tea	

Copy and, if necessary, enlarge your drawings of breakfast ingredients from the book and then cut them out. Ask pupils what they think Meg has for breakfast. Their answers will, no doubt, be vivid and imaginative, recycling many of the ingredients already introduced for Meg's spell. For example, bat hamburger and frog pie!

CASSETTE
To introduce Meg's breakfast ingredients, play the extract, pausing after each item and making sure that you include each sound-effect to help pupils guess the items. Stick the corresponding picture on the blackboard. Explain what a kipper is and that it is eaten in Britain for breakfast. Check pronunciation of the words.

WHAT'S MISSING?
To check comprehension play What's Missing?, as described above.

Optional follow-up activities

BREAKFAST EXHIBITION/DISPLAY
Ask pupils to collect cereal packets with words in English on them (cornflakes, Country Store, muesli, Rice Krispies), as well as egg-boxes, tea and coffee packets, milk bottles, etc. Organize a Breakfast in Britain exhibition in a corner of your classroom. If space is in

short supply you can hang most unbreakable items from a washing-line. Pupils could also look for advertisements in magazines, cut these out and make a collage. These activities will help pupils see how English is used outside the classroom.

STORYTELLING

End this lesson by telling the story up to Meg's spell. Make sure that all pupils can see the pictures in the book and can see you too. If you have already read stories to your pupils, ask them how they think this story will begin. They will probably answer, 'Once upon a time . . .' Encourage your pupils to participate as much as possible by repeating key vocabulary items and phrases. Also encourage them to mime Meg's actions. See that all the pupils join in for Meg's spell. Finish at this point.

CASSETTE

To reinforce comprehension, play the cassette up until the same point so that pupils can enjoy the sound-effects. Make sure you show the corresponding illustrations. Encourage them to participate and mime.

To encourage pupils to predict the ending of the story, ask them to tell you what they think happens after Meg chants her spell.

Lesson Seven

Aim: To read the complete story and to encourage prediction of the ending.

Ask pupils to tell you what they remember of the story from the previous lesson. Get them to chant Meg's spell again and ask what they think happens next. Guide them by asking the following questions, probably in their mother tongue: 'Do you think Meg's spell goes right or wrong?', 'What do you think happens to Bess, Jess, Tess and Cress?'

STORYTELLING

Read the story again, this time all the way through, encouraging your pupils to participate as much as possible. After Meg's spell, you may like to play the cassette recording of 'BOOM! There was a flash and a bang' so the pupils can hear the sound-effects to help them predict. Ask, 'Do you think Meg's spell goes right or wrong?' Read the next page, pointing to the four mice and Mog chasing them. Did anyone predict something similar to the ending?

149

Your pupils may ask to hear the story again. This time you could play the cassette recording encouraging your pupils to participate and mime. Do not hesitate to use the pause button if you want to ask any questions to activate their memories.

PICTURE DICTATION
To revise numbers and some of the key vocabulary items, dictate the following instructions. Each one should be drawn on a new line. Example:

● Draw three tall black hats!
● Draw two broomsticks!
● Draw four cauldrons!
● Draw one moon!
● Draw three stars!
● Draw two cats!
● Draw five eggs!
● Draw two witches!
● Draw five worms!
   etc.

Optional follow-up activities

CULTURAL STUDIES
If you use this story around the time of Hallowe'en, you could organize a Hallowe'en party with your pupils. Related language work could include making invitations, decorations and hats, and organizing games, etc. For ideas see *Copycard* and *Copyparty*.

DRAWING
In collaboration with the art teacher, pupils could draw pictures of witches inspired by *Meg and Mog* to decorate their story envelopes.

MUSIC WORKSHOP
While you read the story your pupils could create the dramatic effects with their voices, percussion instruments or improvise simple musical instruments using classroom objects.

MAKING PUPPETS
Related to handicrafts, pupils could make their own Meg, Mog and Owl puppets. (See *Copyparty* for suggestions.) This would also involve them in revising language related to parts of the body, clothes and colours. Pupils could also turn the story into a shadow

puppet play. They can make all the characters and the setting and one or more children can act as narrator.

MAGIC
In English teach your children some simple tricks.

COOKING
For an English breakfast: porridge or eggs and bacon. For a Hallowe'en party: spider buns or cakes (see *Copyparty*).

INVENTING SPELLS
Depending on the level of your class, pupils could make up their own spells using Meg's as models and substituting certain words. This activity could involve them in useful dictionary work. (See the *Puffin First Picture Dictionary*.) You could also organize a spell competition.

DRAMATIZATION
Pupils could act out the story. If possible, use props such as a cauldron (a wastepaper basket covered in black paper will do), a broomstick, etc. Pupils could provide the sound-effects suggested above. Perhaps they could perform the story for another class.

BOOK CORNER
Bring your pupils' attention to other books (in English or in their mother tongue) on the theme of magic, witches, Hallowe'en, etc. Add other titles from the Meg and Mog series (see page 156) to your book corner.

Meg's Eggs

DINOSAUR QUIZ
You could prepare a dinosaur quiz, if possible in collaboration with the natural science and history teacher, to reactivate your pupils' knowledge of the subject and to prepare them for much of the vocabulary they will meet in the story. The quiz could be done in the mother tongue or in English, depending on your pupils' level. Even quite recent beginners could attempt the quiz in English, trying to work out the meanings of the questions from prior knowledge (what questions would they expect in a quiz about dinosaurs?) from cognates, by looking carefully at the options to work out the question, etc.

DINOSAUR QUIZ

1 When did the first dinosaurs live?
   a 1,000 years ago
   b 1,000,000 years ago
   c 200,000,000 years ago

2 Can you give the names of any dinosaurs?

3 Diplodocus was the longest dinosaur. How long was it?
   a as long as one bus
   b as long as three buses
   c as long as five buses

4 Did dinosaurs eat meat or plants?

5 What is the name of this dinosaur?
   a Tyrannosaurus
   b Stegosaurus
   c Brachiosaurus

6 What was the name of the most ferocious of all the dinosaurs?
   a Tyrannosaurus
   b Stegosaurus
   c Diplodocus

7 What did the Tyrannosaurus eat?
   a water plants
   b cabbages
   c meat

8 Why did dinosaurs disappear?
   a Some new animals came and ate them all
   b The climate got colder and they couldn't keep warm
   c They died of a disease

(Adapted from *The Animal Quiz Book*)

Answers

| 1 | c | 3 | b, about 28 metres | 4 | both | 5 | b | 6 | a |
| 7 | c | 8 | b | | | | | | |

PRONUNCIATION

Repeating the names of the dinosaurs will provide useful practice in pronouncing polysyllabic words and practising stress.

Pronounce each name yourself and ask the pupils how many syllables there are. Divide the word into syllables on the blackboard, repeat the name and ask pupils which syllable is stressed. Mark the stressed syllable with a coloured box. (See illustration below.)

Di/**plod**/o/cus
Steg/o/**saur**/us
Ty/rann/o/**saur**/us

CHANTING SPELLS

Pupils can learn two more of Meg's spells which contain new ingredients: lizards and newts and bacon and eggs.

QUESTIONS

This story contains two useful questions ('Where's my egg? and Who are you?) which your pupils can learn and use in different contexts. In order to practise these you could play the following games:

a Hiding game. Ask each pupil to select six objects they have with them. For example: a rubber, a pencil, a purse, a hat, a pencil-sharpener, a book, etc. Make sure they know the English vocabulary for the items which they arrange on their desks. Then the pupils form pairs. Pupil B closes his or her eyes and pupil A takes and hides one of the objects. Pupil B must ask, 'Where's my pencil?' Pupil A replies, 'Here it is!' Pupils reverse roles and repeat.

b Famous people. Ask five pupils to go out of the classroom. Each one must think of someone famous to be. For example, Batman, Madonna, Mitterrand, etc. They return to the classroom and the pupils ask, 'Who are you?' The pupil must reply, 'I'm Batman!', etc.

COUNTING

Children learn to count up to a hundred. To check and provide practice, play number dictation. For example, dictate the following numbers:

8   15   20   34   46   57   69   72   81   99   100

STORYTELLING
When reading the story, follow the same guidelines as described above.

DRAWING
In collaboration with the art teacher pupils could draw pictures of dinosaurs to decorate the classroom and their folders/envelopes. They could also paint eggs in different colours.

(Associated book: *Dinosaurs*)

Meg at Sea

SOUND-EFFECTS
Record the sound-effects from the cassette. Play these to your pupils and elicit the possible storyline in the pupils' mother tongue. This activity will prepare them for the story in English and sensitize them to the fact that audio clues can play an important role in understanding.

CHANTING SPELLS
Children can learn another of Meg's spells.

SINGING
Teach the song 'London's Burning'.

London's burning. London's burning.
Fetch the engines, fetch the engines.
Fire, fire, fire, fire,
Pour on water, pour on water.

RHYME
Children can learn Meg's rhyme, 'This is the code . . .'

Meg on the Moon

PREDICTING
Use the cover for asking appropriate questions to encourage pupils to predict vocabulary and expressions associated with outer space. This activity will introduce a number of the vocabulary items they will meet in the story. For example:

spaceship	lift-off	splashdown
earth	moon	moon buggy
countdown	crater	lunar module
astronauts	orbit	

HAPPY BIRTHDAY

Teach children 'Happy Birthday'. If it is anyone's birthday in your class the song can be sung to them.

CHANTING SPELLS

Children can learn another of Meg's spells.

COUNTDOWN

An ideal context to revise numbers, this time by counting backwards with Owl for the countdown.

TEATIME

Show pupils the picture of Meg, Mog and Owl having tea on the lawn. Tell pupils about teatime in Britain. If possible, organize a teatime for your class. Teach the action rhyme 'I'm a little teapot' from *This Little Puffin*, page 31.

DRAWING

In collaboration with the art teacher, pupils could draw pictures of the moon, spaceships, astronauts, etc.

GENERAL KNOWLEDGE

Give pupils the following outer space quiz.

OUTER SPACE QUIZ

1   What do we call a person who goes into space?
    a a pilot
    b an astronaut
    c a Martian

2   Which is the furthest planet from the sun?
    a Earth
    b Pluto
    c Saturn

3   Who was the first man to walk on the moon?
    a Georges Pompidou
    b Neil Armstrong
    c Charlie Chaplin

4   How far is the sun from Earth?
    a 17 million miles
    b 52 million miles
    c 93 million miles

5 What sends pictures from space?

  a television
  b telescope
  c satellite

Answers
1 b   2 b   3 b   4 c   5 c
(Adapted from *The Young Puffin Quiz Book*. Associated book *Outer Space*)

Other titles in the Meg and Mog series: *Meg's Car, Meg's Castle, Meg's Veg, Mog at the Zoo, Mog in the Fog, Mog's Box, Mog's Mumps, Owl at School, Meg and Mog Birthday Book*.

Story notes by Gail Ellis and Anne Feunteun

7 Don't Forget the Bacon!

Author and illustrator: Pat Hutchins

Description: An amusing story about a boy who goes shopping for his mother. She tells him a list of items to buy but he forgets some of them and gets into a muddle. In the end he buys all the wrong things!

Layout: The story is told using clear pictures with speech bubbles

and thought bubbles.

There is no narrative text.

Linguistic features: The language of the story consists of a shopping list which is repeated but with some changes. Vocabulary items in the list are replaced by words which rhyme with them. The little boy finds it difficult to remember what is on the list and as a memory aid finds himself rhyming cake with cape, eggs with legs, and so on.

Linguistic objectives

SKILLS

● Listening: remembering the sequence of items; finding words that rhyme

● Speaking: (see language functions and pronunciation features)

157

- Reading: reading labels and simple captions; reading words to match rhymes, using a dictionary
- Writing: copying labels and captions; writing shopping lists; spelling

FUNCTIONS/STRUCTURES
- Giving orders: imperatives using don't and the infinitive
- Counting and describing quantity: for example, a kilo of ——, a pile of ——, a flight of ——
- Making requests: using please
- Checking by asking questions: statements with intonation pattern (ii) below
- Asking about and expressing likes and dislikes
- Irregular past: buy/bought, forget/forgot

VOCABULARY

Nouns: Lexical sets to do with food and types of shop: for example, bacon, cake, eggs, pears and other food items; supermarket, cake shop, junk shop, fruit and vegetable market (market stall). Other words in the story: for example, chairs, legs, stairs.

PRONUNCIATION

- Intonation:
    i) intonation used in 'closed' lists where each item has a rising tone except the last one which has a falling tone

       For example, a cake, six eggs and a kilo of pears

    ii) use of rising tones for checking by asking questions

       For example, a cape for me

    iii) use of high falling tones for expressing strong feelings such as surprise or dismay

       For example, a cake for tea

- Stress:
  Weak forms for a, and, for, of, the (/ə/ /ən/ /fə/ /əv/ /ðə/)

  NOTE: 'the' is pronounced /ðiː/ before vowels and /ðə/ before consonants

  Pronunciation of four vowel phonemes: /e/; /eɪ/; /eə/; /iː/

CONCEPTUAL REINFORCEMENT/CURRICULUM LINKS
● Size and shape
● Maths: numbers and quantities, making and interpreting graphs
● Geography and the environment: shops
● Cultural studies: food in other countries
● Creative activities: making collages, making a theme-based display
● Music and drama: rhymes, role-play

LEARNING TO LEARN
Comparing, classifying, sequencing, hypothesizing, memory training, using charts, surveys and investigations, using dictionaries

Materials
● Pictures of food and food itself (fruit, tins, packets, etc.)
● Photocopies of pictures from the book
● Dominoes
● Written captions
● A map of the world

Lesson One

Aims
● To revise numbers one to ten and vocabulary for food
● To discuss and use strategies for remembering things
● To prepare class for listening to the story.

SHOPPING LISTS
Ask pupils to think of a shopping list for a birthday party for six people. Quickly draw the items on pieces of paper, stick them on the blackboard using Blu-Tack and teach the necessary vocabulary (crisps, cake, etc.). Elicit (using the mother tongue) ways children have of remembering lists of items. For example, associating the word with a mental picture, repeating the word, finding a word that rhymes, writing it down, etc. Ask the class to use any of their usual strategies to remember the items on the board.

KIM'S GAME
Play Kim's Game where you take off one or two items from the board or change the order of items (children close their eyes while you do this) and then ask the class which items are missing or

have been rearranged. Another variation of Kim's Game is to make a list of ten food items, numbering them from one to ten. These can be new words or revision.

one chocolate cake   four chocolate biscuits
two ham sandwiches   five strawberry ice-creams
three hot dogs   six coffee mousses   etc.

Allow pupils a few minutes to memorize the words. Now rub off the words and say any of the numbers from one to ten. The first player to tell you which word on the list corresponds to the number scores a point.

Teacher: What's number four?
Pupil: Hot dogs?
Teacher: Try again.
Pupil: Chocolate biscuits?
Teacher: Yes, well done.

This can then be played in groups after the teacher has provided a model. The children can draw the food items as a reminder if they are unable to write the words in English.

Homework: Ask the children to write or draw a shopping list for their favourite meal. Ask them to start collecting pictures of their favourite foods from magazines and to bring in different kinds of food for a role-play activity in a shop corner. This can be set up in a corner of the room, with some desks and screens to create a shop counter. Use real items of food to make a shop display and plastic money (if available) for the children to practise acting a shopkeeper and a customer selling and buying goods.

Lesson Two

Aims
- To support children in understanding the story
- To practise listening to and recognizing words which rhyme
- To practise four vowel phonemes, weak forms and the intonation of closed lists.

TELLING THE STORY
Read the story showing pictures from the book and substituting kilo for pound in 'a pound of pears'. Discuss briefly the concept of rhyming. Then, using the pictures, go through the shopping list again making sure you use a rising tone for all the items on the

list and a falling tone when you finish with 'and don't forget the bacon!'.

PICTURE MATCHING AND RIDDLES

To check comprehension do a picture-matching exercise on the board where children come up and sort the jumbled-up pictures into the following sets of three:

six eggs	+	six legs	+	six clothes pegs	/e/
a cake for tea	+	a cape for me	+	a rake for leaves	/eɪ/ + /iː/
a kilo of pears	+	a flight of stairs	+	a pile of chairs	/eə/

The children can practise checking, using one of the incorrect answers with a rising tone while the correct answer has a falling tone.

For example,   Six legs?   No, six eggs

This could then be played with pictures and written captions and finally with written captions only.

Now play the riddle game where the teacher says, 'I'm thinking of a word which rhymes with pears,' and the class has to suggest words which rhyme. They might like to find more words which rhyme with the above. For example, a tape for Lee; a group of bears, and so on.

PAIR WORK

Ask the children to read aloud to their partner the shopping list made for homework, adding 'and don't forget the ——' (and a falling tone) for the final item. The children practise using any of the memory strategies discussed in the previous lesson to recall their partner's list. The first child can then say the list again, deliberately leaving out one item. The second child has to remember the missing word. As you monitor the pairs check pronunciation.

Homework: Ask the children to cut out pictures of food from magazines so that a large collage can be made of different kinds of shops and the food you can buy in them. Ask them to start sticking their favourite foods on to a large piece of paper or in a small book, both of which could be cut into the shape of a shopping basket.

Lesson Three

Aim: To teach names of different shops and classify these according to which kind of food is bought there.

SORTING

Tell the story again. Teach the names of different shops using the pictures: a junk shop; a market stall; a cake shop. Suggest other shops such as a supermarket and ask the children what you can buy there. Using pictures of food or the real food in the shop corner ask the children to classify foods according to where you can buy them. Write the name of different shops in columns and ask children to put the picture of food in the correct column.

For example:

supermarket	butcher	cake shop	market stall
eggs	chicken	chocolate cake	a kilo of grapes

Using the blackboard, this can be done with the whole class or if it is turned into a worksheet (with a list of words at the bottom to be sorted) it can be completed individually or in pairs. Remind the children that some food can be bought in several types of shop. For example, fruit or eggs in a supermarket or from a market stall.

CHINESE WHISPERS

In groups of six to eight practise another memory game, Chinese Whispers. Give one child in each group a shopping list which they must remember and whisper to the next child. This child whispers to the next child and so on until the last child is reached. Then ask them to compare this list with the first list and see if it has changed.

LIKES AND DISLIKES

Using the real food or pictures of food that have been collected, make a survey of the class likes and dislikes in food. Teach the question forms and responses, 'Do you like ——?', 'Yes, I do' or 'No, I don't.' The children then complete tickcharts and with your help record the results on a large chart for the whole class.

Tickchart: Foods I like		
	me	my partner
ice-cream	√	×
chocolate cake	√	√
hot dogs	×	√
ham sandwiches	×	×
chocolate biscuits	√	√
pizza, etc.	√	×

This could then be made into a graph using a tallychart, where favourite foods are highlighted.

Tallychart for making a graph	
ice-cream	/ / / / / / / / / /
chocolate cake	/ / / / /
hot dogs	/ / / / / / / / / / / / / / / / / / / /

The results of the graph can be described in simple sentences which the children have to check.

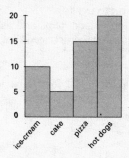

For example,   Seventeen children like hot dogs. Is this true?
                No, twenty children like hot dogs.

This can be done verbally at first but later with written sentences.

Homework: ask the children to bring in food in containers. For example, a box of chocolates, a packet of crisps etc.

Lesson Four

Aim: To teach phrases to describe different quantities or containers
such as:
● a packet of crisps/biscuits/sweets
● a box of chocolates
● a tin of sweets/baked beans
● a bar of chocolate/nougat
● a loaf of bread
● a carton of orange juice

SHOPPING GAME
Teach the above forms using the real food that has been collected.
Check the children are using the weak form /əv/ for 'of'. Practise
asking for items in the shopping game using 'I'd like ———'. This
activity practises new vocabulary and develops the memory. Here
one child (the shopper) says, 'I'd like a packet of sweets, please';
the second child (the shopkeeper) replies, 'Here you are' and the
shopper places the item in a shopping bag. A third child repeats
this and adds another item: 'I'd like a packet of sweets and a loaf of
bread, please', etc. The players can look inside the bag to remind
themselves of the items, although they have to remember the
correct vocabulary and order of the goods. When a player forgets
an item he or she drops out.

SORTING FOOD AND CONTAINERS
Give the class a selection of food items and ask them to sort them
into sets (using drawings or words) according to the container in

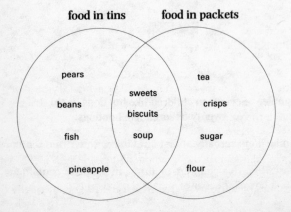

food in tins   food in packets

pears   tea

sweets

beans   crisps

biscuits

fish   soup   sugar

pineapple   flour

which they are normally found (this may differ from country to country). Again, this can be completed on the board with the whole class or can be done individually or in pairs using a worksheet.

Overlapping sets show those items which are found in both tins and packets.

LANGUAGE AWARENESS

The children might like to examine different food labels and find the country of origin. This can be marked on a map of the world with the name of the food next to it. They can then find food containers which are written in different languages, such as packets of cereal or pasta, and make a collage. The children can explain to the rest of the class what the other languages are, find words which are similar in different languages, and so on. They might also like to design their own food label and make a display.

Lesson Five

Free choice

In this lesson the children can select from a variety of activities and work individually, in pairs or in groups.

ROLE-PLAY: SHOP CORNER

In threes or fours the children take turns in the shop corner to role-play shopping by looking at a list, asking for items and having them handed over by the shopkeeper to put in the shopping basket. A sample dialogue is given as an example:

> I'd like a cake and a loaf of bread, please.
> Here you are. Is that all?
> Oh, I forgot the tarts.
> Here you are.
> Thank you. Goodbye.

LISTENING, SEQUENCING AND MATCHING

Individually or in pairs children listen to a tape of the story and sequence the accompanying pictures of eggs, legs, pegs, etc. They then match the pictures with written captions.

DOMINOES

Here the children practise reading and matching words which rhyme, including words from the story. The teacher can make all the dominoes or write word lists which the class copy neatly on to

165

prepared cards as a handwriting exercise in order to make several sets. This can be played in groups of two to four. Simpler rhyming words can be added as well to those in the story. When making the dominoes choose words from different groups:

For example, group one   no, go, so, blow, slow
            group two   eggs, begs, legs, kegs, pegs
            group three   stairs, bears, chairs, hairs
            group four   cake, tape, cape, make, lake
            group five   hat, cat, sat, fat, mat

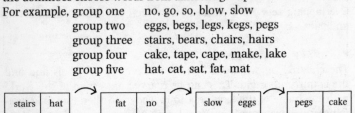

| stairs | hat | | fat | no | | slow | eggs | | pegs | cake |

MATCHING GAME

In this game rhyming nouns used as the subject and object are matched in a sentence using the verb 'likes'. Copy the subject and verb on to one piece of card and the object on to a separate piece of card. (Again, this can be done as a handwriting exercise by the children.)

For example

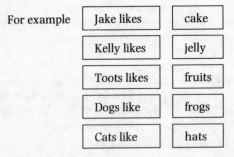

Jake likes	cake
Kelly likes	jelly
Toots likes	fruits
Dogs like	frogs
Cats like	hats

If you have been using other stories with rhymes (for example, *Pat the Cat*, *The Fat Cat*) it would be useful to recycle some of these words.

WORD MACHINES

These can be used to help children develop a working knowledge of possible letter combinations and helps with spelling. The machine changes a word by performing one (or more) operation(s) on it to form a new word. An example with three operations is given below. The children probably need to start by using one operation only, such as 'change the third letter'.

For example:

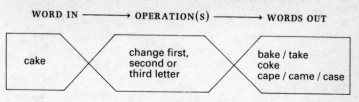

WORD IN ⟶ OPERATION(S) ⟶ WORDS OUT

| cake | change first, second or third letter | bake / take coke cape / came / case |

Words must be checked in a dictionary.

RHYME

A useful rhyme from *This Little Puffin* on the theme of food and shops is 'Five currant buns in a baker's shop' on page 30 (and on cassette).

Story notes by Jean Brewster

8 The Elephant and the Bad Baby

Author: Elfrida Vipont

Illustrator: Raymond Briggs

Description: A highly amusing and moral tale about an elephant who goes for a walk and meets a bad baby. They go into town and visit various shops until the elephant decides the bad baby has forgotten his manners.

Layout: The book is beautifully illustrated by Raymond Briggs with typical street scenes and shop interiors in Great Britain. The illustrations correspond well with the text to aid the pupils' general understanding. The left-hand pages have no text so the teacher can fold the book in half and hold it so that the children can see the illustrations, and you can read the text at the same time.

Linguistic features

Repetition and rhythm: The story has all the elements of the traditional cumulative story: repetition, an infectious rhythm and a predictable ending which encourages participation in the text. This also allows the teacher to omit one or two characters if you feel that the story is too long or to replace unusual ones. For example, a greengrocer for the barrow boy.

Onomatopoeia: 'RUMpeta, RUMpeta, RUMpeta' /rʌmpətə/ (possibly formed by a combination of trumpet, romp, hump and rump to convey sound, action, shape and size) is great fun to imitate and gives pronunciation practice in the following sounds: /r/ /ʌ/ /ə/ and the stressed syllable /rʌm/.

Linguistic objectives

SKILLS
- Listening for general understanding via pictures and by recognizing highlighted keywords when the story is told; listening to instructions
- Speaking: repeating key vocabulary items; asking and answering questions; role-play; songs and rhymes
- Reading: word cues, shopping list

- Writing: vocabulary cards; spelling; copying words, making simple sentences

FUNCTIONS/STRUCTURES
- Giving instructions using the imperative
- Offering something politely using Would you like ——
- Accepting something politely using Yes, please
- Refusing something politely using No, thank you
- Asking for something politely using I'd like ——

VOCABULARY

Nouns

Places to buy food	Shopkeepers	Food
ice-cream stall	ice-cream man	ice-cream
butcher's shop	butcher	pie
baker's shop	baker	bun
snack bar	snack bar man	crisps
grocer's shop	grocer	chocolate biscuit
sweetshop	sweetshop lady	lollipop
fruit barrow	barrow boy	apple
		pancakes

Parts of the body plus trunk and tail

Verbs: simple past
Regular verbs: stretched out, picked up
Irregular verbs: go/went, meet/met, say/said, put/put, come/came, take/took, sit/sat, fall/fell

Draw and add as commands

Adjectives: bad/good, big/small

Time-markers: soon, next, then

Sequencers: first, second, third, next, then

Coordinating conjunctions: so, describing cause and effect; but, describing something contrary to expectation

PRONUNCIATION

- Intonation: Would you like a bun?

  Yes, please!

169

- Individual sounds: /ə/ as in a, an, butcher, baker, and so on

    /ʌ/ as in bun, rumpeta

- Consonant cluster: /sps/ as in crisps
- Stress: RUMpeta, Yes, PLEASE!, ice-CREAM

CONCEPTUAL REINFORCEMENT/CURRICULUM LINKS

Size and shape, cause and effect
Geography and the environment: shops and food
Cultural studies: food and meals in other countries
Creative activities: drawing, cooking, making tickets and posters
Music and drama: singing songs and rhymes, role-play,
    dramatization

LEARNING TO LEARN
Predicting, sequencing, hypothesizing and problem-solving,
memory training

CULTURAL KNOWLEDGE
- Etiquette: the rules of polite behaviour in English, the importance of saying please
- British food items: bun, pie
- British street scenes
- Teatime

Materials
- Individual pictures of the places to buy food, the shopkeepers and the food items. You could either make your own drawings or ask pupils to draw their own – or bring in photographs, pictures from magazines, etc. If it's possible do have real food in the classroom
- Blu-Tack
- Tray or basket
- For optional follow-up activity:
    A boater for the ice-cream man
    A striped apron for the butcher
    A chef's hat for the baker
    A pair of braces for the snack bar man
    A pair of glasses for the grocer
    A frilly white apron for the sweetshop lady
    A cap for the barrow boy
    A checked apron for the bad baby's mother

Lesson One

Aims

● To contextualize the story and introduce the main characters: the elephant and the bad baby.

● To give practice in listening to instructions with visual reinforcement. The main verbs used are draw and add. This activity also introduces or revises trunk and parts of the body: eyes, ears, legs, etc.

PICTURE DICTATION

Each pupil will need a sheet of paper and a pencil. Explain to pupils that you are going to dictate some instructions which they must draw. Do not tell them what they are going to draw. Draw a semi-circle on the board.

Dictate instructions: 'Copy the semi-circle on to the middle of your paper. Draw an eye in the circle on the left side. Draw two big ears. Add a trunk. Add two tusks. Draw four legs. Draw a small tail.'

(See *Copycat*)

Dictate each instruction at least twice. Then draw it yourself on the board for any pupils who have not understood and repeat the instruction again. This will provide immediate feedback for children who have understood and enable those who have not understood to clarify understanding and not get left behind. Point to your own eyes, ears and legs to convey meaning, if necessary. When the drawings are completed ask pupils to show them to each other. Check everyone has an elephant! Check pupils understand trunk by pointing and asking, 'What's this?'

Dictate the final instruction, 'Colour your elephant!'

171

Check passive understanding of vocabulary by asking pupils to come to the board and point to different parts of the body on your drawing of an elephant. 'Stephanie, point to the tail!', and so on.

Introducing the story

Introduce the story by saying, possibly in the mother tongue, 'I'm going to read you a story about an elephant and a bad baby.' Show pupils the cover and ask them to point to the elephant and to the bad baby. Check their understanding of 'bad'. Use the antonym 'good' to help convey meaning and give the appropriate intonations to highlight the difference between good and bad. Ask questions like: 'Were you a bad baby or a good baby?', 'Do you have a bad baby brother/sister?', 'Are you bad/good?', and so on.

ACTION RHYMES

Teach children the action rhymes: 'An elephant goes like this and that' and/or 'The elephant is big and strong' (page 103 in *This Little Puffin* and on cassette).

Lesson Two

Aim: To introduce or revise vocabulary for different places to buy food.

Show pupils the cover of the book again and ask them to tell you who they can see. Say, possibly using the mother tongue, 'The elephant and the bad baby go into town and visit different places where you can buy food. Where do you think they go?' Allow pupils to make suggestions (for example, supermarket, cheese shop, etc.). If their suggestions do not match the places included in the story say something like: 'Yes, but they don't visit the —— today' or 'Yes, they could do, but there isn't a —— in this town' or 'Yes, but it's not open today.' Your pupils will probably suggest the words in their mother tongue. However, this does show that they are thinking in the semantic area of shops, and it provides you with an ideal opportunity to introduce the words in English. When the pupils do suggest a shop that is in the story (for example, baker's shop), repeat it and then get the class to do so too. Stick the picture on the blackboard or wall. Continue until you have introduced all the shops – your pupils may not suggest snack bar and fruit barrow, so give these yourself.

To check comprehension and to give further practice, you could use one or all of the following games, depending on the time available.

Games

WHAT'S MISSING?

Tell pupils to close their eyes. Remove a picture. Tell pupils to open their eyes and say which picture is missing. For example, the butcher's or the butcher's shop!

SEQUENCING

It is useful to have the pictures on the board in the order they appear in the story. Jumble them up and ask pupils to stick them on the board in the correct order. For example, 'Christel, put the ice-cream stall first!', 'Michel, put the butcher's shop second!', and so on. You could use this opportunity to introduce 'next' and 'then'. For example, 'Next, put the butcher's shop!', 'Then put the baker's shop!'

This activity could also be used to introduce or revise prepositions and directions: 'Christel, put the ice-cream man in the top left-hand corner!', 'Michel, put the butcher's shop next to/on the right of/on the left of/above/below the ice-cream stall!', and so on.

MEMORY GAME

You could use a variation of the memory game 'I went to market and bought . . .' in the following way:

Pupil 1: I went to the butcher's shop and bought a pie

Pupil 2: I went to the butcher's shop and bought a pie, to the baker's shop and bought a bun

Pupil 3: I went to the butcher's shop and bought a pie, to the baker's shop and bought a bun, to the grocer's shop and bought a chocolate biscuit . . .

and so on.

For Lessons Three and Four jumble up the shopkeepers and food items. Say, 'Sylvie, put the bun/baker in the baker's shop!', and so on.

Vocabulary techniques

Optional: Tell your pupils to write the words in their exercise or vocabulary books, grouping them in the same way as on page 169, and to draw the corresponding pictures. Alternatively, pupils could make vocabulary cards (6 × 2.5 cm) for self-testing. They can write the English word on one side and either draw a picture on the other or write the word in their mother tongue.

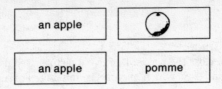

| an apple | ⊘ |

| an apple | pomme |

Lesson Three

Aim: To introduce or revise vocabulary for shopkeepers.

Start with the butcher's shop. Ask, 'Who works in the butcher's shop?' Pupils suggest words. Repeat the word butcher and check pronunciation. Say, 'André, put the butcher in the butcher's shop,' and he selects the relevant picture and sticks it in the butcher's shop. Continue with: 'Who works in the baker's shop?' and 'Who works in the grocer's shop?' Practise pronunciation of /ə/.

'Who works in the sweetshop?' Pupils may say sweeter! (This would show that they are attempting to work out a rule for themselves: that is, words for people who work in shops end in 'er'.) Say, 'Good try!' or 'Well done!' and then teach the words: sweetshop lady. Say, 'If this is the sweetshop lady, who works here?' (pointing to the snack bar man). Finally, point to the fruit barrow and teach barrow boy.

Check understanding and give further practice of these words by playing the above games.

Lesson Four

Aim: To introduce or revise vocabulary for food items.

Ask, 'What do you think the elephant gets at the ice-cream stall/at the baker's/at the butcher's?' Repeat until all food items have been introduced. Explain that buns and pies are typical British food. If possible, buy or make some for the children to taste.

Check the understanding of and give further practice of these words by playing the above games.

ACTION RHYME
Teach the action rhyme, 'Five currant buns in a baker's shop' on page 30 in *This Little Puffin*.

174

Lesson Five

Aims

- To develop listening for general understanding using context and picture clues and by recognizing vocabulary already introduced.
- To involve pupils actively in the storytelling process by encouraging them to join in and predict.

STORYTELLING

If necessary, revise the main vocabulary items and get pupils to arrange pictures on the blackboard in the order in which they appear in the book.

Ask pupils to sit in a group on the floor in front of you and make sure each child can see the pictures.

Read the story. Mime actions where appropriate. For example, 'So the elephant stretched out his trunk and took a ——' When you come to the baker's shop pause after 'Would you like a ——?' to encourage the children to participate and use the vocabulary items previously introduced. Pause again after 'with the ice-cream man, the butcher, and the ——'. Continue in this way. When you come to the grocer's shop, pause after 'And the Elephant said to the Bad Baby ——' Pupils may now be able to repeat the phrase, 'Would you like ——' Also encourage them to imitate 'rumpeta, rumpeta, rumpeta'. Pause after 'But you haven't once said ——!' Allow pupils to guess the missing word in their mother tongue or in English. Pause again after 'And they all said, Yes, ——!'

Read the story again if pupils request it.

Lesson Six

Aim: To practise offering and accepting politely.

ROLE–PLAY

- Practise pronunciation and intonation by getting pupils to repeat:

  'Would you like ——' and the response. 'Yes, *please*!'

- Choose two children to demonstrate the following dialogue. Pupil A has the food items on a tray or in a basket. Ensure that pupils make eye-contact with each other and use the appropriate gestures.

175

Pupil A: Hello!
Pupil B: Hello!
Pupil A: Would you like ——? (*Pupil chooses item from tray or basket.*)
Pupil B: Yes, please! Thank you.
Pupil A: Goodbye!
Pupil B: Goodbye!

Working in pairs, the class then acts this out. The dialogue can be varied according to the level of your pupils. For example,

i)   pupils say Good morning/afternoon/evening
ii) pupils can say No, thank you!
iii) introduce prices to revise numbers
     Pupil A: 'That will be six p, please' or 'Six p, please.'
     Pupil B: 'Here you are. Here's tenpence.'
     Pupil A: 'Thank you. Here's fourpence change.'
iv) Teach the structure for asking for something politely: 'I'd like a/an/some —— please!' Allow pupils to include food items of their own choice.

Optional follow-up activities

DRAMATIZATION
The story can be acted out with pupils playing the different characters in the story. This will be a memorable experience for them, especially if you can provide the props mentioned above. The children could also make tickets, posters, and so on, and then act the story for another class.

CULTURAL STUDIES
Teatime: Tell your pupils about English teatime. Show them the picture from the book again. Activities could include laying a table, making pancakes, offering and drinking tea ('Would you like a cup of tea?'), organizing an English teatime with sandwiches and cakes. Teach one or all of the following action rhymes from *This Little Puffin*: 'I'm a little teapot, short and stout' (page 31), 'Mix a pancake' (page 25), 'Slice, slice, the bread looks nice' (page 27). (These are on cassette.)

GRAMMAR
Discover the rule! Write the following sentences on the blackboard and ask pupils to copy them:

	pie?
	bun?
Would you like *a*	chocolate biscuit?
	lollipop?
	cup of tea?

	ice-cream?
Would you like *an*	apple?

Ask: 'Why is it *a* bun but *an* apple?'

Pupils explain the rule for using *a* or *an*. (*An* comes before a vowel.)

PAIR WORK

Pupils practise offering the following items (or ones of their choice) to their partners. Alternatively, they could write the sentences in their exercise books.

'Would you like a/an ——?'
'Yes, please!/No, thank you!'

```
orange   pear   banana
    hamburger   egg
  sweet   cake   lemon
    sausage   apricot
```

DRAWING

Show the pictures of the street scenes again. Discuss similarities and differences with the pupils' own countries. They then draw their own versions of a British street scene. Or a large drawing of the town could be made to decorate the classroom by allocating different places (park, factories, shops) to different groups of pupils to draw. Pupils could also draw teatime scenes.

SPELLING/SHOPPING LISTS

Ask pupils to think of a shopping list for a tea party for six people. Write and then draw the items on the board. Allow the pupils to look at the list for a few minutes and then rub it off. Now dictate the shopping list.

For example: 12 buns
6 packets of crisps
6 ice-creams
6 apples
tea
chocolate biscuits
6 lollipops

(*The Elephant and the Bad Baby* is on cassette.)

Story notes by Gail Ellis

9 *My Cat Likes to Hide in Boxes*

Author: Eve Sutton

Illustrator: Lynley Dodd

Description: Written in the style of a nursery rhyme, the story uses repetition and story-building techniques to describe cats from different countries, with their various interests. The infectious rhythm and humour of the story make it ideal for group work.

Layout: The drawings on the left-hand pages illustrate the two new lines which are systematically added to the beginning of the rhyme on the right-hand pages.

Since text and illustrations are separate, the teacher can fold the book in two, so that the pupils can see the pictures while the story is being read.

NOTE: The book is structured in such a way that one or two characters can be left out if the teacher thinks the text is too long for the pupils' level.

Linguistic features

PRONUNCIATION: the text encourages the pupils to practise a number of rhyming phonemes, as well as intonation and rhythm.

VOCABULARY: the nature and variety of the actions described in the text, and the use of rhyme, mean that role-play and mime can be used to facilitate the learning of new vocabulary.

Linguistic objectives

SKILLS
- Listening for general understanding via pictures and by recognizing highlighted keywords when the story is told; listening to instructions; developing an awareness of words which rhyme
- Speaking: repeating key vocabulary items; asking and answering questions
- Reading: charts; matching; pupils' stories
- Writing: creating stories based on the original

179

FUNCTIONS/STRUCTURES
● Describing location and origin using 'in' and 'from'
● Expressing likes and dislikes
● Asking and answering Yes/No and Wh– questions

VOCABULARY
The vocabulary in the story falls into three groups which rhyme;
countries, verbs and objects.

Countries/city	Verbs	Objects
(My cat . . .)	hide	box
France	sing/dance	
Spain	fly	aeroplane
Norway	get stuck	doorway
Greece	join	police
Brazil	catch	chill
Berlin	play	violin
Japan	wave	fan

PRONUNCIATION

● Phonemes (Lessons One, Four and Five)

[ɑ] as in dance, France
[eɪ] as in Spain, aeroplane, Norway, doorway
[i] as in Greece, police
[ɪ] as in Brazil, chill, Berlin, violin
[æ] as in cat, Japan, fan
[aɪ] as in my, hide

● Intonation and stress: But My cat likes to hide in boxes (Lessons
Four, Five and Six)

NOTE: The text, written in the past simple, can be put into the
present simple. For example:

Original text
The cat from . . .
France liked to sing . . .
Spain flew an aeroplane . . .
Norway got stuck . . .
Greece joined the police . . .

Adapted text
The cat from . . .
France likes to . . .
Spain flies . . .
Norway gets stuck . . .
Greece joins the . . .

180

Original text	**Adapted text**
Brazil caught a very bad . . .	Brazil has got . . .
Berlin played the violin . . .	Berlin plays . . .
Japan waved a big blue fan . . .	Japan waves . . .

CONCEPTUAL REINFORCEMENT/CURRICULUM LINKS
- Spatial context
- Geography and the environment: using a map

LEARNING TO LEARN
Comparing, classifying, predicting, memory training, using charts.

CULTURAL INTEREST
Pupils find the geographical nature of the text very attractive. The 'typical' elements presented in each illustration allow for discussion of the different countries 'visited' in the book.

Time Needed
Each of the following activities can be implemented during thirty- or forty-five-minute lessons, depending on the time you have available, as well as on the level of your pupils and how interesting they find the activity.

NOTE: More time may be needed for Lesson Three. (You may have to do it over two lessons.)

Materials
- Vocabulary cards with the name of a country in English on one side and in the pupil's mother tongue on the other side (Lesson One).

- Drawings of the book's illustrations (you could ask the pupils to colour them in) which can be used independently of the text (Lessons Two and Five).

- Handwritten copies of the text opposite the Japanese cat. You will need one copy for each pair of pupils.

- Two packs of cards which the children can make using small index cards. The names of the six countries and a city are written on one pack, the words which rhyme with those countries are written on the other (Lesson Four).

- Two packs of cards, like those above, each containing one line

from each couplet (Lesson Five). For example:
Pack A: The cat from Norway
Pack B: Got stuck in the doorway

● A map of the world (Lessons One and Six).

General Procedure
The work on *My Cat Likes to Hide in Boxes* is divided into six lessons representing three steps:

● Lessons One, Two and Three: these are lessons which prepare the pupils for the text by introducing context, keywords and aspects of pronunciation.

● Lessons Four and Five: these are devoted to reading aloud by the teacher, using the pictures as visual aids. Gradually, the class is invited to become more actively involved in the storytelling.

● Lesson Six: the text is used as a starting-point for more personalized activities.

NOTE: Even if the storytelling does not begin until Lesson Four, it is important that the pupils are introduced to the book from the start, making them constantly aware of both the context and the meaning of their work. This is why you should refer to the illustrations as much as possible during the first three lessons.

Lesson One

Aim: To introduce the names of countries in English.

Procedure

1 Show your pupils the picture of the dancing French cat and ask them: 'What country is it?'
    You now answer: 'It's France.' (You should not expect your pupils to reply at this stage.)
    ● As you reply, point to France on the map of the world (which will have been put on the board before the lesson). You could also show the pupils each new country you introduce by using stickers or coloured drawing-pins.
    ● If possible, while you are pointing out different countries at the board, ask your pupils to do the same using their geography books.

2 Now, show your pupils the Japanese cat wearing a kimono. Ask the same question as before. Your pupils will almost certainly answer in their native language. You now answer, pointing to its location on the map: 'It's Japan.'
 ● Concentrate on the difference between the pronunciation and accentuation of the word in the mother tongue and in English.

3 Repeat the procedure for the Greek cat.

4 So as to remain within the context of countries, introduce 'Germany' for the cat from Berlin, before introducing the name of the city.

5 Since the pictures for the Spanish, Norwegian and Brazilian cats are not as helpful as they might be, introduce photos of bull-fighting or Amazonian tribes to illustrate typical characteristics of each of these countries.
 ● As before, highlight the mother tongue/English differences in pronunciation.

6 In order to reinforce this last point, ask your pupils to make little vocabulary cards with the name of each of the countries written in their mother tongue on one side and in English on the other side. When they choose a card, they must explain the differences in spelling and in pronunciation between the two.

7 To introduce the notion of continuous rhyme in the text, write the names of the six countries and a city on the board (or the first four, if you do not have enough time). The pupils try to recognize the name of a country by listening to the last syllable or sounds only. You say: 'Close your eyes. Listen, please. –ance– What country is it?' (France)
 Continue the game with: –ain 'Spain'; –way 'Norway'; –eece 'Greece'; –zil 'Brazil'; –lin 'Berlin'; –pan 'Japan'
 You can then invite a pupil to replace you asking the questions.

8 *Optional:* Ask your pupils to close their eyes. Take away one of the stickers or drawing-pins you have used on the map of the world. Ask the question: 'Which country is missing?'
 Children with an insufficient knowledge of geography can refer to an atlas.

Lesson Two

Aims
- To revise names of countries
- To introduce the cats
- To introduce the prepositions 'from' and 'in'

Procedure

1 Show your pupils the cover of the book and, pointing at the cat, ask: 'What's this?'

   Your pupils might know the English word; if they do not, you answer: 'It's a cat.'
   - Ask the following questions to create a link between the book and your pupils' personal experience. (If necessary, you can use the word dog for pupils who do not have cats):

     'Have you got a cat?'
     'What's his/her name?'
     'What colour is this cat?' (showing them the cover)
     'What colour is your cat?'
     'My cat is grey/black/brown.' (Insist on the stressed form of 'my'.)

2 Next, show your pupils one of the illustrations where the cat is obviously hiding. Point to the cat. Say: 'This is my cat.'

   Then point to the box and say:
   'What's this?'
   'It's a box.'
   'Where's my cat?'
   'Oh, look, my cat's in a box!'

3 Come back almost to the beginning of the book, to the picture of the French cat, leaving aside the picture of 'my cat'. Ask your pupils, showing only the illustrations: 'What country is it?'

   This time, they should be able to reply: 'It's France.'

   You say: 'Yes, this is the cat from France.'

4 On the next double-spread, say: 'Oh, this is my cat. What's this?' (showing them the box)

   Your pupils should be able to reply: 'It's a box.'

   You say: 'Oh yes, my cat's in a box.'

5 Continue in this way until you reach the Japanese cat. In the middle of the book, invite the participation of the whole class by introducing gaps into your answers which your pupils must complete:

'What country is it?'
'It's Greece.'
'Yes, this is the cat . . .' (*the whole class*): 'from Greece.'

'This is my cat. What's this?'
'It's a box.'
'Oh yes, my cat's . . .' (*the whole class*): 'in a box.'

6 To reinforce the difference between 'from' and 'in', make a grid on the board with simple drawings of the seven countries and their names (see model below). Make sure that each box in the grid is also large enough to contain a copy of the illustrations without covering the names.

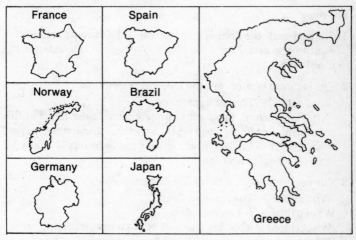

- Show the group the copies of each of the cats in succession (except for 'my cat') and ask them:
  'Who's this?
  'It's the cat from France.'

- One pupil comes to the board:
  'Julie, put the cat from France in Brazil, please!'

- Show your pupil exactly what she must do.

- Repeat this exercise with other pupils, using all the cats. Then summarize, using the grid as the basis for a kind of nursery rhyme that the class can repeat:
  'The cat from France is in Brazil,
  'The cat from Spain is in Greece,
  'The cat from Berlin is in Japan,' etc.

7 *Optional:* If you have enough time, draw two columns on the board and play True or False. You say:

'The cat from France is in Norway. True or false?'

The pupil at the board looks at the grid and puts a cross in the appropriate true or false column. This game can also be used as the starting-point for the next lesson.

Lesson Three

Aims
- To present verbs and their respective objects
- To give practice in expressing likes and dislikes

Procedure

1 Starting with the French cat, introduce the various activities of each of the cats. Leave the 'My cat' pages to one side for the time being.

2 The cat from France. Ask the following questions:

'Who's this?' – 'The cat from France.'

'What's he doing?' (You will definitely have to use mime at this point, and the children will reply in their mother tongue. Repeat their answer in English, inviting your pupils to repeat after you, 'Yes, he's singing and dancing.')

3 The cat from Spain. Ask the following questions:

'Who's this?' – 'The cat from Spain.'

What's this?' – 'It's an aeroplane.'

'What colour is it?' – 'It's red.' – 'Yes, it's a red aeroplane.'

'What's he doing?' (*mime*) 'He's flying an aeroplane.'

4 The cat from Norway. Ask the following questions:

'Who's this?' – 'The cat from Norway.'

'What's this?' (*pointing to the door*) 'This is a doorway.'

'Peter, come to the board. Please go to the doorway.'

'Look, the cat from Norway is fat.' (*mime*) 'He's stuck in the doorway.' (*mime*)

5 The cat from Greece. Ask the following questions:

'Who's this?' – 'The cat from Greece.'

'What's this?' (*pointing to the cap*) 'A cap.'

'What's he doing? Is he a taxi driver?' (*your pupils will give various answers in their mother tongue: a soldier, a ticket inspector ... If they do not think of the police, mime a policeman/woman directing the traffic*) 'Yes, he joined the police.'

186

6 The cat from Brazil. Ask the following questions:

'Who's this?' – 'It's the cat from Brazil.'
'What's this?' (*pointing to the handkerchief*) 'It's a handkerchief, a big white and red handkerchief.'
'What's this?' (*pointing to the bowl of water*) 'It's water. It's hot water.'
'Why is the cat from Brazil doing this?' (*mime a sneeze*) 'Yes, he's caught a very bad chill.'

7 The cat from Berlin. Ask the following questions:

'Who's this?' – 'It's the cat from Berlin.'
'What's he wearing?' – 'Shorts, leather shorts.'
'What's he drinking?' – 'Beer.'
'What's he playing?' – 'He's playing the violin.'
'Do you play the violin, Mary?' (*ask other pupils the same question, introducing different instruments; the piano, the flute, the guitar . . .*)

8 The cat from Japan. Ask the following questions:

'Who's this?' – 'It's the cat from Japan.'
'What's this?' – 'It's a fan.'
'What colour is it?' – 'It's blue.'
'Is it a small or a big, blue fan?' – 'It's a big, blue fan.'

9 Use the following game to revise the above features: divide the class into two groups, making sure there are an equal number of boys and girls in each group.

● Give the following instructions to both groups:
'Two girls: play the violin.'

● If two girls stand up and pretend they are violinists, their group wins a point. Here are some other possible instructions:
'Sing and dance.'
'Fly an aeroplane.'
'Get stuck in the doorway.'
'Join the police.'
'Catch a very bad chill.'
'Wave a big, blue fan.'

187

10 To introduce, 'Do you like ——?', give your pupils copies of a chart like the following one:

Name:		
Do you like:	Yes	No
Chocolate Television To sing and dance		

- Get one pupil to come to the board and ask him or her one or two of the questions; record the answers in the appropriate boxes using a tick (√).
  'Natasha, do you like chocolate?'
  'Philip, do you like television?' etc.

- Then ask the whole group questions, instructing them to use a tick to record their answers to the questions in the left-hand column as you read them out. Here is a list of questions you could ask (start with easy words they are already familiar with, then introduce vocabulary from the story):
  'Do you like chocolate?'
  'Do you like television?'
  'Do you like football?'
  'Do you like gymnastics?'
  'Do you like to sing and dance?'

- When you have finished asking the questions, get your pupils to exchange lists with their neighbours. They must then read what their neighbour likes (do *not* introduce the negative 'he or she doesn't like').
  'Mary likes to wave a fan.'
  'Oliver likes television.' etc.

- Point to the first 'My cat' picture, the one with the green background, and say:
  'This is my cat. My cat likes to hide in boxes' (*if necessary, mime the meaning of 'to hide'*).
  'Helen, have you got a cat?' – 'Yes.'
  'What's his name?' – 'Fred.'
  'My cat likes to hide in boxes, and Fred?' – 'Yes, he likes to hide in boxes.' Continue to ask pupils questions about their pets, using the 'My cat' pictures.

Lesson Four

Aims
- To make your pupils aware of rhyming sounds
- To start reading part of the story aloud

Procedure

1 Write two lists of words on the board, one containing the names of the countries in the story, the other with the rhyming words in the wrong order. Ask pupils to close their eyes, and say: 'Dance . . . What country sounds the same?'

- When your pupils have found the answer, ask one of them to come to the board and draw a line between the words 'France' and 'dance'. Repeat this procedure for the other words in the lists.

- At the end, go through the rhyming words again, making sure your pupils pronounce them correctly.

2 Introduce the following game:

- Ask your pupils to work in pairs. One of them writes the names of the seven countries on seven cards the size of playing cards. The other does the same, using the rhyming words.

- When they have finished, each pupil keeps his or her cards, shuffles them and then spreads them out on the table, face down. Each player then picks up one of his or her own cards and reads out the word written on it.

- If the words rhyme, the two cards are put to one side and no longer feature in the game. If they do not rhyme, both cards are put back on the table, face down but away from the other cards. In the subsequent rounds each player must try to remember whether the card which rhymes has already been drawn and, if so, which card it is. If the player finds the correct card, he or she keeps the two cards. Each player must try to collect more cards than the others.

- Obviously, to give all players an equal chance, they must take it in turns to read their word out first.

3 Start telling the story, showing the class the pictures as you read.

- For the moment restrict yourself to the pages concerning the seven cats, leaving the 'My cat' pages and the last two pages featuring all the cats together to one side.

- Take advantage of the reading to encourage pupil participation: pause before each of the rhymes, letting them find the correct word. For example:

  'The cat from Norway
  Got stuck in the –' (*the class*) 'doorway.'
  'The cat from Greece
  Joined the –' (*the class*) 'police.'

Lesson Five

Aims
- To increase the pupils' familiarity with the text, encouraging oral expression and active participation
- To tell the whole story

Procedure

1 Attach copies of the pictures, in no particular order, to the board. Read aloud again the part of the story you told in the previous lesson, and ask your pupils to come to the board and put the pictures in the correct order.

2 Try to reconstruct the text with the whole class, using the pictures in the correct order or at random. To reconstruct the text, you could say the first line and your pupils the second line of the rhyme, or you could simply give a keyword (the verb or the rhyme).

3 One pupil comes to the board and, addressing another pupil, says:
'The cat from Japan . . .'

- The other pupil has to mime the activity of the cat in question and say the second line. You could repeat this process for the rest of the story.

- Alternatively, the pupil at the board could ask a classmate to guess which cat he or she is miming.

4 Play a card game using the two packs of seven cards your pupils have prepared. The first pack contains the first lines of the couplets (for example, 'The cat from Brazil'); the second pack contains the second lines (for example, 'Caught a very bad chill'). Ask pupils to work in groups of three. The two packs are mixed together and the fourteen cards are dealt to the three players. The aim of the game is to pair up the rhyming couplets:

Pupil A: Have you got 'The cat from France'?

Pupil B: Yes. (*the card is given to pupil A*)

As long as Pupil A receives positive answers, he or she can continue asking B or C questions:

Pupil A: Have you got 'Flew an aeroplane'?

Pupil C: No. (*now, it is C's turn to ask questions*)

5 Go back to the book and tell the whole story. Before starting, you can explain the word 'clever' (which appears at the end of the text) by contrasting it with 'stupid'.

'Look at all these cats (*pointing to the pictures on the board*) Are they stupid?' – 'No, they are clever' (*mime the word*).

6 During the reading ask the class to chant the refrain in unison: 'But **my** cat likes to hide in boxes.'

Lesson Six

Aim: To summarize and recycle all newly acquired language items by applying them within a more personalized, creative context

Procedure

1 Write the following two lists on the board:

Morocco	Navy
the moon	umbrella
Italy	balloon
Amsterdam	sleep all day
Peru	piano
Venezuela	tram
Bombay	flu

2 Work on the pronunciation of the names of countries and towns in the left-hand list by pointing to them on the map of the

world. Then do the same with the right-hand list using mime and drawings, if necessary, to explain the chosen words.

3 Ask your pupils to match the rhyming words, once you are sure they have mastered their pronunciation. Read the pairs of words. Your pupils must tell you whether or not they rhyme. For example:
'Morocco/tram' – 'No!'
'Moon/balloon' – 'Yes!'

● You could ask volunteers to read the words. Draw lines (or ask a pupil to draw them) between the rhyming words as they are discovered.

4 Explain to your pupils that they now have everything they need to write their own text, using the original as a guide. The left-hand list provides them with the cats' places of origin and the first part of the rhyme, the right-hand list provides them with the end of the couplet. All they need to do is to guess the part that is missing: what the cats do. The words in the above lists have been chosen carefully to enable your pupils to recycle vocabulary from the original text. The children should produce the following:

'The cat from Venezuela
Waved a(n) (big blue) umbrella.
But my cat likes to hide in boxes.
The cat from Morocco
Played the piano.
But my cat likes to hide in boxes.
The cat from Peru
Caught very bad flu.
But my cat . . .
The cat from Italy
Joined the Navy.
But my cat . . .
The cat from Amsterdam
Got stuck in a tram.
But my cat . . .
The cat from the moon
Flew a balloon.
But my cat . . .
The cat from Bombay
Liked to sleep all day.
But my cat . . .'

● Pupils should work in pairs to accomplish this task. Give them a copy of the text concerning the cat from Japan. This should help them to create their own text. While your pupils work, go around the class, checking they have understood the exercise and giving them any help they may need.

5 When the text has been written, ask a couple of volunteers to come to the board to read it, each pupil reading a line in turn, except for 'My cat likes to hide in boxes', which they should read together. You can also divide the class into two groups for a collective reading of the text, each half reading a line in turn, and the whole group reading the refrain.

6 *Optional:* Pupils can create their own book, based on the original, illustrating the text they have devised.

(*My Cat Likes to Hide in Boxes* is on cassette.)

Story notes by Eileen Sorley

10 Little Red Riding Hood

(in *The Fairy Tale Treasury*)

Author: Charles Perrault

Illustrator: Raymond Briggs

Description: This well-known fairy-tale is a favourite with children. It is rich for storytelling and lends itself well to being acted out. These notes show how the tale can be turned into a play to assist the pupils to achieve the linguistic objectives outlined below.

Assumption: The children will probably know the story in their mother tongue.

Linguistic features

Repetition: 'Grandmamma, what big —— you have!'
'All the better to —— you with, my dear.'

NOTE: This version of *Little Red Riding Hood* uses the word 'great'; we suggest you use 'big'.

Linguistic objectives

SKILLS
- Listening to instructions, for general understanding
  i) via pictures and prior knowledge, ii) by recognizing high-lighted keywords and phrases as the story is retold
- Speaking: asking and answering questions, role-play, repeating key vocabulary items and phrases as the story is told, songs and rhymes, dramatization
- Reading: charts, matching words to describe family relation-ships, family trees, word cards for Snap game, script (optional)
- Writing: labelling (family tree and parts of the body), writing invitations, tickets and programmes, copying captions

FUNCTIONS/STRUCTURES
- Giving instructions using imperatives
- Asking for and giving information using Wh– questions
- Asking for and telling the time
- Greetings

194

VOCABULARY

Family relationships: mother (mamma), grandmother (grand-mamma), grandchild/granddaughter

Food: custard, pot of butter (Different versions of the story include other food items.)

Parts of the body and corresponding verbs: arms/hug, ears/hear, eyes/see, teeth/eat

Opposites: little/big, country/town, girl/boy, pretty/ugly, mother/father, grandmother/grandfather, ill/well, fast/slow, good/bad, wicked/kind, happy/sad

PRONUNCIATION

● Intonation: Falling intonation on Wh– questions:

Who's this?

Where are you going?

What have you got . . .?

What's the time, Mr Wolf?

● Individual sounds: /ɪə/ as in ear and hear
/i/ as in teeth, see, eat
/aɪ/ eyes
/ə/ as in better to /betətə/

● Sentence stress: 'Grandmamma, what big **ears** you have!'
'All the better to **hear** you with my dear!'

CONCEPTUAL REINFORCEMENT/CURRICULUM LINKS
● Size and shape, cause and effect
● Maths: telling the time
● Geography and the environment: food, clothes
● Creative activities: drawing, making masks, making tickets, pro-grammes
● Music and drama: singing songs, role-play, dramatization

LEARNING TO LEARN
Classifying, predicting, memory training, using charts

Suggested procedures

Time

The following suggestions can be carried out as separate lessons of approximately thirty minutes, depending on the time available and the level and interests of your pupils. It is intended that each lesson end with a retelling of the story (to the point you have reached) which should contain more and more recognizable language. The play will take a minimum of two to three hours to prepare.

Materials

- A basket for Lesson Two
- Card for game in Lesson Four
- Simple reproductions of the drawings in the book to help pupils situate the different stages of the story (These can also be used as prompts when acting out the play.)
- Blu-Tack to stick pictures up on the board
- Props for the play: basket with food, a cape for Little Red Riding Hood, a scarf for Grandmamma and a mask for the wolf, if possible (See *Copyparty* for instructions on how to make masks.)

Lesson One

Aims

- To refresh pupils' memory of the story
- To teach or revise vocabulary for family members and relationships and to practise asking for and giving information

Show pupils the picture of Little Red Riding Hood and the wolf and ask them to tell you what they remember about the fairytale and who the main characters are. (Their answers will probably be in the mother tongue.) This should elicit vocabulary for family members. For example: mother, grandmother, and so on.

FAMILY PHOTOGRAPHS

Ask pupils to bring a family photograph or ones of individual family members to class. Ask one pupil to tell the others who the people in the photo(s) are. For example: This is my mother. This is my grandmother. Teach vocabulary items when necessary.

196

Working then in pairs, pupils ask and explain to each other who the people are in their photo(s):

Pupil A: Who's this?
Pupil B: This is my father.
Pupil A: Who's this?
etc.

Storytelling

LISTENING TASK

Before you read the first paragraph of the fairy-tale to your pupils, tell them that two family members are mentioned. Which ones? Read the first paragraph. Check that pupils heard 'mother' and 'grandmother'. Read the paragraph again, encouraging pupils to participate where possible.

Optional follow-up activities

FAMILY RELATIONSHIPS

Ask pupils to copy the following diagram into their exercise books or have copies ready for them. If appropriate, you could include other family members. For example: aunt, niece, step-mother, etc.

My Family

Members   *Relationships*

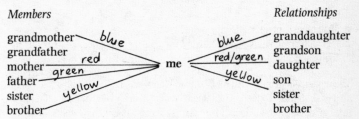

Make sure pupils understand that the left-hand column refers to family members and the right-hand column to the relationships with them. Ask them to draw lines to members of their family, using a different colour for each person. Pupils then draw lines to their relationship with these people in the right-hand column using the same colour. (See the example above.)

FAMILY TREE

Ask a pupil to name the members of his or her family and to draw a model of their family tree on the blackboard.

Family Tree

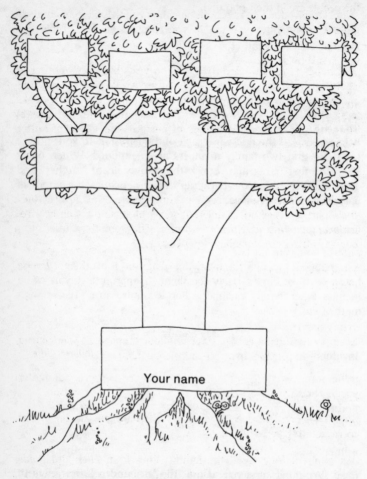

(From *My Family*, Puffin Step Ahead)

Ask pupils to copy the family tree above (adapting it for their family) and, if possible, to stick on family photos – or to draw pictures of them – and to write their names below.

ACTION RHYME

You could teach the action rhyme 'This is the father short and stout' on page 14 of *This Little Puffin* (and on cassette).

Lesson Two

Aim: To introduce or revise 'ill' vocabulary for food items and the phrase 'What have you got in your basket?' and the reply 'I've got ——'

Ask pupils why Little Red Riding Hood visits her grandmother, to elicit the word 'ill'. Ask pupils what they would take their grandmother if she was ill. They will probably suggest: flowers, books, magazines, fruit, etc. Introduce the food items in the tale by showing pupils the illustrations of custard and a pot of butter. You may need to make larger drawings of these.

ROLE-PLAY

Pupils write the names or draw pictures on pieces of card (without their partners seeing) of different foods of their own choice, but including custard and a pot of butter. They put the cards into a basket and act out the following dialogue:

Pupil A: What have you got in your basket?
Pupil B: I've got —— (*taking one item out at a time*)

STORYTELLING

Read paragraphs one, two, three and four on page 146, encouraging pupils to participate by repeating food items.

Lesson Three

Aim: To teach or revise vocabulary for parts of the body with corresponding verbs

Ask pupils if they recall the famous lines from *Little Red Riding Hood:* 'What big arms you have', 'All the better to hug you with!', etc. to elicit words for parts of the body and the corresponding verbs. Show the illustration of Little Red Riding Hood and the wolf to help them remember.

Ask one pupil to come to the front of the class. Using him/her as a model say, 'Touch your head!' If you are introducing these vocabulary items for the first time, convey the meaning by touching your own head or drawing a picture of a head, etc. Go through other parts of the body in the same way. Next, give similar instructions to the whole class.

199

SIMON SAYS

The game Simon Says is a good way to check comprehension and give further practice. The pupils mime the actions only when the command is preceded by the words 'Simon says . . .'. Those who mime when they shouldn't are 'out'. Pupils could also give the commands. Use appropriate actions to convey meaning or prepare simple pictures. Examples: 'Simon says, touch your ears!', 'Simon says, hug your neighbour!', 'Simon says, eat an apple!', 'Simon says, close your eyes!', 'Simon says, brush your teeth!', 'Simon says, put up your arms!', 'Simon says, skip!', 'Simon says, gather nuts!', 'Simon says, run after butterflies!', 'Simon says, pick flowers!', etc.

STORYTELLING

Read the story to page 150 (line 14), encouraging the pupils to repeat the lines 'What big arms you have!', etc.

Optional follow-up activities

ACTION RHYME

To give more practice you could teach the action rhyme 'Heads and shoulders, knees and toes' on page 125 of *This Little Puffin* (and on cassette).

LABELLING

Ask pupils to copy a simple drawing of a person into their exercise books (see page 201). Put the following words in any order on the blackboard: head, feet, arms, eyes, neck, legs, knees, shoulders, nose, mouth, ears, toes, hands, fingers, (you can, of course, limit these, depending on time available and pupils' level) and ask them to label their drawing. (For an example see *Start Testing Your Vocabulary*, page 7.)

Lesson Four

Aim: To teach or revise vocabulary through opposites (see page 195) and to revise vocabulary introduced in Lesson Three

GAME: SNAP

Teach target vocabulary and check pronunciation. Use simple drawings to convey meaning (see page 205). Ask pupils to copy words on to pieces of card (about 5 × 3 cm) so each has about

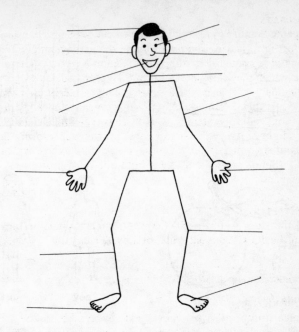

twenty-two (or fewer depending on time available and level of pupils). In pairs, they play Snap. Make sure they shuffle their cards well. Each pupil in turn puts down a card and says the word. When an opposite appears (for example big/little) the pupils must say 'Snap.' The pupil who says it first picks up the cards and the game continues until one of the players has no cards left.

PICTURE DICTATION
Using the words introduced above and in Lesson Three, dictate instructions for drawing a picture in the following way: 'Draw a little girl. She's pretty. She's happy. She's got little arms, little teeth, little ears and big eyes. She's in the country. Draw some flowers and some butterflies.' Pupils could also dictate a picture to the teacher, class or another pupil. (For instructions on how to draw see *Copycat*.)

STORYTELLING
Retell the story up to page 150 (line 14).

country

town

little   big

boy   girl

ill   well

Lesson Five

Aim: To revise asking the time and the word 'eat'

GAME

Pupils play 'What's the time, Mr Wolf?' Ask pupils to repeat the question after you, making sure they use a falling tone on 'time' and a rising tone on 'Wolf'. One pupil plays the wolf and stands at the far end of the class with his or her back to the other children lined up across the opposite end of the room. The pupils ask,

202

'What's the time, Mr Wolf?' and take steps towards him according to the number in his answer: 'Seven o'clock', 'Two o'clock', etc. The aim of the game is to try to touch the wolf before he shouts, 'Time to eat you!', turns round and chases after the other children who must run back and touch the wall in order to be safe. If the wolf catches someone they take his place.

STORYTELLING
Retell the story up to page 150 (line 14).

Lesson Six

Aim: To finish the story and develop listening for general understanding via prior knowledge of the story, visual clues and by recognizing keywords and phrases as the story is told. Although your pupils will probably not understand everything, comprehension of specific vocabulary and structures will take place during the acting stage.

STORYTELLING

1 Stick the illustrations on the blackboard in the order in which they appear in the book and elicit vocabulary from your pupils. For example: girl, grandmamma, wolf, custards, etc. Ask the children if they can remember the end of the tale. What happens to Little Red Riding Hood, the grandmother and the wolf?

2 Read the tale, pointing to the appropriate drawings on the blackboard, disguising your voice for the different characters and using any gestures, sound-effects and expressions to liven up the story and to sustain suspense.

Encourage your pupils to participate by repeating and predicting the lines, 'Grandmamma, what big —— you have!', 'All the better to —— you with, my dear.' Make sure they stress the noun and corresponding verb. They can also point to their own arms, ears, eyes and teeth as they repeat the lines to reinforce meaning. This will help build up their confidence and prepare them for the acting stage.

Lesson Seven

Aim: To develop comprehension and express in simple English (see suggested script on pages 205 and 206) what they can understand through acting out the tale.

Acting

- Retell the story, using the pictures and script together and getting your pupils to repeat. This initial rehearsal should be very controlled to iron out any pronunciation difficulties. Work on the falling intonation of the Wh– questions. Tell your pupils to imagine their voice is going down a flight of stairs, so they need to start high and gradually go down. They could also mime going down stairs as they repeat. Also work on the sentence stress in the lines 'What big —— you have!', etc. Encourage pupils to make the appropriate expressions and gestures as they say them. This will make them more memorable. They can memorize the lines through oral repetition.

Optional: You may like to give your pupils a copy of the written script.

- Allocate roles and act out a scene three or four times with different pupils. The first time the teacher could play one of the characters to set the pace. Make sure pupils make eye-contact with the person they are speaking to as they sometimes have a tendency to look at the teacher to seek reassurance as they say their lines. If possible, use the props mentioned above.

In large classes an excellent way to discourage any boredom that could arise from rehearsing is to have prompters or understudies for each role. Or you can divide the class into different theatre troupes, each troupe getting a chance to act and so learning from the others.

Suggestion: Why not have the children perform for another class or even in front of their parents, as working towards a performance heightens motivation. If possible, the performance could be videoed and shown to other classes.

Suggested script
Children sometimes have difficulty in learning certain lines so you may need to adapt the script accordingly. Participation is just as important as achieving linguistic objectives.

The script on pages 205 and 206 represents a simplified version of the tale.

CHARACTERS: Mamma, Little Red Riding Hood, Wolf,
　　　　　　 Grandmamma, Huntsman

SCENE ONE (Mamma, Little Red Riding Hood)

Mamma (putting items in basket): Go, my dear, and give this to
　　Grandmamma *(hands basket to LRRH)*
Little Red Riding Hood: Yes, Mamma. Goodbye.
Mamma: Goodbye.

SCENE TWO (LRRH, Wolf)
(LRRH enters, skipping and singing)

Wolf (slyly): Hello.
LRRH (surprised): Hello.
Wolf: Where are you going?
LRRH: To see Grandmamma.
Wolf: What have you got in your basket?
LRRH (showing basket): Custard and a pot of butter.
Wolf (rubbing his tummy): Mmmm. Goodbye!
LRRH: Good-bye.

SCENE THREE (Grandmamma, Wolf)
*(Grandmamma is sitting in a chair, centre stage. Wolf knocks on the
door)*

Grandmamma: Who's there?
Wolf (disguising voice): Little Red Riding Hood.
Grandmamma: Come in.
*(Wolf enters abruptly and makes munching sounds as though he's
eating Grandmamma)*

SCENE FOUR (Wolf, LRRH)
*(Wolf, wearing Grandmamma's scarf, is sitting in the chair. LRRH
knocks on the door)*

Wolf (disguising voice like Grandmamma's): Who's there?
LRRH: Little Red Riding Hood. I've got some custard and a pot of
　　butter.
Wolf: Come in.
LRRH (enters and looks a bit suspiciously at the Wolf): Grandmamma,
　　what big arms you have!
Wolf: All the better to hug you with, my dear!
LRRH: Grandmamma, what big ears you have!

205

Wolf: All the better to hear you with, my dear!
LRRH: Grandmamma, what big eyes you have!
Wolf: All the better to see you with, my dear!
LRRH: Grandmamma, what big teeth you have!
Wolf: All the better to EAT you with, my dear! (*jumps up and makes munching sounds to eat LRRH who screams and disappears behind the chair*)

SCENE FIVE (Huntsman, Wolf, LRRH, Grandmamma)
(*Grandmamma and LRRH are hiding behind the chair. Wolf is sleeping in the chair*)

Huntsman (enters): Someone's snoring. (*looks around and spots the Wolf*)
LRRH and Grandmamma: Help! Help!
Wolf (wakes up): The huntsman!
(*Huntsman 'cuts' Wolf in the back. LRRH and Grandmamma jump out from behind the chair*)
LRRH and Grandmamma: Oh, thank you, Huntsman!
(*Huntsman drags Wolf offstage. Grandmamma and LRRH open contents of basket together*)

Optional follow-up activities

1 Making invitations, programmes and tickets. Children can make invitations to the play for parents, friends and other classes. They could also design a programme and tickets for the play. These activities provide a motivating way of practising writing and reading.

2 Making books. Pupils could create their own version of *Little Red Riding Hood* in the form of an illustrated book with simple captions. They could work individually, in pairs or in groups. Afterwards they could exchange books. This activity would provide writing and reading practice.

(*Little Red Riding Hood* is on cassette.)

Story notes by Leslie Young

11 Pat the Cat

Authors and illustrators: Colin and Jacqui Hawkins

Description: The story of an amusing cat called Pat.

Layout: The large. clear drawings lend themselves to easy, quick comprehension and interest. Cut-away pages reveal a rhyming word in large, black type and the bubbletalk and comic-style presentation have great appeal to the young learner.

Linguistic features: An original and funny introduction to pronunciation and intonation, the language of position and rhyme and spelling. Cut-away pages introduce pupils to nine rhyming words (five concrete nouns, two proper nouns, one adjective and one verb) simply by changing a phoneme: c–at, f–at, etc. These words are repeated by characters in the story in a bubble of cartoon-like, rhyming conversation, and by a narrator who addresses the listener/reader directly through simple questions and statements. The conversations are easy to repeat and to memorize and the story can be acted.

The tale provides a motivating context for pronunciation practice of individual consonants and vowel sounds (see Phonetic Bingo). It can also be used to present a range of intonation patterns for: expressing disbelief or surprise, disagreement, questioning, showing happiness or disappointment/unhappiness and anger.

Level of class
It is possible to use this book with a variety of different levels.
LEVEL ONE: Using only the basic –at words.
LEVEL TWO: Using the basic vocabulary and rhyming
conversation.
LEVEL THREE: Using the narration and the above two features.

These notes suggest how the book can be exploited at Level One and at Level Three. However, many of the activities and techniques could be used at all levels, depending on time available.

Level 1

Preparation and material

You will need a space in the classroom where the children can sit in front of you, ideally with a minimum of distractions around (games, books, etc.) so that their interest is directed towards you and the book.

An instant follow-up is useful, so prepare an adjacent area of tables or desks with a selection of coloured crayons, pencils and scissors.

Time

A forty-to-fifty-minute lesson

- five minutes' introduction time
- fifteen minutes for the teacher to read the story
- ten minutes rereading the main words, with help and suggestions from pupils
- ten to twenty minutes for a follow-up activity

Introduction

For a group of ten to sixteen small children, have them sit in front of you on the floor, making sure they can all see the book. Use a small, low chair for yourself.

Before opening the book, talk generally about the cover picture. This discussion will probably take place in the mother tongue, but introduce in English the following questions and answers.

What's this?	A cat.	A hat.
What's his name?	Pat.	
Have you got a cat?	Yes/No.	
What's your cat's name?		

Page by page

1 Read the title *Pat the Cat* aloud. Pupils repeat the words.
2 Ask, 'What's this?' Direct pupils' attention to the word 'cat'. They repeat it. Say, 'Hi!' (or 'Hello!') Pupils reply, 'Hi, Pat!' or 'Hello, Pat!'
3 Ask, 'Is he thin?' Mime 'thin': put your hands close together. 'Is he fat?': spread your hands wide apart.
  Direct pupils' attention to the word 'fat'. Repeat while opening out your hands wider and wider.
4 Say, 'This is a mat/This is a cat/This is a hat.' Ask pupils to listen and put up their hands when they hear the new word. Repeat

'mat' several times and get pupils to repeat it. Say, 'hat/cat/mat' and point to each picture when you say the words.

5 Ask pupils in their mother tongue what is happening: 'Is the hat moving? Why?'

Use the same procedure as on page 4, but in this order: hat/cat/mat and point to each picture. Pupils repeat 'hat'. You can ask them to put their hands in front of their mouths and feel the aspirated/h/ – like breathing on a window-pane to make it misty.

6 Say, 'bat/hat/cat'.

Ask pupils to show you the bat. Say, 'Hello, Tat!' Pupils repeat.

7 Say, 'rat/hat/cat'. Pupils repeat 'rat'.

Ask pupils to show you the rat. Say, 'Hello, Nat!' Pupils repeat the greeting.

8 Say, 'Where's the rat? In the hat?' Direct pupils' attention to the word 'sat' and mime sitting down. Ask a pupil to say and mime 'sat'.

9 Ask pupils what the rat's name is. Did anyone read it correctly? Pupils repeat 'Nat'. Say, 'Pop!' and point to the hat. Ask what has happened.

10 Say, 'mat/cat/hat'. Direct pupils' attention to the hole in the hat. Ask pupils what the cat's name is. Pupils repeat 'Pat'.

If pupils ask you to read the book again, just reread the words in thick black print, showing them how two letters remain the same and the first letter changes. Get pupils to repeat the words after you.

Pupils may notice the caterpillars on each page. Say, 'one caterpillar/two caterpillars' where and when necessary.

Optional follow-up activities

GAME

Copy these drawings on to separate cards two or three times, depending on the number of pupils: cat/mat/hat/bat/rat. Show pupils a card and the pupil who says the word first wins the card. When all the cards are distributed, use in the opposite sense. Say, 'Can I have a cat, please?' and hold out your hand for the card, and so on.

DRAWING

Using a large sheet of paper, draw a cat with the help of the pupils. Use the relevant vocabulary, for example: eyes, ears, whiskers, etc., as it is drawn and finally ask them to draw or copy their own versions. While they are drawing, use the vocabulary by asking, 'Where are the eyes?', etc.

COLOURING

Give pupils a traced drawing to colour and cut out. They could label this with the –at words.

SONGS AND RHYMES

There are many songs and rhymes about cats. See for example: *This Little Puffin*, page 158, for 'Pretty little pussy cat' and *The Mother Goose Treasury*, page 163, for 'Pussy cat, pussy cat'.

Level 3

Linguistic objectives

SKILLS

- Listening to instructions and for general understanding via visual clues and by recognizing highlighted keywords and phrases as the story is told
- Speaking: pronunciation of individual words in Phonetic Bingo, questions and answers, dramatization
- Reading: individual words in Phonetic Bingo, sentences in version 2 of the Emotion Game.
- Writing: simple captions, rhyming vocabulary

FUNCTIONS/STRUCTURES

Asking for and giving information:
- What is it? It's a ——
- What's its name? His/her name is ——
- What's this? It's a ——
- I've got a ——
- Do you know ——? Yes, I do/No, I don't.
- Where is/Where are ——?/It's ——/They're ——

VOCABULARY

Nouns

Parts of the body	Animals	Clothes	Miscellaneous
head	cat	hat	pan
ears	bat	bag	cup
eyes	rat	cap	pen
nose	caterpillar		nut
mouth	bug		map
whiskers	hen		net
legs			sum
tail			man

210

Verbs: wears, sits

Prepositions: on, in, under

Time markers: while, now

PRONUNCIATION
- Intonation: Expressing emotions (see page 222)
- Individual sounds: /æ/ as in cat, hat, etc.

  /ʌ/ as in cup

  /e/ as in pen

  /h/ as in hat, hole

  /r/ as in rat
- Stress: I **do** like my hat.

CONCEPTUAL REINFORCEMENT/CURRICULUM LINKS

- Size and shape, spatial context
- Geography and the environment: using a map
- Cultural studies: famous people from other countries
- Creative activities: drawing, making masks, making collages, making tickets, invitations, posters
- Music and drama: dramatization

LEARNING TO LEARN
Comparing, classifying, sequencing, memory training

Materials
- Bingo boards
- Word and picture cover-cards for Bingo
- Pictures of famous people
- World map

Introduction

Aims
- To introduce the main character, Pat, and to give practice in listening to instructions and in asking for and giving information
- To introduce or revise words rhyming with Pat.

PICTURE DICTATION
Pupils will need a sheet of paper and a pencil. Tell them to start their drawing at the top of the sheet of paper. Make sure they

understand the instructions: 'draw' and 'add'. Dictate instructions for drawing a cat.

Instructions:
Copy the head.
Add eyes and a nose.
Draw a mouth and whiskers.
Now draw a body.
Add two legs and a tail.
Colour your cat.

Repeat each instruction three to four times and, if necessary, use gestures/mime to help convey meaning.

When the drawings are completed, ask pupils, 'What is it?' Encourage the reply, 'It's a cat.' Tell pupils to give their cat a name and to draw a speech bubble in which they can write, 'My name's ——' Tell them not to show their partner. Draw a cat on the blackboard and think of a name for it. Invite pupils to ask, 'What's its name?' Teach/revise the reply, 'His/her name is ——'

GROUP WORK
In groups, using their pictures, pupils ask and answer the above question, 'What's its name?'

Using the cover of the book, introduce *Pat the Cat*. Ask pupils questions, for example,

Have you got a cat?
What's its name? etc.

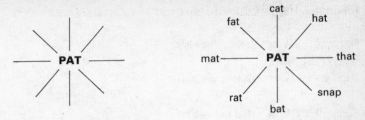

VOCABULARY: WORD STARS

This activity can be used to revise or introduce words rhyming with Pat.

Ask pupils to turn over their drawings and copy the above diagram from the board.

Discuss briefly the concept of rhyming. Ask pupils to write on their word star any words they know that rhyme with Pat by changing the initial consonant only. They may add other words with the same sound. Some children will do this activity randomly, remembering words already encountered. For example: bat, rat, hat, etc. Others may work through the alphabet systematically until they recognize English words.

If these words are new, introduce them by showing pictures and then saying the word. Pupils repeat and practise pronunciation. Ask them to arrange the words on their word star.

SORTING

Ask pupils to sort the words according to grammatical category (for example, concrete nouns, proper nouns, adjectives, etc.) or meaning (for example, clothes, animals, etc.).

Storytelling

The story can be read at the beginning and end of each of the following lessons. When reading it, use your own voice for that of the narrator and disguise it for the different characters. Invite pupils to participate in the story, especially when the narrator or characters interact with the listener. For example:

Narrator: Do you know Pat the cat?
Pupils: Yes, we do!
Pat: Hi!
Pupils: Hi, Pat! (or Hello, Pat!)

Use facial expressions, gestures, intonation and stress to help convey meaning. For example:

Pat: I **do** like my hat.

Narrator: Who's **that** in Pat's hat?

Pat: 'Who's **that** in my hat?

Caterpillars: 'Who's **that** in the hat?

When reading the story for the first time, the aim is for the pupils to listen for general comprehension. The more they hear the story, the more they will understand and be able to participate. Introducing the story early on provides a memorable context for the language activities that follow.

PHONETIC BINGO

This game is a form of Bingo which aims to sharpen pupils' perception of English sounds and to sensitize them to the sound pattern of English through auditory discrimination. It also revises the above vocabulary and introduces other nouns of three letters.

The eighteen concrete nouns selected for the game are similar-sounding words consisting of three letters and which focus on the vowel sounds /æ/, /ʌ/ and /e/. Many of the words may already be familiar to your pupils, so the game will provide revision practice. Where possible, minimal pairs have been included, for example: hat/hut, bag/bug, etc.

/æ/	/ʌ/	/e/
bag	bug	
bat		
cap	cup	
cat		
hat	hut	hen
man		
map		
mat		
	nut	net
pan		pen
rat		
	sum	

Version 1
This version of the game uses twelve of the above words, including those from *Pat the Cat*. It requires pupils to listen attentively to the word and match it with both the written and visual equivalents.

1 Vocabulary
  Draw and enlarge the pictures on page 217. Cut these up. Show each picture to the pupils and ask, 'What's this?' Insist on the reply, 'It's a ——' Stick the picture on the blackboard and practise pronunciation.

TEAM GAME: LISTEN AND TOUCH
Divide the class into two teams. Each team stands in a line before the blackboard so that one member from each team is facing the pictures on the board. Call out a word. The first pupil to touch the picture wins a point for their team. The two pupils then go to the back of the line. Continue until each pupil has had a turn. The team with the most points is the winner.

2 The game
  a Copy the board on page 217 for each pupil.
  b Each child will need twelve word cover-cards with the name of an object written on each (See page 218.)
  c Ask pupils to cover any four squares on their board by placing the matching cover-card *face down* over the picture. Each pupil's board should now have eight different pictures showing. Ask them to arrange the remaining eight cover-cards *face up* on their desks.
  d You will also need a set of word cards. Shuffle your cards. Lay them face down in front of you. Pick up a card and read out the word. The first time you play the game, tell pupils you will repeat the word twice. When they are familiar with the rules, read out the word only once.
  e If you read out cat, pupils must cover this picture with the corresponding cover-card which is laid with the word *facing up*.
  f Continue calling out words from your cards until one of the pupils has covered all the squares on their board. The first player to do so shouts 'Bingo!'
  g This player must check that his or her board is correct by *reading back* the words that are face up. If they are right, he or she wins.

215

Version 2
This version uses all eighteen words.

a Introduce or revise the remaining six words (see page 217).

b If you have a class of over sixteen pupils, you may need to divide them into groups to play the game. Prepare boards with nine pictures for each pupil. To make the boards, number each column on page 217.

Copy and cut up the strips and make boards based on variations of these pictures. For example:

1	2	3		1	4	5		4	3	5		4	5	2
mat	bag	hen		mat	rat	man		rat	hen	man		rat	man	bag
pan	cat	pen		pan	cup	cap		cup	pen	cap		cup	cap	cat
hat	bug	bat		hat	hut	nut		hut	bat	nut		hut	nut	bug

4	6	5		2	4	3		2	5	6		5	1	2
rat	sum	man		bag	rat	hen		bag	man	sum		man	mat	bag
cup	net	cap		cat	cup	pen		cat	cap	net		cap	pan	cat
hut	map	nut		bug	hut	bat		bug	nut	map		nut	hat	bug

5	3	1		5	6	3		3	2	6		3	5	2
man	hen	mat		man	sum	hen		hen	bag	sum		hen	man	bag
cap	pen	pan		cap	net	pen		pen	cat	net		pen	cap	cat
nut	bat	hat		nut	map	bat		bat	bug	map		bat	nut	bug

3	6	4		6	2	4		6	3	1		6	5	4
hen	sum	rat		sum	bag	rat		sum	hen	mat		sum	man	rat
pen	net	cup		net	cat	cup		net	pen	pan		net	cap	cup
bat	map	hut		map	bug	hut		map	bat	hat		map	nut	hut

Other variations could be devised. If possible, make the boards on card and cover them in plastic.

c Using different coloured paper, copy picture cover-cards and put these into a hat.

d Take out a card and call out the word. Any player who has the picture on his or her board must say, 'Bingo! I've got a cat.' The first pupil to say this correctly is given the card and places it on their board *face up* over the corresponding picture. Keep a record of the cards you call out.

e Continue calling out words until one of the pupils has covered all the squares on the board. The player to do so shouts 'Bingo!'

f This player must check their board is correct by telling you which words have been called out. If correct, he or she is the winner.

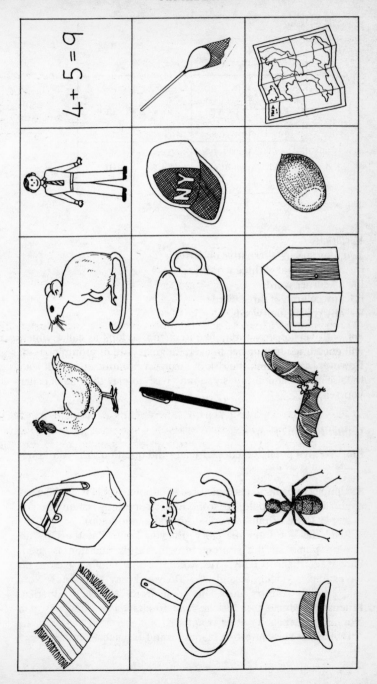

MAT	BAG	HEN	RAT
PAN	CAT	PEN	CUP
HAT	BUG	BAT	HUT

Variations

You may specify alternative objectives:

i)   any diagonal of three words
ii) all corner words
iii) any column of three words
iv) any row of four words.

For both versions, you may like to choose a pupil as caller which will encourage him or her to exercise great care in pronunciation. However, if you think the risk of incorrect pronunciation will lead to false claims and disputes you may wish to play the role of caller yourself.

Game: Famous People

Aim: To give pupils practice in using the question, 'Do you know ——?'

Ask pupils to bring to class pictures of famous people from different countries (these could be from English-speaking countries, for example: Great Britain, America, Australia, and so on).

Read the line from the story 'Do you know Pat the Cat?' to remind pupils of the context in which this question is used. Encourage them to reply, 'Yes, we do!' Show pupils a picture of, for example, Madonna, and ask, 'Do you know Madonna?' Now ask, 'Which country does she come from?' to elicit America. Practise pronunciation. Ask a pupil to show you America on a world map. Repeat for other countries.

Divide the class into two teams, A and B. Each team must sort their pictures of famous people into countries. Then one member from Team A asks a pupil from Team B, 'Do you know a famous person from Great Britain?' He or she must name a person. The pupil from Team A must give the picture to the pupil in Team B who sticks it on a world map or on the board under the heading of the country. Then a member from Team B asks a pupil from Team A, and so on. The team with the most points is the winner.

COLLAGE

Pupils could make collages using their pictures of famous people. Cut out shapes of, for example, English-speaking countries and pupils stick their pictures on these, depending on where the people come from. The collages can be used to decorate the classroom.

Prepositions

Aim: to give practice in understanding and producing the prepositions: on, in, under.

Read the lines from the story containing the prepositions 'on' and 'in'. Check pupils understand the meanings by giving instructions. For example: 'Stephen, put the pencil on Mary's desk!', 'Bobby, put the pencil in your bag!', and so on. Now introduce under. Take an object and say, 'Look, the pencil is under the table', etc.

ACTION GAME

Show pupils the following actions for 'on', 'in' and 'under' to help them memorize these prepositions. Clench fists and put:

  i your right fist *on* your left fist
 ii your right hand *in* your left hand
iii your right fist *under* your left fist.

Now call out the prepositions at random and the children must respond by showing you the corresponding action.

ACTIVITY: PICTURE DICTATION

Give pupils a copy of the worksheet on page 220. Dictate the following descriptions and ask pupils to draw and number each object, one to six, on their worksheet.

1 There's a cup *on* the table.
2 There's a rat *in* the hat.
3 There are two caterpillars *under* the table.
4 There's a cat *on* the mat.

5 There's a bug *under* the table.
6 There are two pens *in* the bag.

Check by asking the following questions:
Where's the cup/rat/cat/bug?
Where are the caterpillars/pens?

Encourage pupils to reply: It's on/in/under the ——
                                    They're under/in the ——

PAIR WORK
Divide pupils into pairs, A and B. Give pupils a copy of the pictures
on page 221. Pupil A draws items one to four and Pupil B, five to
eight wherever they like on their picture without showing their
partner.

A

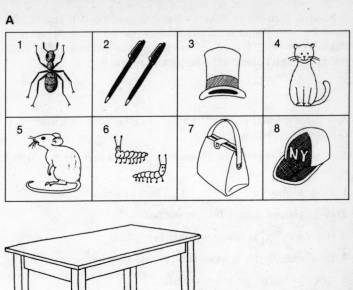

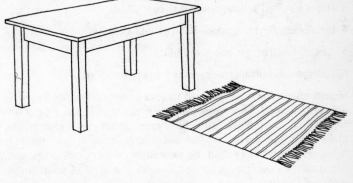

B

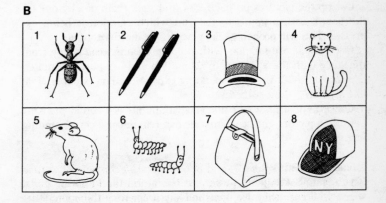

Pupil A then asks, 'Where's the rat?' and Pupil B replies, 'It's
—— the ——' Pupil A then draws the rat on his or her picture.
Pupil B now ask, 'Where's the bug?', and so on. When they have
finished, pupils compare their drawings to check.

Emotions

Aim: To sensitize pupils to how facial expressions and intonation
can convey meaning.

Throughout the story the characters express a number of different
emotions:

1 Surprise/disbelief: Is that a cat?/A bat? In a hat?

2 Disagreement/denial: fat? I'm not fat!

3 Happiness/self-satisfaction: I do like my hat.

4 Puzzlement/interrogation: Who's that in my hat?

5 Anger: Bad Tat, get out of my hat!

6 Unhappiness/dismay/anger: Look at my hat, Nat!

Depending on the way you read the story, certain lines can express
different emotions. For example, when Pat says at the end, 'Look
at my hat, Nat!' This could be anger, dismay or unhappiness.
Make sure you decide beforehand which emotion you think is
being expressed here and be consistent with your intonation.
Alternatively, depending on the level and interest of your pupils,
you could discuss the variations with them.

Cut up the pictures on page 224 and stick them one by one on
the board, asking pupils to tell you which emotion is being expressed. This will probably take place in the mother tongue.

Once pupils are familiar with the expressions, read a line from
the story with the appropriate intonation and ask pupils to match
the emotion with the corresponding expression. For example, 'I do
like my hat.' 'Number three!'

Continue in this way until you feel pupils are confident. Now
point to a picture and see if anyone can remember a corresponding
line.

THE EMOTION GAME
If your pupils are going to act out this story, the following game
will help them memorize lines and say them with the appropriate
intonation.

Version 1

You will need a pack of cards for each group of three or four pupils. On each card draw one of the facial expressions.

Each player begins the game with ten points.

1 Shuffle the cards and place them face down in the middle.
2 Player number one takes the top card and repeats a line from the story corresponding with the emotion.
3 The other players must guess what the emotion is. If someone guesses correctly, that pupil and the 'actor' each gain a point. If the pupil is wrong they both lose two points. If no one has guessed after two turns then the card goes back into the pack and player number two takes a card. The winner is the pupil with the most points when everyone has had two turns.

Version 2

This version will help pupils with their reading. In pairs, one pupil has a copy of lines from the story and the other a copy of the facial expressions (see page 224). Pupil A reads out a line and Pupil B must show the corresponding picture. They then change over. Alternatively, Pupil B shows an expression and Pupil A must read a line corresponding with the emotion shown.

COLLAGE

Pupils could collect pictures and photographs from magazines and newspapers of real people showing different expressions and make these into a collage. They can, of course, include other emotions.

Dramatization

If children have enjoyed listening to *Pat the Cat*, you may be surprised how much of it they already know by heart. Developing the story into a play will be a very memorable experience for them. It can be acted out in groups of six:

- A narrator
- Pat the Cat
- Caterpillar 1
- Caterpillar 2
- Tat the Bat
- Nat the Rat

The script can be adapted according to the level of your pupils and the time available by leaving out some of the lines.

You will need the following props: a hat and a mat.

A

Who's that in Pat's hat?
I do like my hat.
Is that a cat?
Do you know Pat the Cat?
Fat? I'm not fat!
A bat? In a hat?
Bad Nat, get out of my hat!
A rat? In a hat?
Bad Tat, get out of my hat!
A rat? In a hat?

B

Costumes could simply consist of masks for the cat, the cater-pillars, the bat and the rat. These could be made as part of the handicraft and drawing lessons. (See *Copyparty* for instructions.)

It is always motivating for pupils to perform a play in front of another class or at an open day. If this is possible, they could also make invitations and posters, etc. You may also be able to film/video your pupils, so that they can view the play themselves. This helps them develop their confidence and learn to evaluate their per-formance.

Other books in this series: *Jen the Hen, Mig the Pig, Tog the Dog, Zug the Bug.*

Story notes by Hilary Cormack and Gail Ellis

12   Mr Gumpy's Motor Car

Author and illustrator: John Burningham

Description: The story of Mr Gumpy's eventful day in the country, accompanied by his animal friends and two children. Everyone wants to come for a day's outing but nobody wants to push when the car gets stuck in the mud! An appealing adventure that may be familiar to many children – and one which ends happily.

Layout: Delicate pastel and ink drawing, generally on the page opposite the text. Smaller ink drawings accompany the text printed in large, clear letters and these provide logical links between the text and the coloured drawings.

Linguistic features

- A story with a beginning, a middle and an end: a direct sequence of events to exploit the concept of measurement.
- Short conversational phrases in everyday English provide practice in rhythm and stress and an introduction to the use of dialogue.
- A selection of delightful onomatopaeic words: action and noise words which are tempting to mime and reproduce.
- It is possible to shorten the text for younger learners, emphasizing only the keywords and relying on the drawings as complementary explanation.

Linguistic objectives

SKILLS

Listening: listening for understanding, using visuals and picking out keywords

Speaking: (see language functions and pronunciation features)

Reading: reading labels and simple captions

Writing: copying direct speech, writing simple captions to accompany pictures

FUNCTIONS/STRUCTURES
- Describing ability using can

225

- Asking permission using may
- Talking about intentions using will
- Making predictions using going to/might
- Making suggestions using let's
- Comparing using comparative forms –er

VOCABULARY
The keywords can be classified into four lexical sets:

Animals: rabbit, cat, dog, pig, sheep, chickens, calf, goat

The weather: nouns, for example: clouds, rain, mud
        adjectives, for example: cold, lovely, muddy, dark
        verbs, for example: shine

Parts of a car: engine, hood, wheels, tyres

Movement words: for example: slither, chug, churn, grip, slip

Other verbs: for example: push, look, stick, stop

PRONUNCIATION
- Intonation and stress: It's going to **rain**

        May we come **too**?

        push

        Not **me**

- Diphthongs: /aɪ/ in drive/ride
             /eɪ/ in came
             /əʊ/ in home

Past tense + /t/:	jumped, looked, pushed
Past tense + /d/:	chugged, piled, strained

CONCEPTUAL REINFORCEMENT/CURRICULUM LINKS

- Spatial context
- Geography and the environment: weather and seasons
- Creative activities: drawing, making models
- Music and drama: singing songs and rhymes

LEARNING TO LEARN
Comparing, classifying, using charts, surveys and investigations, memory training

Time

The following suggestions can be used as separate lessons of thirty to forty minutes. The book and recording will take three or four lessons.

Classroom organization

For the story-reading, recording and games a cleared space where the children can sit on the floor around you is the most practical. Desks or tables should be available for any writing or drawing activities.

Materials

- Poster collage of the weather
- Page of weather squares
- Pictures of animals in the book
- Written labels of parts of a car
- Cardboard templates of cars
- Cassette
- Photocopies of drawings
- Written captions to accompany the drawings

Other Puffin books used:
Weather (Pienkowski), *Puffin Song Book* (Woodgate), *Cars* (Rockwell), *Copycat* (Kilroy).

Lesson One

Aim: To introduce weather vocabulary

Show pupils the prepared collage of the weather. Pointing to each one, say, 'rain', 'sun', 'clouds', etc.

Ask one pupil to look outside. Then choose another to point to one of the pictures and to ask, 'Can you see the sun?' or 'Can you see the rain?' The pupil should reply with 'Yes' or 'No'. Repeat this with other pupils.

FLASH CARD GAME

Each child has a page of the weather drawings (see opposite) to colour and cut out for the flash card game. The teacher gathers all the cards together. One by one the cards are shown to the pupils seated on the floor. The first child to say the word correctly gets the card. The winner is the pupil with the most cards. Pupils can replace the teacher to show the cards.

228

WEATHER CHART

Prepare a large squared sheet of paper with the name of the month written at the top and numbers marking the days.

At the beginning of each lesson choose a pupil to reply to the questions: 'Can you see clouds?', 'Can you see the sun?' You can point to the original collage as a reminder. After the reply, 'yes', the pupil chooses the appropriate drawing from the others, colours it and glues it on the date square. (Keep a personal calendar list and tick off each child's name as they have a turn.)

For revision and additional interest

Fold in two the Puffin book *Weather* by Jan Pienkowski so that the pupils can see the coloured window on the left-hand side. Repeat the original questions: 'Can you see the rain?', etc. Then ask the children to predict what might be drawn on the other page.

Lesson Two

Aim: To introduce the names of the animals in the story

MAKING A FARM

Show pupils the animal picture cards one by one. Ask, 'What's this?' and use the reply, 'It's a cat.' Mix up the cards and repeat the question for each card, asking different pupils to reply. Look at each card again, repeating, 'It's a pig.'

Ask for suggestions as to where all the animals might be found. Encourage pupils to describe a farm. Have a large sheet of paper prepared and ask them to help draw farm buildings. Choose pupils to place the picture cards in the appropriate buildings. Use the words farm, here and there.

DRAWING

Ask pupils to draw a farm with the animals they would like to keep. Ten minutes before the end of the lesson re-group the children and ask them to display their drawings and say the names of the animals they have drawn.

SONG 'OLD MACDONALD'

Before listening, ask pupils to say the names of animals that they can now recognize. Then play a recording of 'Old Macdonald had a Farm.' Use the picture cards after listening. Ask, 'Is there a cat?' and 'Is there a pig?'

Lesson Three

Aims
- To introduce the vocabulary to describe a car
- To revise all the vocabulary learned so far
- To practise asking Wh– questions

DOING A SURVEY

Ask some of the pupils how they come to school. Introduce 'on a bicycle; by bus; on foot; by car; by train'. Ask the children to work together in groups of six to find out how everyone in the group comes to school. This information should be recorded on a chart:

Name	on a bicycle	by bus	on foot	by car	by train
Sophie			✓		

RIDDLE GAME

When each group has finished, the teacher can play a guessing game saying, 'I'm thinking of someone who comes to school on foot. Who is it?' After four or five tries the children can then play this game themselves in their original groups of six.

LABELLING A CAR

Draw a large picture of a car on the board (or have one already prepared on a large piece of paper). Elicit, where possible, the following words: window, hood, engine, wheels, tyres, doors. Have ready labels with these words and ask volunteers to stick them on the drawing with Blu-Tack.

Lesson Four

Aims:
- To read the story and encourage comprehension through using the context and visuals
- To encourage participation of the pupils in the storytelling
- To revise vocabulary already acquired

Introducing the story
Before reading the story, use the cover picture to introduce it by
asking questions such as:
● Which animals are in the car?
● How many wheels can you see?
● Where are they going?
● Who is driving?
● What might happen next?

When telling the story, use gestures or sound-effects to explain the
meaning of words such as squash and chug.

MAKE A CARDBOARD CAR
Have available a rectangular piece of stiff card for each pupil,
crayons and scissors. Fold the card in half along its longest side
and ask the children to draw a car on the front. You could make
some templates of different car designs by drawing a shape on stiff
card and cutting it out. The children who are not very confident
about drawing a car could then use this to draw around. (See
Copycat for further guidelines.)

Ask the children to draw a driver and passengers in the win-
dows.

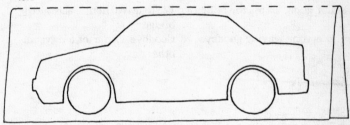

FOLLOW-UP SONG
Sing and mime the story 'The Wheels on the Bus . . .' from *This
Little Puffin* (page 73).

Follow-up book: *Cars* (Rockwell).

Lesson Five

Aims
● To revise the story
● To familiarize the pupils with written captions from the story

Sequencing and matching exercise

If necessary tell the story again. Ask the pupils which pictures or events they remember the most. Put the set of pictures and their accompanying captions on the board using Blu-Tack. Ask individual pupils to try to sequence the pictures. Revise the language of the story as each picture is put in its correct place. When this is completed the pupils will be more familiar with the story and the language contained in the pictures. Now ask individual pupils to come to the blackboard and match the picture with its written caption or speech bubble.

Pictures	**Captions**
1 Children and animals	May we come too? All right. But it will be a squash.
2 Car on the cart track	It's a lovely day. Let's take the cart track.
3 Dark clouds	I think it's going to rain.
4 Car going up the hill	You will have to get out and push.
5 All of the animals	Not me!
6 Car in the mud	Now we're really stuck.
7 Everyone pushing	Don't stop. We're nearly there.
8 Car going across the bridge	We'll drive home across the bridge.
9 Everyone waving goodbye	Goodbye. Come for a drive another day.

Lesson Six

Aims

● To encourage the pupils to retell the story and record it on cassette
● To prepare the class for making a big book.

Rewriting the story

If necessary tell the story again and then divide the class into four groups so that each group can work on producing a rewritten version of the story. Each group can work on a different section of the story. For example:

Group 1: pages 1–7   up to 'and they all piled in'.
Group 2: pages 8–13   up to 'I think it's going to rain.'
Group 3: pages 14–23 up to 'They all got out and pushed.'
Group 4: pages 24–30 up to 'Come for a drive another day.'

The pupils might like to use the captions above for their part of the story, illustrating it with pictures they draw themselves.

Ask each group to practise describing the pictures they have drawn to make part of the story. When they are ready, ask the groups to come out in turn to tell the whole story again. Using the completed work above, volunteers can be asked to retell their part of the story on cassette. The rest of the class can start sticking their drawings and captions on to large sheets of paper which will make a big book when it is all put together. Make sure the pages are numbered and that there is a cover. Another class might then like to listen to the recording while the teacher shows them the pupils' book.

Story notes by Hilary Cormack and Jean Brewster

13   Mr Biff the Boxer

(in the Happy Families series)

Author: Allan Ahlberg   *Illustrator:* Janet Ahlberg

Cassette: Read by Martin Jarvis

Description: Mr Biff the Boxer is a lively modern story about the physical training, match and eventual friendship between two boxers: Mr Biff and Mr Bop. The story is wonderfully illustrated and there is an accompanying cassette.

Layout and linguistic features of the story
The text is interspersed with several coloured illustrations which sometimes include speech bubbles. The narrative contains a great deal of direct speech which, along with the visuals, helps to make the story more accessible. The story is suitable for older children in the upper primary classes.

Linguistic objectives

SKILLS
Listening: for the gist, using visuals, for detail (to fill in a chart), for sequencing pictures
Speaking: retelling the story (see Functions and Pronunciation)
Reading: family trees, charts
Writing: details in charts

FUNCTIONS/STRUCTURES
- Describing actions: present continuous
- Introducing family members: this is my ——
- Describing past events or habits: regular simple past, for example: helped, stopped, moved
  irregular past, for example: drank, ate, slept
- Giving commands: imperative form
- Predicting: will
- Comparing: as (adjective) as, for example: as fit as a fiddle

234

● Use of adjectives in superlative forms, for example: the toughest

VOCABULARY

Family members: for example, dad, mum, sister, brother

'Boxing' words: for example,

i) *nouns:* boxer, champion, trainer, fight, referee, time-keeper, draw

ii) *verbs:* box, biff, bop, train, win

'Food' words: for example, diet, cream cakes, a bottle of beer, jam tart, fish and chips, roast chicken

Adjectives: for example, tough, fit, terrible

Describing location: to the left/right, forward

PRONUNCIATION

Individual sounds: short vowel /ɪ/ as in fit, win, fiddle, sit

diphthong /aɪ/ as in fight, right

Stress: weak forms of words, for example, for /fə/; the /ðə/; of /əv/;

Sentence stress:

for example, Mr Biff was **not** tough.

Mrs Biff helped to toughen him up **too**.

'I feel **terrible**.'

Intonation: i) falling tone to show feelings

for example, 'I feel **terrible**'

ii) falling tone when asking Wh– questions

for example, 'How do you **feel**, Dad?'

iii) rising and falling tones when making lists

for example, 'I'd like three cream **cakes** and a bottle of **beer**.'

'You can have three **carr**ots and a glass of **wat**er.'

CONCEPTUAL REINFORCEMENT/CURRICULUM LINKS

● The environment: sports and food

● Science: healthy eating

- Creative activities: making a collage
- Cultural studies: famous people from other countries
- Music and drama: chants, miming, dramatization

LEARNING TO LEARN
Comparing
Predicting
Classifying
Using charts and surveys

Materials
- Pupils' family photos
- Drawings from the book
- Scissors
- Coloured pencils
- Stapler
- Blank family trees
- Cassette of the story
- Name tags

Suggested procedures

Preparation activities

1 **Sports**
   a Ask the pupils what sports they play (for example, football, rugby, tennis, gymnastics, judo). Introduce running, skipping and boxing.
   b *Miming activity:* one pupil mimes a sport in front of the class. Others guess what it is: 'You're playing football' or 'You're running.'

2 **Family members**
   a Using a family photo (preferably the teacher's) introduce family members: mum, dad, daughter, son, sister, brother
   b A good way to concretize this exercise is to provide simple drawings or name tags of an imaginary family (such as the Biff family from the book). Distribute name tags or drawings to pupils who come up in front of the class. One of the family members can then introduce the others. For example, Betty Biff (the daughter) can say:
      'This is my mum, Mrs Biff.'
      'This is my dad, Mr Biff.'
      'This is my brother, Billy Biff.'

Each family member can say hello to the class or even shake hands with the pupil to whom he or she is being introduced.

c Encourage the pupils to bring in their family photos the following day. They can then talk about who is in the photo: 'This is my mum', etc.

Telling the story
1 The story can be told either by reading it and showing the illustrations, or by playing the accompanying cassette. The children generally like the cassette as the different characters are well represented vocally.

2 In either case it's useful to point to the appropriate illustrations and to use any additional gestures to help the children while the story is being told.

NOTE: The pupils need not understand every word in the story. The goal of the storytelling is twofold: 1) to practise listening for the gist 2) to provide a base to work from. The pupils will have the opportunity to learn the story in a later activity (see Follow-up activity).

Follow-up activity: Making a class book
If the pupils are encouraged to compile their own book, it will make the story-learning process easier and much more fun.

Procedure

1 Review the book by asking your pupils about all the characters and events in the story.

2 Depending on the number of pupils you have, distribute the lines (on pages 239–40) in no particular order, either to individuals or to small groups. Ask them to illustrate the sentence(s) they have been given.

3 Once they have completed this task, tell the story again, asking pupils to hold up the appropriate illustration.

4 Tell the story a third time, having the pupils repeat each line and hold up the appropriate illustration. Encourage any gestures such as flexing muscles. Suggest voice-disguising, too. Get pupils to act out the chant as they sing it.

5 Ask pupils to assemble their illustrations in the correct order. You may wish to number them on the back to make this task easier.

6 Ask each pupil to design a cover. The class can then choose the one they like most, and the book can finally be stapled together.

7 Pupils are now invited to tell the story while one pupil stands at the front of the classroom and turns the pages of their own book.

Here's Mr Bop. He's fit and he's tough.

Here's Mr Biff. He's not fit and he's not tough.

Big fight! Mr Biff against Mr Bop.

Betty and Billy Biff said: 'Our daddy will win!'

Running with Billy . . .

Skipping with Betty . . .

In the tummy!

Mrs Biff said: 'Three carrots, dear!'
Billy and Betty Biff said: 'How are you, Dad?'
'Not very well.'

One day, Billy and Betty said: 'How are you, Dad?'
'Fit as a fiddle!'

The fight!
'On my right, Mr Bop!' (*cheers and applause from pupils*)
'On my left, Mr Biff!' (*cheers and applause from pupils*)

Ding-ding!
(*chant*)
Lean to the left
Lean to the right
Stand up
Sit down
Fight, fight, fight!

(*same as before*)

Bang!

10, 9, 8, 7, 6, 5, 4, 3, 2, 1, out!

'How are you?'

'Not very well. How are you?'
'Not very well.'

Mmm – we're hungry!

Woof-woof! Us, too!

Optional follow-up activities

DRAWING A FAMILY TREE
Draw a family tree on the blackboard (like the one below) and

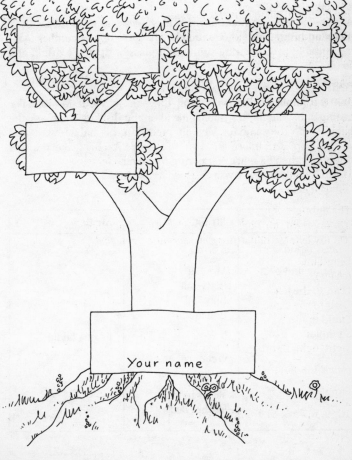

Your name

complete it for one of the pupils – or for yourself – explaining, 'This is my father, John; This is my sister, Ann; This is my grandfather, Eric', etc. Ask the pupils to draw their own family tree using the model on the board. When this has been completed, one pupil can describe his or her prepared family tree to a partner who listens carefully to the description and fills in a blank family tree. When this has been checked, the pupils reverse roles so that in the end each pupil has completed a family tree of his or her partner.

MAKING A BOOK OF SIMILES

Discuss some of the more common similes such as:

● as cool as a cucumber
● as cold as ice
● as fit as a fiddle, etc.

Ask the children to find out more examples and to illustrate their meaning humorously. For example, a picture of a cucumber looking suitably cool, wearing shorts, sun-glasses, sipping a drink, and so on.

COMPARING MR BIFF AND MR BOP

Ask the pupils to list everything they know about Mr Biff. For example, his family, his habits, his likes and dislikes. Then ask the pupils to do the same for Mr Bop, predicting his habits, likes, and so on, from the information in the story. A chart like the one below can then be made comparing the two boxers.

	Mr Biff	Mr Bop
Occupation	a boxer	
Family and pets	Mrs Biff Betty Biff Billy Biff Bonzo Biff	
Fitness		fit as a fiddle
Likes	cream cakes bottles of beer	
Habits	sleeps in a feather bed	

FAMOUS SPORTSMEN/WOMEN

Encourage the children to find out about the routines and training famous sportsmen and women have to pursue. (This will be read about in the children's mother tongue first.) They can then extract the information to make simple charts outlining their family details, daily routines, likes and so on, as in the chart above.

HEALTHY EATING

Using the information the children probably know from other lessons, ask them to work out a healthy diet suitable for an athlete, footballer, ballet dancer, and so on. They will need to think about vitamins (fruit and vegetables), protein (meat, dairy products, lentils), carbohydrates (bread, potatoes, pasta), sugar (chocolate) and fats (butter, cream). Then ask them to make a list for two days (or more) of all the food they eat. They can then work out which food groups these belong to and whether they have a healthy diet or not. They might like to make a poster or collage of different kinds of food.

Other Happy Families stories on cassette:
Mrs Plug the Plumber, Master Salt the Sailor's Son, Mrs Wobble the Waitress, Mr Cosmo the Conjuror, Mrs Lather's Laundry.

Story notes by Jean Brewster and Lesley Young

14   *The Turnip*

(in *The Fairy Tale Treasury*)

Author: Aleksei Tolstoy

Illustrator: Raymond Briggs

Description: This simple traditional Russian tale is about a farmer who grows a giant turnip which is too big for him to pull up by himself. He asks for help and more and more people – and animals – are needed to pull the turnip out of the ground.

Layout: The story is illustrated with vivid pictures which could act as further visual aids or 'story props' for the teacher. These can be used when telling the story to the whole class and also by the children for retelling the story.

Linguistic features

Repetition: The story contains one or two repeating actions, using the past simple tense, which are reinforced by the addition of a repeating dialogue. The simple storyline is developed with six characters which allows for reinforcement of the vocabulary and structures introduced. The cumulative effect of the story allows the children to participate and to predict events, while the pictures give support when they retell the story.

Pronunciation features: The six different characters encourage the use of different voices when telling and retelling the story; these changes can include variations in pitch and speed. The words which are repeated can also be emphasized through altering the volume, stress and intonation.

Linguistic objectives

SKILLS

Listening:
- for general understanding via pictures
- for detail to recognize keywords

- to recognize pronunciation features associated with keywords. For example, prominent stress, loudness, pitch movement, longer length of vowels

Speaking:
- retelling the story
- predicting the next action/dialogue
- (see language functions below)

Reading:
- distinguishing narrative from dialogue through use of speech marks
- matching speech bubbles to characters
- reading for detail in order to sequence events
- simple labels on a diagram

Writing:
- copying simple captions for a picture or diagram
- labelling sets of objects according to size

FUNCTIONS/STRUCTURES
- Recounting past events using simple past tense:
  - i) regular verbs: for example, call, plant, pull, want and –ed
  - ii) irregular verbs: for example, come/came, fall/fell, grow/grew
- Describing size: determiner 'much' and adverb 'too'
- Comparing size: comparative forms for example, big/bigger
- Giving commands: imperative without 'to', for example, come, grow
- Describing a consequence or result: clause using 'so'
- Contrasting: clause using 'but'

VOCABULARY
Verbs: come, fall, grow, plant, pull, want
Nouns: cat, dog, man, mouse, soup, turnip, woman
Adjectives: big, enormous, little, strong
Determiners: much
Adverbs: again, too

CONCEPTUAL REINFORCEMENT/CURRICULUM LINKS
- Size and shape, time, cause and effect
- Maths: size and time
- Environment: gardening, plants we eat

- Science: conditions needed for growing seeds
  growth in seeds and plants
- Creative activities: drawing and printing, making masks,
  making a theme-based display, cooking, making tickets etc.
- Music and drama: Singing songs and rhymes, dramatization

LEARNING TO LEARN
Comparing, classifying, predicting, sequencing, hypothesizing and
problem-solving, using charts and surveys

Materials
- Pictures of a turnip at different stages of growth
- Cut-out figures of all the characters pulling each other
- Speech bubbles on card
- Paper-plate masks of characters for retelling
- Russian doll (the kind where a smaller doll fits into a larger one
  and so on).
- Objects to rank in order of size. For example, shells, boxes
- Containers for growing seeds (optional)
- Packets of seeds

Lesson One

Aims
- To introduce the concept of growing to prepare children for the
  story
- to begin telling the story

Preparation for the story
Show children a packet of seeds. Talk about growing and planting
in the mother tongue but ensure that the English words for 'seed',
'plant', 'grow', 'small', 'big' and 'bigger' are introduced. Show
children a real turnip or a picture of one. Introduce the six
characters and get the children to identify them: old man, old
woman, granddaughter, dog, cat, mouse.

Telling the story
It will probably be easier to tell a revised version of the story (a
suggested version is on page 251). Tell the story using some
pictures of the individual characters. These can be attached to a
blackboard or a piece of paper with Blu-Tack and could be placed
on a background scene showing the farm, a house and a field.

Homework: Ask the children to bring a paper plate and different sizes of one or two everyday items (for example, boxes, bottles or shells).

Lesson Two

Aims
- To reinforce the concepts of size and to introduce the comparative
- To retell the story

COMPARING

Show children the Russian doll, if you have one. Use it to reinforce the idea of size and comparison saying, 'Here's a big doll. Here's a smaller one.'
(Fit the smaller doll inside the bigger one.)

Repeat with as many dolls as there are. If you do not have a Russian doll, you could use cardboard boxes of different sizes.

To rehearse the sentence patterns, repeat this activity with one child fitting the items inside each other. Encourage the children to join in.

MAKING MASKS

Remind children of the story by using the pictures of the turnip getting bigger and bigger. Ask for the names of the six characters. Give each child a paper plate and ask them to choose which character they would like to be. They can then make a mask by drawing a face and cutting out holes for the eyes, nose and mouth for the people. (They can add ears and whiskers for the animals.) Thin elastic is then knotted through a hole on each side of the plate to keep the mask in place. Retell the story asking the children to say their character's lines when appropriate.

CLASSIFYING

Begin making a collection of small, medium and large boxes, shells or bottles. Classify them into three sets, labelling them small, big and bigger.

Homework: Ask the children to finish off their masks.

PART 2

Lesson Three

Aim: To encourage children to retell the story

USING THE MASKS
Ask for volunteers to come out to the front wearing their paper masks so that they can re-enact the story. The teacher narrates the storyline while the children supply the dialogue. The story props can be available in the right sequence to act as prompts.

COMPARING SIZE
Using the boxes collected by the class, sequence them in order of size. Pick up two boxes and ask, 'Which one is bigger?' or 'Is this one bigger than that one?' The pupils should reply, 'No, it's smaller.'

You can then ask a child to fit the smaller box inside the bigger box, or place the boxes in a row. In groups the children could practise asking and answering these questions with collections of boxes.

DRAWING AND WRITING
Let the children choose a scene from the story. For example, the turnip getting bigger and bigger or some of the characters pulling the turnip. Provide two captions for them to copy on to their picture or help the children write their own captions.

Caption 1   The turnip grew big and strong. It grew bigger and bigger and bigger until it was ENORMOUS.
Caption 2   'One, two, three, PULL,' said the old man. And they all pulled.

Homework: Ask the children to bring in vegetables of different kinds and any packets of seeds.

Lesson Four

Aim: To describe and compare different kinds of vegetables using 'but'

LABELLING PLANTS
Discuss some of the different vegetables brought in by the class, making sure that they know the English names for them. Draw and label a simple diagram on the blackboard showing a plant with a root, a stem and leaves, a flower or a pod. Check that the

246

children can remember these words, then write them at the side and rub off the labels. Ask volunteers to come and rewrite the label in the correct place.

PARTS OF VEGETABLES
Look at the vegetables brought in by the class and ask the children to name the vegetable and say which part of it we eat.

For example: root   turnip, potato, carrot
              leaf   lettuce, spinach
              pod or cob pea, sweetcorn, bean
              fruit   aubergine, cucumber, pepper

This can be made into a chart (see below).

What do we eat?				
	root	leaves	pod	fruit
tomato	×	×	×	√
lettuce	×	√	×	×
aubergine	×	×	×	√
carrot	√	×	×	×

The children may be able to add a clause using 'but', saying which part we do not eat.

Using this chart rehearse the following sentence patterns so that the class can make sentences such as:

This is a potato. We eat the root but not the fruit.
This is a lettuce. We eat the leaves but not the root.

The children could also write short sentences following this model. They could write some examples which are true and some which are false for other children to check.

For example: A tomato: we eat the leaves. True or false?
              A carrot: we eat the root but not the leaves. True or false?

This can be continued for homework.

247

Lesson Five

Free choice

RETELLING THE STORY

● One or two groups may choose to retell/re-enact the story with a different fruit or vegetables, for example, a pumpkin or a tomato, using masks or pictures. They might like to put together a picture book to accompany their spoken version of the story. The book could be made in the shape of the fruit or vegetable they select.

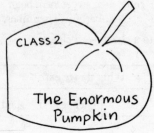

LISTENING AND SEQUENCING

● A pair or group can listen to the story on cassette and sequence the pictures as they listen. For example, they find the picture of the old man pulling the turnip and add on the picture of the old woman pulling him, etc.

MATCHING

● Pairs or groups can listen to or read the story and match a 'speech bubble' written on card to the correct picture
For example: Matching the picture of the granddaughter with the speech bubble

248

COMPARING AND SORTING

A group may like to put all the boxes or shells collected in order of size from small to big and to label them using three captions: small, big, bigger. If there is a really big example the word enormous could be added. The children can have a competition to see who can fit the largest number of objects into the same-sized box and then list the contents of the boxes with the highest number of objects.

GROWING SEEDS

The class may like to plant some seeds which grow very quickly into small plants. They can copy a caption: Grow, grow little seed. Grow big and strong. The seeds can be grown in used eggshells filled with soil. The children can draw faces on the eggs and after a short while the leaves of the growing plants will look like green hair!

INVESTIGATING CONDITIONS FOR GROWTH

Some children might like to experiment with seeds grown in different conditions: in the dark for too long: with too little water; with too much water, etc. (The seeds would need to have been planted two weeks before.) The pupils can then compare the results, writing sentences such as: a) These seeds grew badly. The soil was too dry/wet. It was too dark. b) These seeds grew well. Everything was just right.

VEGETABLE PRINTING

A group of children might like to do some vegetable printing. Cut the vegetable in half (a potato or turnip would be a good choice). Cut out a shape on the cut side, dip it in some paint and then press lightly on to paper to make a pattern.

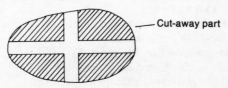

Cut-away part

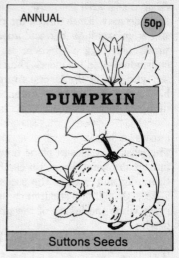

DESIGNING SEED PACKETS
Some children might like to design some seed packets. They could choose an English brand-name, for example: Suttons Seeds, Hurst, Thompson & Morgan, Cuthbert, Unwins, Johnson. They also need to include the price, the name of the plant, and the fact that it is an annual (it dies in the winter). Display the finished products in the classroom.

COOKING: MAKING TURNIP SOUP
If possible make this at school or give a list of instructions for a simple recipe pupils can make at home

Ingredients
1 onion   ½ litre of water
4 turnips   salt and pepper

SONGS AND RHYMES
Useful songs and rhymes on the theme of growing and planting from *This Little Puffin* include:
- 'Flowers grow like this' (page 43)
- 'Oats and beans and barley grow' (page 83)
- 'Do you plant your cabbages?' (page 85)
- 'We are going to plant a bean' (page 48)

Revised version of the story

Once upon a time an old man planted a little turnip and said, 'Grow, grow, little turnip, grow big and strong.' And the little turnip grew up strong and big. It grew bigger and bigger and bigger until one day it was ENORMOUS.

The next day the old man wanted to have some turnip soup, so he went to pull up the turnip. He pulled and he pulled again, but he couldn't pull it up. He called to the old woman, 'Come and help me, please. I can't pull up the turnip. It's too big.'

So the old woman came and she pulled the old man. He pulled the turnip. They pulled and pulled again but they couldn't pull it up. So the old woman called to her granddaughter, 'Come and help us, please. We can't pull up the turnip. It's too big.'

The granddaughter pulled the old woman. The old woman pulled the old man. And they pulled and pulled again but they couldn't pull it up. Then the granddaughter called to the black dog, 'Come and help us please, dog. We can't pull up the turnip. It's too big.'

So the black dog pulled the granddaughter, the granddaughter pulled the old woman and the old man pulled the turnip. And they pulled and pulled again but they couldn't pull it up. The black dog called to the cat, 'Come and help us please, cat. We can't pull up the turnip. It's much too big.'

So the cat pulled the black dog, the dog pulled the granddaughter, the granddaughter pulled the old woman, the old woman pulled the old man and the old man pulled the turnip. They pulled and pulled again but they still couldn't pull it up. The cat called to the mouse, 'Come and help us please, mouse. We can't pull up the turnip. It's ENORMOUS!'

So the mouse came and pulled the cat, the cat pulled the dog, the dog pulled the granddaughter, the granddaughter pulled the old woman, the old woman pulled the old man and the old man pulled the turnip.

'One, two, three, **pull**!'

And they pulled so hard the old man fell over, the old woman fell over, the granddaughter fell over, the dog fell over, the cat fell over and the mouse fell over. But what do you know? This time the turnip came out at last. The next day they all had lovely turnip soup.

Story notes by Jean Brewster

15   The Fat Cat

Author and illustrator: Jack Kent

Description: A repetitive/chain story about a cat which eats a great number of people and animals, and ends up (Red-Riding-Hood-like) having its stomach cut open by a woodcutter, so releasing all the occupants. Has the pleasing nasty-nonsense-impossible element which appeals to young children.

Layout: Well illustrated in a clear, direct style of coloured drawing. Patterned layout, for the most part, with the cat meeting the next person on the left-hand page and eating them on the right-hand one of each double-page spread. We never actually see the characters being eaten, and on the last page there is an uncaptioned illustration of the cat with a bandaged stomach, not really hurt at all.

Linguistic features
A cumulative folk tale which enables pupils by repetition to join in and predict what happens next in the story. It is told mainly in the narrative past simple with one past continuous (was cooking), one present perfect (has happened), one past perfect (had gone), one future simple (I'll be), one going to future (I am going to eat you), one present simple (you are) and one conditional (would look after). The position of the word 'also' in the cat's repeated statement, 'And now I am going to also eat **you**', is unusual. You may prefer to change this to 'I am also going to eat you', which sounds more natural.

Linguistic objectives

SKILLS
Listening: an ideal story for controlled listening work, patterned as it is by a strongly repetitive refrain and highlighted by focus illustrations of each new item.

Speaking: the patterning allows the story to be broken down into its few basic elements for repetition by learners, which then merely requires addition of new elements as they occur.

Reading: the learners will find it easy first to follow the patterns, then later to produce them themselves, matching lexical and pictorial clues to what they read.

Writing: labelling (naming of characters and objects belonging to them), gap-filling and sequencing.

FUNCTIONS/STRUCTURES
- Narration (sequencers and past simple)
- Inquiries about recent actions (what and present perfect continuous)
- Observations on excess (verb to be and so and adjective)
- Describing people and possessions (noun and with and noun, for example, a parson with a crooked staff),
- Polite agreement to do something (future simple of to be and glad)
- Listing (chaining: I ate the gruel *and* the old woman *and* the pot *and* —— *and*)

VOCABULARY
This can be classified into:

Characters: The fat cat, the old woman, Skohottentot, Skolinkenlot, the five birds in a flock, the seven girls dancing, the lady with a pink parasol, the parson with a crooked staff, the woodcutter

Objects (belongings): gruel, the pot, the pink parasol, the crooked staff, the axe

Linking/sequencing words: when, afterwards, next, later, a little later

Exclamations of surprise: Gracious! Heavens! Dear me! My!

Intensifier: So

Other vocabulary: The pictures also include various other items mostly connected with the house (fire, chimney, fork, spoon, plate, chair, mug, stool, window) and the village (house, roof, tree, fence, windmill, flower, church) which can be practised.

PRONUNCIATION
Intonation: 'What **have** you been eating, my little **cat**?'

Stress
In each of these lines there is a rise.

'I ate the gruel

and the pot

and the old wǒman, too,

and Skohǒttentot,

and Skolìnkenlot

and five BǏRDS in a flock

and seven gìrls dancing

and the lǎdy with the pink pàrasol

and the pàrson with the crooked SТAFF.

And nǒw I am going

to also eat you.'

'You are so fat.'

CONCEPTUAL REINFORCEMENT/CURRICULUM LINKS
● Size and shape
● Creative activities: making masks, a frieze, puppets
● Music and drama: singing songs and rhymes, dramatization

LEARNING TO LEARN
Predicting, sequencing, memory training

Cultural knowledge
Little Red Riding Hood may already have introduced the carnivore/
woodcutter motif to many children. This kind of cumulative story
is common in most European cultures. Gruel is a fairly universal
food, if somewhat old-fashioned.

Materials
● Drawings
● Visuals
● Objects (for example, a bag, a pen)

Suggested procedures
The sequence of activities suggested below involves children progressively making the story their own, and builds their confidence
with the language. The order and activities suggested are not
intended to be rigidly followed, but rather to act as a framework
for adapting to your own situation.

Preparatory activities (before the story is told)

a Introduction of characters: elicit what you can (old woman, girl, cat, bird should be easiest, if those words have already been taught), and introduce the others (woodcutter, lady, Skohotten-tot, Skolinkelot, parson). This may be done using copies of large outline drawings of their pictures in the book which can be cut out and coloured in.

b Introduction of the concept of fatness. This can be done using blown-up drawings from the books, your own drawings on the board or magazine pictures. It is a good idea to introduce the idea on a comparative basis: a thin man, a fat man, etc.

c Introduction of the concept of listing (the intonation) through familiar objects. For example: 'Look what I've got in my bag. I've got a pen, and a book, and a ball and an apple and also a key (or whatever words they know).' They should listen and then repeat this and then practise it using their own possessions.

d Introduction of the past simple for telling stories, if this is not known already. You can do so by comparing what one does every day and what one did yesterday, and by using the language pupils will meet in the text, and a time line. There are only three regular verbs here (looked, asked, jumped), while the others are irregular (was, had, said, ate, came back, went, met, took, cut) but at least they are all fairly frontline in terms of their usefulness. The only difficulties seem to be the use of looked ('it looked so good') and came ('came back'). Perhaps some explanation in the mother tongue might help here. Otherwise, the following is one way to introduce them: Write on the board

YESTERDAY   EVERY DAY

and make sure the learners understand the words. Then write: I go to school. And say, '*Every day* I go to school'; get the learners to repeat. Then write: I went to school. And say, '*Yesterday* I went to school.' Get the pupils to repeat this.

This procedure can be repeated for each of the new verbs. Some visuals might help (*meet*, for example, might be helped by a picture of two people shaking hands; *cut* by you cutting something with a knife or pair of scissors). Then try to get the learners to offer some sentences of their own using these verbs.

e Introduction of the vocabulary related to the story which will probably be new to the learners (gruel, neighbour, pot, flock, lady, parasol, parson, crooked staff, axe). These words can be introduced with visuals, and possibly with a mother-tongue explanation if they are difficult concepts (gruel, parson). The children can be asked to draw the new words and to label them, either in their own books or larger labels to put on the wall. The latter is good for ready reference and can make an interesting revision activity if the labels are removed and the children are asked to replace them next lesson.

f The introduction of 'I'll be glad to' as a way of agreeing to do something for someone. This can be done as follows: give a pupil your bag and then return to your desk. Say to the child: '[Maria], will you bring me my bag, please?' and indicate what you are asking for by gesture. Then get the child to say, 'I'll be glad to' and to bring the bag. Repeat this. Role-reverse with the child asking you. Repeat with different objects and possibly with different verbs. If you wish, this could be the point to practise the reported form in the story ('and asked the cat if he would look after the gruel'). You can say '[Maria], will you give me that pen, please.' Maria: 'I'll be glad to.' You say, 'I asked Maria if she would bring me my bag.' You might feel the will–would use here fits into the present–past scheme described earlier, although plainly one cannot match it to the habitual present as there (**d** above).

Lesson One

Aims:
- To arouse expectations
- To let the learners hear the story

Introduction
Show the class the cover of the book and ask, 'Who is he?', expecting the answer 'the cat' and/or 'the fat cat'. Elicit 'fat', if it isn't forthcoming. Point to the title and repeat 'the fat cat' a few times. Get pupils to repeat this chorally and then individually.

Open the book to the first double-page spread where the text starts and show the class the picture there. Ask, 'What can you see?', expecting answers like 'the cat', 'the old woman' and 'the pot'. Ask what is in the pot (gruel) and if the cat is fat (no). Elicit whatever is not given.

Ask what other objects pupils can see (spoon, plate, seat, window, fire, fork).

Ask what they think the woman is saying to the cat and what the cat replies.

Focus
Read the whole story, very expressively, showing the children the pictures as you read.

Conclusion
Ask the children to try to retell the story with the help of the pictures. Some or all of this may be done in the mother tongue but try to encourage and help pupils to use the English words they know already.

Lesson Two

Aims
- To aid comprehension of the story
- To begin production of the language involved

Introduction
Show pupils the cover again, and ask, 'Who is he?' They should all say 'the fat cat'.

Ask, 'Who remembers what he did?' and try to elicit answers that he ate lots of people.

Preparation
On the board Blu-Tack pictures of the main characters and objects in the story in order of appearance (the old woman, the cat, the gruel, the pot, Skohottentot, Skolinkenlot, five birds in a flock, seven girls dancing, a lady with a pink parasol, a parson with a crooked staff, a woodcutter with an axe). Ask the children who they are and label them. Then get them to repeat the names with you, then chorally, then individually. Take the labels away and see if the pupils can manage without them.

Then give each child a picture of one of the key elements (listed above). Check they know what they have by asking, 'Who has (got) the seven girls dancing?' and expect the learners to hold up their pictures. Try it for each element.

Focus
Tell the children that you are going to read the story right

257

through, and that each time you mention one of the characters those pupils with that element should hold up their picture.

Read the story from the beginning, pausing slightly and checking who is holding up what after each item has been mentioned. You might repeat the story if the pupils aren't getting it right.

Conclusion
Give each of the learners all of the characters, and tell them that this time they have to put them in the order the fat cat eats them. When you have read the story you can check by circulating. Then ask for a consensus and put the characters up on the board with the labels under them.

The children can then stick the pictures into their own books and label them.

Lesson Three

Aims
● To increase production
● To start the learners telling the story

Introduction
Tell the story up to page 5. Then ask the learners to listen very carefully while you read what the cat said:

'I ate the gruel,
and I ate the pot, too.
And now I'm going to also eat you.'

Repeat it several times with full expression.

Focus
Ask the children to repeat each line after you chorally and, occasionally, individually until they can say the whole piece by themselves.

Then carry on the story until you get to the next 'And the cat said:'. Encourage the learners to tell you what they can remember, although noting that it is slightly different this time. Read and get them to repeat as before.

Continue in this way, allowing pupils to try with each of the listings – before reading it and getting them to repeat – and to do the new one by themselves until you get to the last one which goes backwards. (It may help to have the 'cast' on the board in picture, word or picture and word form to point to when they get stuck. You should aim to get the children listing with a good rhythmic swing and the correct intonation.)

Conclusion
Give them the last list the cat says (to the woodcutter) with the items blanked out and ask pupils to fill them in in the correct order:

'I ate the ——
and the ——
and the ——, too,
and ——
and ——'
etc.

You might care to put in the first letter of each item to assist them.

Lesson Four

Aim: Further production of key items

Introduction
Read the story through with the class chorally listing 'I ate the gruel', etc.

Now read the story yourself as far as the meeting with Skohotten-tot and get the learners to repeat. Then produce: 'What have you been eating, my little cat? You are so fat', paying attention to the intonation and stress as suggested on pages 253–4.

Focus
This time when you read the story, let the whole class say the question and the listing for each character.

Then get half the class to be the cat and half to be the other people who ask the repeated question. You act as narrator, filling in the rest of the story.

Conclusion
On the board list as many foods as they know. Then ask them to choose what they would like to have eaten from this list and to take it in turns to ask the question: 'What have you been eating, my little girl/boy? You are so fat' and to reply, for example, 'I ate the gruel and the bread and the potatoes and the cheese and the meat. And now I'm also going to eat **you**.' This could be done with

the class moving about and stopping when you clap your hands and then asking or telling the nearest person. In this way they talk to four or five different people.

Lesson Five

Aim: To enact the story
Organize the class into groups of eight and allocate a part to each child. (Remember that the cat has most to say and should be a good speaker.)

Introduction
Read the story and, when you get to the spoken parts, get the characters from the groups to say them with you.

Focus
Now read the story again, but allow pupils to say the spoken parts and act it out as a group. You might need to help with initial stage-managing here: decide where each group's kitchen is, where the road is, and get the people to meet in order, etc.

Conclusion
Practise this a few times, then let each group show the others what they've worked out.

It might be fun to perform it for another class. You could go on to make masks or costumes or even puppets. Stick puppets are easiest: a cut-out character stuck on cardboard and Sellotaped to a long stick.

Optional follow-up activities

FRIEZE
This story lends itself very nicely to the production of a class frieze. The cat gets progressively fatter, with drawings of the things and the people he has eaten under each picture of him. There would be ten pictures: nine of the things and the people and the tenth of the woodcutter letting them all out.

SONG/RHYME

Pussy cat, pussy cat	Pussy cat, pussy cat
Where have you been?	What did you there?
I've been up to London	I frightened a little mouse
To visit the Queen.	Under her chair.

GAME: THE PARSON'S CAT

In its true form, the players sit in a circle and have to provide an adjective describing the parson's cat in alphabetical order. For example: The parson's cat is an amiable cat, the parson's cat is a black cat, the parson's cat is a curious cat, etc.) When someone repeats a word already given, takes too long or just can't think of an adjective, he or she is out. If you use adjectives known to the children – obvious ones like colours and simple descriptives (big, small, fat, thin, long, short, nice, pretty, ugly, happy, sad, etc.) – and give each child one or two of them, the game could be adapted to go round simply in correct alphabetical order.

Story notes by David Hill

16   *The Snowman*

Author and illustrator: Raymond Briggs

Description: A moving yet amusing story about a little boy who builds a snowman. One magical night the snowman comes alive and the two become friends. Now a classic, the story relates well to the themes of the weather, the seasons and Christmas. It could be introduced in November, December, January or February.

Layout: The wordless story is told in a series of strip format pictures in soft muted colours. As the illustrations are sometimes rather small, the book is best used with groups of not more than fifteen pupils.

Linguistic features: The pupils can build up the story orally by making their own interpretations of the narrative and illustrations. This enables them to exercise their imaginations and to become personally and creatively involved in the story as they identify with the characters.

A text is suggested on pages 274 and 275 which incorporates the linguistic objectives outlined below.

Linguistic objectives

SKILLS
● Listening for gist as the story is told; listening for detail via instructions
● Speaking: asking and answering questions
● Reading: matching words; reading numbers for telling the time; reading charts
● Writing: labelling pictures/diagrams

FUNCTIONS/STRUCTURES
● Asking for information using Yes/No and Wh– questions
● Asking for permission using can
● Asking for and telling the time
● Greetings
● Showing someone round a house using this is the ——
● Expressing ability using can
● Expressing likes and dislikes

VOCABULARY

This includes items from the following lexical areas:

- parts of the body
- the weather
- clothes
- colours
- numbers
- rooms in a house
- furniture
- toys
- adjectives: happy/sad, hot/cold

PRONUNCIATION

- Intonation: What colour is ——?

    What's the time?

    This is the ——.

    Can I ——?

    Can you ——?

    Do you like ——?

- Individual sounds: /kən/ as in I can skateboard.
    /ɑ/ as in can't, scarf, arms.
    /əʊ/ as in snow.

- Stress: I CAN'T skateboard.

CONCEPTUAL REINFORCEMENT/CURRICULUM LINKS

- Colours, size and shape, time, cause and effect
- Maths: telling the time
- Geography: weather and seasons, games
- Cultural studies: festivals in other countries
- Creative activities: drawing, making collages, models and Christmas cards

LEARNING TO LEARN

Comparing, classifying, predicting, sequencing, using charts and surveys, memory training

Materials
- Drawn copies of some of the illustrations from the book
- Card and paper fasteners to make a clock (Lesson Four)

Lesson One

Aims
- To introduce *The Snowman*
- To revise or introduce vocabulary for parts of the body and clothes

PICTURE DICTATION

Explain to the pupils that you are going to dictate some instructions which they must draw, but do not tell them they are going to draw a snowman. Explain the meaning of draw and add. Repeat each instruction at least three or four times and, when necessary, mime or point to your own eyes, etc., to convey meaning. After the third or fourth repetition draw the item yourself on the blackboard (see below). This will provide immediate feedback or reinforcement for any pupils who are unsure and will prevent

264

anyone getting left behind. (Instructions: Draw a circle. Add two eyes. Add a nose. Add a mouth. Add a body. Draw two arms. Draw two legs. Add a hat. Add a scarf. Add three buttons.)

Ask pupils what they have drawn. Teach snowman. Allow pupils to compare their pictures.

To check comprehension of vocabulary items, ask pupils to come to the blackboard and respond to your instructions. For example, 'Yacine, show me the snowman's nose!', etc.

Pupils could colour their pictures and stick them on to their story envelopes.

Show pupils the cover of the book and tell them they are going to work on a story about a snowman.

Lesson Two

Aim: To introduce or revise further vocabulary for clothes and colours and to practise asking for information.

Hold up the cover and ask pupils, 'Who's this?' to revise the word snowman and the vocabulary for parts of the body and clothes. Show them the first page of the story and introduce the little boy. Ask pupils to give him a name.

Choose a pupil in the class who is wearing a pullover, jeans and boots to revise or teach this vocabulary. Ask, 'What's this?' and point to the pullover. Pupils will probably reply in their mother tongue. Teach the English word and get them to repeat 'pullover'. Do the same for the other items. Check by asking individual pupils to show you different clothing items. For example, 'Sarah, show me your pullover!', etc. You could also revise colours at this stage. 'What colour is it?' 'It's red.' 'Yes, a red pullover', and so on.

Make drawn copies of the first page. Cut them up so each pupil has ten individual pictures. (Pupils could do this themselves, but it saves time to do it yourself.) Put the pictures in an envelope which each child labels: The Snowman: Clothes. They can store this in their A4 Snowman story envelope.

LISTENING AND ARRANGING

Ask pupils to put their pictures on their desk. Tell the first page of the story. As you do so, the pupils must show the corresponding picture and arrange it in the correct order. They can then number their pictures.

Suggested text

Once upon a time there was a little boy called ——. One morning in —— (*month*) he woke up and looked out of the window. 'Ah! It's snowing!' he said. He got dressed quickly. He put on his red pullover and his blue jeans, and said to his mother, 'Can I go outside, please?' And she said, 'Yes, ——.' He put on his black boots and his red hat and ran into the garden.

Retell the story so far, inviting pupils to participate by repeating key vocabulary items and phrases. For example: the boy's name, the month, 'It's snowing!', his red pullover, his blue jeans, 'Yes, ——', his black boots, his red hat. To encourage pupils to predict, ask them what they think the little boy does next.

Optional follow-up activities

COLOURING AND LABELLING
Pupils may like to colour their pictures and label them with the vocabulary for clothes (see the example above). These could then be used again in the following pair-work activity.

Pupil A: What colour is ——'s pullover?
Pupil B: It's green.
etc.

Alternatively, you could give the following instructions: 'Colour Brian's hat red!' or 'Show me Brian's blue jeans', etc.

ASKING FOR PERMISSION
Depending on the level of your class, you could teach the language

for asking for permission. Refer to the story where the little boy asks his mother. 'Can I go outside, please?' Practise the pronunciation: the weak can /kən/ and the rising tone. Now ask pupils to make up sentences referring to situations in the classroom. For example, 'Can I open the window, please?', 'Can I borrow a pen, please?', and so on.

Lesson Three

Aim: To revise or introduce further vocabulary for clothes.

Select other illustrations of clothes (see suggestions on page 266). Copy these for each pupil to add to their Clothes envelope. They already have pictures of pyjamas, a pullover, jeans, boots, a hat and gloves. This will encourage them to build up their own personal lexical sets for vocabulary learning. Teach new vocabulary items and check pronunciation.

Check their understanding by saying, 'Show me a hat!', 'Show me a tie!', etc. You could also instruct pupils to colour their pictures: 'Colour the snowman's trousers black!', etc.

Retell the story from the beginning encouraging pupils to participate and asking them what they think the little boy does when he goes out into the garden. Introduce the next two pages which could include new language such as snowball, tangerine and coal (revise hat, scarf and buttons). Teach the expression, 'He's smiling.'

Retell the story including the next two pages.

Suggested text

. . . and ran into the garden. First, he made a small snowball for the head and then a larger one for the body. He gave him a scarf and a hat, a tangerine for a nose, and lumps of coal for buttons and eyes. Finally, he drew a mouth. —— was very happy and said, 'He's smiling.'

Lesson Four

Aim: To revise or introduce numbers and language for telling and asking the time.

Revise the numbers one to ten and introduce eleven and twelve if these are new.

NUMBER DICTATION

To practise, dictate the following numbers: two, five, nine, twelve, eight, four, eleven. Ask pupils to read out the numbers for checking.

MAKING A CLOCK

Make a clock by cutting out a cardboard circle of approximately 20 cm (big enough for all the class to see). Write the numbers on it. Cut out two hands and attach these, using a paper fastener. If there is more time children could make their own clocks as an activity linked to mathematics and handicrafts.

Introduce midnight and the expression, It's one o'clock. Move the hands on your clock to different times. For example, five o'clock, eight o'clock, etc., and ask pupils to tell you the time. Introduce the question, 'What's the time?' Move the hands to different positions and ask, 'What's the time?' Pupils reply, 'It's —— o'clock.'

If pupils have their own clocks they can do this in pairs. They could also ask you, 'What's the time?' You reply and pupils move the hands on their own clocks.

Optional follow-up activity: Time Dictation
Give pupils a worksheet such as the one below. Pupils ask, 'Number

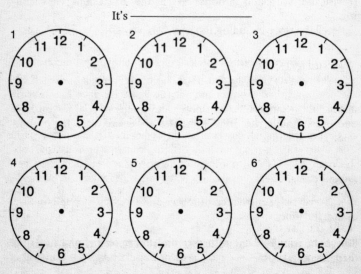

What's the time?

It's ————————————

One: What's the time?' You reply. Pupils then draw the hands on the clock face corresponding to your reply. (Continue in this way until Number Six.) To check, pupils can show you the time on their own clocks or on yours.

Copy the four pictures from the book that show the time: eight o'clock, nine o'clock, eleven o'clock and midnight. Cut up these drawings and give them to pupils in envelopes which they label The Time. Introduce the next pages and, as you tell the story, pupils show you the corresponding pictures.

Suggested text
Soon it was time for bed. —— brushed his teeth and at eight o'clock he looked out of the window at the snowman. His mother said, 'Good-night ——' and at nine o'clock he was asleep. At eleven o'clock he woke up and got out of bed and looked out of the window at the snowman. He was still there! He went back to bed but couldn't sleep. At midnight he got up. He put on his dressing-gown, went downstairs and opened the door . . .

Ask pupils to tell you what they think happens next.

Retell the story from the beginning, encouraging pupils to participate as they become more and more familiar with the story and memorize the language.

Lesson Five

Aims
- To introduce or revise vocabulary for rooms in a house and furniture items
- To introduce greetings and language for showing someone round a house.

Ask pupils to tell you the names of the different rooms in their homes. Teach the English words as the need arises.

Give pupils envelopes containing copies of the main rooms in the story (sitting-room or living-room, kitchen, upstairs, parents' bedroom, ——'s bedroom, downstairs, garage) which they can label Rooms. Check vocabulary by saying, 'Show me the kitchen!', and so on.

TRUE OR FALSE?
To check comprehension further and to revise (or introduce) the expression 'This is ——' play True or False? Hold up a drawing of

a room and say, for example, 'This is the kitchen.' Children reply 'True', or 'False'. Alternatively they could say 'Yes' or 'No'. 'Right' or 'Wrong'. Pupils could also play this game in pairs.

GREETINGS

Show pupils page 6 of the story and ask them to tell you what they think the snowman and the little boy are saying. Teach How do you do! and explain that this expression is very formal and usually used by people meeting each other for the first time, usually accompanied by a handshake. Explain that it is rarely used by children. It is far more natural for the little boy simply to say 'Hello!' However, pupils will enjoy practising How do you do! in pairs, accompanied by a handshake.

SHOWING SOMEONE ROUND A HOUSE

Ask pupils what they would say to someone visiting their home for the first time. Elicit possible dialogue: for example, 'This is the ——.'

PAIR WORK

For practice, ask pupils to sketch their own homes and to explain to their partners what the different rooms are. 'This is the ——', etc.

Teach the vocabulary for furniture/appliances as it comes up. For example, television, radiator and freezer. How many other vocabulary items you introduce at this stage will depend on the time available and on the level of your pupils.

Optional follow-up activities
To provide pupils with a further lexical set, copy pictures of furniture in the story and put these in an envelope which pupils can label Furniture.

Suggested text
Snowman: How do you do!
Little boy: Hello, Snowman! I'm ——. Sssh! Come in!
Snowman: Thank you ——.
Little boy: This is the sitting-room! This is the television! This is the radiator! This is the kitchen! (*Then they go upstairs.*)
Little boy: Sssh! This is my parents' bedroom! (*And the snowman dresses up in their clothes. He puts on a tie, a pair of glasses, a pair of trousers and a hat!*)

270

Little boy: Come on! This is my bedroom! (*And they play with
——'s toys. Then they go downstairs.*)
Little boy: This is the garage!

(*The snowman is feeling hot so he climbs into the freezer to cool down.*)

Retell the story, encouraging pupils to participate.

Optional follow-up activities
To check vocabulary for the house, see *Start Testing Your Vocabulary*
(page 40) for a labelling activity.

Lesson Six

Aim: To revise or introduce vocabulary for toys and for expressing
ability.

Show pupils the two pages when the snowman and the little boy
go into the boy's bedroom. Pointing to the skateboard ask, 'What's
this?' Teach the English word when it arises. Ask, 'Can you
skateboard?' and teach the reply 'Yes, I can'/'No, I can't.' Introduce other toys, a punch-ball, a torch and balloons. Ask, 'Can you
box?', etc. Introduce other abilities related to toys by asking pupils
what they can do. For example, ride a bicycle, play cards, etc.

CLASS SURVEY
Draw a chart on the blackboard like the one below:

	Sarah	Mohamed	Lucy	Nicholas
skateboard	√			
box	×			
ride a bicycle	√			
play cards	√			

etc.

Get a pupil to come to the front of the class and ask, 'Sarah, can
you skateboard?', etc. Sarah must reply, 'Yes, I can'/'No, I can't'
and mark a tick or a cross on the chart.

GROUP WORK
This chart could also be used as a questionnaire. Give each child a

copy without including pupils' names. Each pupil must interview four others, completing the chart themselves. To monitor this activity join in yourself.

Returning to the story, ask pupils what they think the little boy and the snowman are saying: 'Look, I can skateboard!', 'I can't skateboard!', 'I can box!', 'I can't box!', etc. Contrast the weak can /kən/ and the stressed can't /kɑnt/.

Suggested text
Little boy: Come on! This is my bedroom! Look, I can skateboard!
Snowman: Let me try! Ooooh! I can't skateboard!
Little boy: Are you all right?
Snowman: Yes, I think so!
Little boy: Look, I can box!
Snowman: Oooooh! I can't box!
Little boy: Oh, poor Snowman. Look, this is my torch!
(*And they play with balloons in the light of the torch.*)

Lesson Seven

Aim: To revise or introduce language for expressing likes and dis-likes

Show pupils the two pages where the snowman first enters the house. Point to the picture of the snowman turning away from the fire and ask pupils what they think he is saying. Possible sugges-tions: 'I don't like the fire', 'I don't like hot things.' Now point to the picture of the radiator and again ask pupils what they think the snowman is saying. They may suggest: 'I don't like the radiator', 'I don't like hot things.'

Continue in this way pointing out the hot water, the cooker, the ice cubes and the fridge. Ask pupils what they think the snowman is saying: 'I like ice', 'I like the fridge' or 'I like cold things.'

Ask pupils what else they think the snowman likes or dislikes. For example: ice-cream, cold water, the snow, frozen food, the sun, etc.

TRUE OR FALSE?
Check comprehension by playing True or False? 'The snowman likes the sun!', 'The snowman doesn't like ice-cream!', etc.

Optional follow-up activities

SORTING
Pupils could collect pictures/or draw pictures of hot and cold

things and sort these into groups according to the snowman's likes and dislikes.

The snowman likes . . .	The snowman doesn't like . . .
cold	hot

PAIR WORK

Using the chart above, in pairs pupils can compare their items by saying, 'The snowman likes ice-cream', 'The snowman doesn't like the sun.' They can add different items mentioned by their partner to the chart.

CLASS SURVEY

Teach the phrase 'Do you like ——?' and the reply 'Yes, I do'/'No, I don't.' Draw a chart on the blackboard like the one below:

	Mary	Yacine	Meddy	Virginia
the sun	✓			
ice-cream	✓			
balloons	✗			
television	✓			
the snow etc.			✗	

Conduct a class survey in the same way as described above.

Retell the story, encouraging pupils to participate, up to the point where the snowman takes the little boy by the hand. Ask pupils what they think happens next.

Lesson Eight

Aim: To finish the story

Retell the story to the point you reached above and ask pupils to tell you what they think happens next. They may have seen the back-cover page and predict that the boy and the snowman fly up into the sky.

Optional follow-up activities
If you have the cassette, play the song and ask pupils to imagine what they think happens.

Continue with the story. When the two land on the pier, ask pupils what they think the snowman is saying. Prompt them by asking what time it is and pointing to the sun. Continue with the next two pages eliciting possible dialogue. Show the next two pages and ask pupils what they think the little boy will find when he goes outside. Did anybody predict the ending? Is it a happy or sad ending? Why? Do they think the story was a dream?

Suggested text
Once upon a time there was a little boy called ——. One morning in —— (month) he woke up and looked out of the window. 'Ah! It's snowing!' he said. He got dressed quickly. He put on his red pullover, and his blue jeans, and said to his mother, 'Can I go outside, please?' And she said, 'Yes, ——.' He put on his black boots and his red hat and ran into the garden.

First he made a small snowball for the head and then a larger one for the body. He gave him a scarf and a hat, a tangerine for a nose, and lumps of coal for his buttons and his eyes. Finally, he drew a mouth. —— was very happy and said, 'He's smiling!'

Soon it was time for bed. He brushed his teeth and at eight o'clock he looked out of the window at the snowman. His mother said, 'Good-night ——' and at nine o'clock he was asleep. At eleven o' clock he woke up and got out of bed and looked out of the window at the snowman. He was still there! He went back to bed but couldn't sleep. At midnight he got up. He put on his dressing-gown, went downstairs and opened the door.

'How do you do!' said the snowman. —— couldn't believe his ears! 'Hello, Snowman! I'm ——. Sssh! Come in!' said ——. 'Thank you,' said the snowman. —— showed him round the house. 'This is the sitting-room. This is the television! This is the radiator!' 'I don't like hot things,' said the snowman. 'Come on, then,' said ——. 'This is the kitchen! This is the cold water!' The snowman turned on the hot water. 'I don't like hot things,' he said. —— gave the snowman some ice. 'I like cold things. I like the fridge!' he said. Then they went upstairs. 'Sssh!' said ——. 'This is my parents' bedroom!' And the snowman dressed up in their clothes. He put on a tie, a pair of glasses, a pair of trousers and a hat! 'Come on!'

said ——. 'This is my bedroom. Look, I can skateboard!' 'Let me try!' said the snowman. 'Oooooh! I can't skateboard!' 'Are you all right?' said ——. 'Yes, I think so!' replied the snowman. 'Look, I can box!' 'Oooooh! I can't box!' 'Oh, poor Snowman,' said ——. 'Look, this is my torch!' And they played with balloons in the light of the torch.

Then they went downstairs. 'This is the garage!' The snowman was feeling hot so he climbed into the freezer to cool down. They had something to eat and then the snowman took —— by the hand.

They ran into the garden, across the snow and up, up into the air. They were walking in the air! They were flying! They flew for miles through the cold moonlight air. It was wonderful! Then the snowman said, 'It's six o'clock! We must go back!' —— thanked the snowman and said good-night. At last he went to sleep. When he woke up the sun was shining. He ran downstairs and across the sitting-room without saying good-morning to his parents and into the garden.

Optional follow-up activities

VIDEO
If you have access to the video, show this to pupils and ask about the differences between the video and the story.

DRAWING
In collaboration with the art teacher, pupils could create their own story in a series of strip format pictures inspired either by *The Snowman* or by a story of their own choice.

MAKING A SNOWMAN
Pupils could make their own snowman or snowwoman.

CHRISTMAS CARDS
Pupils could make Christmas cards decorated with scenes from the story. (See *Copycard*.)

RESEARCHING
Pupils could find out about and compare winter climates around the world. For example, in other English-speaking countries. This could be integrated into a geography class.

VOCABULARY
Encourage pupils to revise their vocabulary by testing themselves using their own personal lexical sets.

COLLAGE

Pupils could collect pictures of hot and cold things and make two large collages to decorate the classroom.

Associated books and cassettes:

Copycat for drawing activities

Copycard for Christmas cards, etc.

Copyparty for masks, models, etc.

This Little Puffin for related songs and rhymes. (See page 57 for weather games.)

Nursery Books by Jan Pienkowski: *Colours, Numbers, Weather, Faces, Time*

The Snowman cassette: Snowman Enterprises 1986

The Snowman video: Snowman Enterprises 1982

Other books by Raymond Briggs

Father Christmas

Father Christmas Goes on Holiday

The Fairy Tale Treasury (with Virginia Haviland)

The Mother Goose Treasury (traditional nursery rhymes)

Story notes by Gail Ellis

Resource books

Other Puffin and Penguin English books referred to throughout the story notes are:

Copycat: A Drawing Book useful for picture dictations; *Copycard*, *Copyparty*, *Copythat*, *Copytoys* useful for creative activities such as making cards, invitations, and models

Nursery series by Jan Pienkowski. It introduces basic vocabulary: *ABC*, *Colours*, *Faces*, *Farm*, *Food*, *Homes*, *Numbers*, *Shapes*, *Sizes*, *Time*, *Weather*, *Zoo*.

This Little Puffin, Finger Plays and Nursery Games. Musical games and action rhymes and songs organized by theme. Melodies are provided where appropriate.

The Mother Goose Treasury. A collection of traditional nursery rhymes selected and illustrated by Raymond Briggs.

Start Testing Your Vocabulary. A selection of varied activities for practising and consolidating basic vocabulary.